PRAISE FOR *BRAVE FACE*

★ "Razor-sharp, deeply revealing, and brutally honest."
—*BOOKLIST,* starred review

★ "An important message to other queer teens: your life is a gift, and support is out there." **—*PUBLISHERS WEEKLY*, starred review**

"By turns funny and heartbreaking but *always* gut-wrenchingly honest." **—*BOOKPAGE***

"Hutchinson's raw honesty pierces readers. . . . *Brave Face* is a bold, banner announcement that there is a future for everyone."
—*SHELF AWARENESS*

"As much a book about coming out as it is a book about simply coming to be, *Brave Face* is the bravest memoir I've read in years. Illuminating, brutally honest, poignant, and sometimes laugh-out-loud funny, this isn't a book just for queer kids; it's a book for any teen (or adult) who feels left out, rejected, confused, and scared about their place in the world."
—KATHLEEN GLASGOW, *New York Times* bestselling author of *Girl in Pieces*

"Shaun David Hutchinson has long been one of our brightest lights and best storytellers. In *Brave Face*, he shares all the sh*t he had to survive to get there—and how we can too. Brutal and essential."
—SAM J. MILLER, award-winning author of *The Art of Starving*

"Shaun David Hutchinson's account of his teenage years is as honest and compelling as his young adult fiction. People of all ages will find comfort and hope in this powerful, beautifully written memoir."
—BRANDY COLBERT, Stonewall Book Award–winning author of *Little & Lion*

"Shaun David Hutchinson has been hammering out one brilliant book after another, and *Brave Face* is his most honest and courageous one yet. This profound memoir is a triumph—a full-throated howl to the moon to remind us why we choose to survive and thrive."
—BRENDAN KIELY, *New York Times* bestselling author of *Tradition*

"Fearless and resonant, Hutchinson's memoir explores personal darkness with profound candor and earned wisdom. Courageous, devastating, and beautiful." **—CALEB ROEHRIG, author of *Death Prefers Blondes***

"Shaun David Hutchinson's *Brave Face* is an unforgettably profound memoir. A gut punch with moments covered in raw emotion. Its exploration of depression, family relationships, acceptance, sexuality, old wounds, and pain remind all of us that it's okay to not be okay. That we are not alone, even in our darkest hours."
—JULIAN WINTERS, author of *Running with Lions*

ALSO BY
SHAUN DAVID HUTCHINSON

The Past and Other Things That Should Stay Buried

The Apocalypse of Elena Mendoza

Feral Youth

At the Edge of the Universe

We Are the Ants

Violent Ends

The Five Stages of Andrew Brawley

fml

The Deathday Letter

BRAVE FACE

a memoir

SHAUN DAVID HUTCHINSON

Simon Pulse
New York London Toronto Sydney New Delhi

SIMON PULSE
An imprint of Simon & Schuster Children's Publishing Division
1230 Avenue of the Americas, New York, New York 10020
First Simon Pulse paperback edition May 2020

Also available in a Simon Pulse hardcover edition.

For information about special discounts for bulk purchases, please contact
Simon & Schuster Special Sales at 1-866-506-1949 or business@simonandschuster.com.
The Simon & Schuster Speakers Bureau can bring authors to your live event.
For more information or to book an event contact the Simon & Schuster Speakers Bureau
at 1-866-248-3049 or visit our website at www.simonspeakers.com.
Cover designed by Sarah Creech
Interior designed by Mike Rosamilia
The text of this book was set in Chaparral Pro.
Manufactured in the United States of America
2 4 6 8 10 9 7 5 3
The Library of Congress has cataloged the hardcover edition as follows:
Names: Hutchinson, Shaun David, author.
Title: Brave face : a memoir / by Shaun David Hutchinson.
Description: First Simon Pulse hardcover edition. | New York : Simon Pulse, 2019.
Identifiers: LCCN 2018044085 (print) | LCCN 2018044456 (eBook) |
ISBN 9781534431515 (hardcover) | ISBN 9781534431539 (eBook)
Subjects: LCSH: Hutchinson, Shaun David. | Suicidal behavior—Patients—Biography. |
Self-destructive behavior. | Manic-depressive illness. | Gays—Biography.
Classification: LCC RC569 (eBook) | LCC RC569 .H88 2019 (print) |
DDC 616.85/84450092 [B]—dc23
LC record available at https://lccn.loc.gov/2018044085
ISBN 9781534431522 (pbk)

For anyone who's ever felt a little queer.

You're not alone.

Please be aware that *Brave Face* includes the following content:

Suicidal Ideation

Attempted Suicide

Self-Harm

Sexual Assault

The Trevor Project

www.thetrevorproject.org

or call TrevorLifeline at 1-866-488-7386

National Suicide Prevention Lifeline

www.suicidepreventionlifeline.org

or call 1-800-273-8255

The It Gets Better Project

www.itgetsbetter.org

To Write Love On Her Arms

www.twloha.com

Trans Lifeline

www.translifeline.org

or call 877-565-8860 (US) 877-330-6366 (Canada)

The Jed Foundation

www.jedfoundation.org

CONTENT WARNING, PART 1

I'LL KEEP THIS SHORT. A LOT HAPPENS IN THIS MEMOIR. There's drug use, sex in the backseat of a Mustang, discussion of homosexuality, alcohol use, a smidge of profanity, and a little petty theft. Those, of course, aren't worthy of a content warning. Those are just the hundred million pieces that make up a life, and I'm not ashamed of them. But I'm also going to talk about depression, about cutting and burning myself, and about my attempted suicide. I'm not ashamed of those things either, but they might be tough for some of you to read, and I want to make sure you're aware of what's coming.

I'm also going to use words that will probably make you uncomfortable. Words like "faggot" and "fag" and "homo." I know these words hurt to read. They're not pleasant to write, either, but they're part of my story. There were a lot of misconceptions about what being gay meant in the 1990s, and I absorbed them all. Many of my attitudes and beliefs were a result of internalized homophobia and are not beliefs I hold today.

I should also warn you that I was selfish, arrogant, and kind of screwed up when I was younger. I made a lot of mistakes. And while I had my reasons for many of the things I did, they're not excuses. There are no excuses for the ridiculous crap I did when I was younger, and if I could apologize to every single person I hurt, I would. It's fine to hate teenage me a little, but trust me, no one will ever hate that arrogant little prick more than he hated himself.

As you're reading, it's okay to put the book down if it becomes too much or if you need a break. I took lots of breaks while writing. Just remember that no matter how dark it gets along the way, I'm working on this from the light at the other end of the tunnel, and I'll be waiting for you there.

THE TRUTH

THANKFULLY, I WAS ABLE TO PIECE TOGETHER TIME LINES and events from old e-mails and journals that I managed to hold on to. I've changed the names of all schoolmates and friends as well as many identifying details. Some of the people portrayed are composites. When it came to re-creating conversations, I've done my best to recall the flavor of the conversation, because it's not always possible to recall something from twenty years ago word-for-word.

One thing I do want to point out is that memory isn't always accurate. I gave a speech for the 2016 *School Library Journal* Leadership Summit, where I discussed some of my personal history with suicide and depression. In it, I mentioned how my mom had been tested in the hospital as a potential match for liver donation. Later, after my mom watched the speech, she told me that I'd gotten it wrong. She'd never been tested; she'd only talked to the doctor about being tested.

That's not how I remembered it, though. So as I started writing this memoir, I wondered what was more important: what actually happened or what I remembered happening.

I think the answer depends on who's doing the telling. How *I* remember events is more important to this memoir than how someone else remembers them, and someone else's recollection isn't necessarily the objective truth either. For example, I don't remember my mom crying when she came to the emergency room after my suicide attempt. Her strength and stoicism set an example for me later in my life. If I found out that she *had* actually cried in the ER, it wouldn't change the effect my original belief ultimately had on me.

Therefore, while I've done my best to verify dates and other objective truths, the majority of this memoir is how I remember events. Anything I've gotten wrong is on me.

Finally, this memoir contains e-mails, journal entries, and some of my early writing. Even though it's incredibly embarrassing, I've left all my awful grammar and spelling errors intact except where doing so rendered the passage too confusing to read. Please don't judge me.

PART 1

THE WRONG WORDS

JOURNAL ENTRY

1997

Every day, at least once, I silently wish I wasn't gay. See, basically, being gay involves choices and fears. The choice is how to go about finding love. The fear is that I never will.

I feel so alone because I'm surrounded by people who can never understand exactly how I feel.

I know that I'm gay and I can't do anything about the life I have to lead, but neither can I do anything with the life I have.

No matter what angle I try to look at things, the truth is that I'm a coward. I talk and strut, but what do I ever accomplish? I don't know, it just seems like I'm running in an endless circle. I don't want to look back on my life and regret the path I took. I look at my life presently though, and I hate and I hate and I hate . . .

VOCABULARY LESSON, PART 1

Eighth Grade, 1991 to 1992

I KNEW WHAT IT MEANT TO BE A FAGGOT, BUT NOT WHAT IT meant to be gay.

I was thirteen, in eighth grade at St. Mark's Catholic School. Thankfully, this wasn't a building filled with nuns who beat our knuckles with rulers. Our science teacher and vice principal was a woman with short hair who'd served in the military, rode a Harley to school, and taught us about both puberty and evolution. We attended daily religion class, which is where I did my homework for my other classes, and had mass once or twice a month, but I didn't mind.

Despite not being Catholic, I liked St. Mark's. It was nothing like my previous school, where I'd been frequently sent to the administrator's office for counseling with the vice principal, who would beat my ass with a sandal and then pray for my eternal soul, which she made sure I knew she believed was hell bound. I hated that school so much that I faked fevers by going to the bathroom and running hot water against my forehead. I also scraped a pencil eraser across the crook of my arm until it bled and frequently jumped from the top of a metal geodesic dome on the playground in an attempt to break my ankle. My only friend was a boy who once ate a spider during a fire drill.

My experience at St. Mark's was different. I learned how to cultivate friendships, how to fit in without being miserable, how to make people laugh. And I learned some new vocabulary words.

In the mornings before school, I sat in front of the library, which was situated at the far end of a parking lot between the main school building and the church. Younger kids chased one another around or threw footballs, but I was an eighth-grader and too cool for that. Instead, I killed time reading. After falling in love with Robin McKinley's *The Blue Sword*, I searched out and devoured as many fantasy novels as I could get my little hands on. My appetite was insatiable. And when I couldn't find books I hadn't read, I reread old ones.

One morning near the beginning of the school year, I was lounging on the steps, my back to a column, reading *The Eye of the World* by Robert Jordan. I didn't hear Kurt approach, didn't know he was there until his shadow fell across me, and I didn't think anything of it until he slapped the book out of my hand so hard the cover tore off.

"Faggot." He stood over me with his hands on his hips, staring down.

I'd never been bothered while reading before. In fact, I was known for sneaking books behind my textbooks when I was bored. I wasn't popular, but I wasn't unpopular, either, and I certainly wasn't a faggot.

Albert was a faggot. Albert was a tall, thin boy with delicate features and long eyelashes whose hair was always perfect and whose uniform was always impeccably neat. Albert was best friends with girls and hung out with them instead of with us.

Tito was a faggot. Tito was my mother's hairdresser, and she sometimes took me to him to get my hair cut too. He was a flamboyant Mexican man who fluttered around his shop, spoke with a lisp, and carried his hands with a characteristic limp wrist.

Hollywood was a faggot. Hollywood was a character in the 1987 movie *Mannequin*, which tells the story of an uninspired young man on the verge of losing his job designing window displays for department stores, and the mannequin who comes to life and does the work for him. She saves his job, they fall in love, barf, the end. Hollywood is a fellow window dresser who is played for laughs by Meshach Taylor. From his campy demeanor and dramatic gasps to his flamboyant collection of glam sunglasses, he's nothing but a joke. Hollywood has no backstory, no life, and serves no purpose in the movie other than to be laughed at and to help the hero get the girl. Hollywood was every gay stereotype rolled up into one poorly written character.

Hollywood was a faggot, Tito was a faggot, Albert was a faggot, and "faggot" was the worst insult to fling at an eighth-grade boy.

"Fuck you," I said. Slowly, I rose to my feet. Kurt was bigger than me, but I was taller. All I wanted to do was pick up my book and go back to reading about a world of magic, where a person's deeds defined them, but I couldn't let Kurt's challenge pass. There was no one else from our class around, but that didn't matter.

"Faggot," Kurt said again, and then he walked away.

I retrieved my book, and the cover, which I later decided not to tape back on. It was the cover, I believed, that had set Kurt off, and I made the decision to stop reading where anyone might see me so that no one else thought I was a fag. I also decided Kurt had to learn a lesson. So I casually whispered to the right people that I'd seen Kurt being friendly with Albert. *I* never called Kurt a fag, but soon other kids did. Soon Kurt was the butt of jokes. Soon boys he'd been friends with conspired to throw him in the Dumpster at the edge of the PE field. And Kurt never called me a faggot again.

No one did.

I knew nothing of sexuality, nothing of sex except that it sounded kind of gross. I knew nothing of love. Nothing of being gay. To me, being gay and being a faggot were the same. They were the worst thing a person could be. They were what I never wanted to become, and I'd do anything to ensure I never did.

FUTURE SELF, PART 1

August 1992

"I WANT TO BE A LAWYER."

My mom was scared. She was driving slowly, stuck in traffic alongside everyone else who'd waited until the last minute to flee the monster hurricane that had targeted South Florida. Hurricane Andrew might have been the first hurricane of the season, and he might have come late, but he was not playing games. My mom had been born and raised in Florida, as had I, so she didn't scare easily when it came to hurricanes, but Andrew was projected to tear right through our neighborhood, and she'd finally made the call to take me and my two stepbrothers to my aunt's house north of us.

"Why?" my mom asked.

I shrugged. "To help people."

"Then you'd want to be a defense attorney?"

"Yeah," I said. "A public defender."

"You won't make much money that way."

"I guess not, but I love to argue, and you don't need a lot of math to be a lawyer."

My mom laughed. It was good to see her laugh despite the fact that a force of nature, a thing over which she had no control, was threatening to tear apart the life she'd built. My mom had worked for a law firm until she'd fallen down a flight of steps and hurt her back so badly that she'd been declared legally disabled. She'd escaped a small town, escaped a bad marriage to my biological father, and had built a life she was proud of. She was raising me and my brother, Ryan, had remarried, and was helping to raise my stepdad's two sons. No matter what the universe threw at her, she fought to protect the life she had and the life she wanted.

But no one can fight a hurricane.

I was fourteen when Hurricane Andrew hit, wobbling slightly to the south and sparing my hometown, but devastating Homestead. While most of my friends from St. Mark's graduated eighth grade and went to a nearby Catholic high school, I decided to jump ship and attend my local public school. I honestly don't know why. Maybe I was ready for a new adventure, maybe I wanted to reinvent myself. Leaving the kids I'd spent four years with and starting over at a new school was a terrifying decision, but it also felt like the right one. I said good-bye to my friends and never saw any of them again.

I was excited to start high school. I'd signed up for classes and had gone shopping for supplies, but Hurricane Andrew screwed everything up. I was maybe the only person who was actually disappointed that the first week of school had been canceled, because I'd spent all summer dreaming of how my first week would unfold. It'd be like a John Hughes movie, more *Sixteen Candles* than *The Breakfast Club*. I wished I was Jake or Bender, but I was probably going to wind up more like the characters played by Anthony Michael Hall—nerdy, eager, and badly dressed. I was okay with that because the cool kids still accepted him in their own way.

I saw my future self make friends and go to homecoming games and get drunk at parties and go to prom. I saw my future self graduate high school and head off to college. Fall in love and get married. Attend law school and build a career defending the vulnerable. Have children and grow old and die happy, surrounded by people I loved.

"You can do it," my mom said. "I believe you can do anything you set your mind to."

"Really?"

"Of course."

My mom always told me the truth, even when I might have preferred she didn't. So I believed her when she said I could do anything and become anyone. I believed there were no doors closed to me, no challenges I could not defeat, no obstacles I could not overcome if I worked hard, fought bravely, and moved through life with integrity. I wasn't a good student. Teachers were constantly saying that I was smart but that I wasn't living up to my potential. I'd come to believe that my failures were a result of me just being lazy.

We studied the thirteen original US colonies in Mrs. Baker's eighth-grade social studies class. Mrs. Baker had never liked me, and I'd definitely never liked her. She was a bully, and I hated bullies, so I took advantage of every opportunity to undermine her. I asked uncomfortable questions that I knew she wouldn't want to answer—questions about the colonists' complicity in the mass murder of native tribes and about how American exceptionalism was an idea founded on the backs of slaves—and played the class clown whenever possible. When Mrs. Baker announced we'd be taking our comprehensive exam on the thirteen colonies, she made sure to fire a shot at me.

"The exam will be on Monday, giving you all weekend to study, though I'm sure that won't bother Mr. Hutchinson, since no amount of studying can help him." She sneered at me, and a couple of people snickered. Oh damn. I'd been called out by Mrs. Baker.

"I can ace the test," I said.

"This is a test about the thirteen colonies, not about napping."

"Okay," I said. "We'll see."

The exam would require knowing everything about those original colonies. When they were founded, who founded them, their major imports and exports, their locations, the country the founding colonists came from. The exam was something of a legend at St. Mark's, known to make or break a student's grade for the semester. So, of course, instead of spending the weekend studying, I set an alarm to wake me up two hours early on Monday morning. I sat outside on my patio, and I memorized everything.

"I'm impressed," Mrs. Baker said when she handed back the exams. She'd eyed me skeptically on test day when I'd been the first to finish. "Not only a ninety-eight, but also the highest score in the class." She paused at my desk. "You must have studied a lot."

I could have taken the win. I could have accepted the praise and let it go. But I didn't. "I played *Super Mario* all weekend," I said. "I didn't start studying until Monday morning."

Yeah, I know. I was a dick. But I also believed, like my parents and my teachers, that I could do anything I set my mind to, and that when I failed it was because I was lazy and not living up to my potential.

I believed that the future I envisioned for myself was achievable. I just had to try harder. I just had to want it badly enough.

So even as Hurricane Andrew bore down on South Florida and threatened the future my mother had worked so hard to build, my future felt bright and perfect and possible.

THE FUNNY FREAK

Fall 1992

HIGH SCHOOL WAS *NOT* LIKE A JOHN HUGHES MOVIE, WHICH was probably for the best. Those movies had issues—they were racially and culturally insensitive at best, misogynistic, homophobic, and they used rape as a punch line. I was, however, still basically an Anthony Michael Hall character. Nerdy, awkward, overwhelmed. All the students at St. Mark's had been able to fit into one two-story building, but my high school was a sprawling campus full of confusing hallways and buildings that seemed to shift and move at random like the staircases at Hogwarts. There were more students in my class than there'd been in all the classes at St. Mark's combined, and I was a nobody in a great horde of somebodies.

I'd made a couple of friends. There were Debbie and Allison in my English class, the two Dans I sat with at lunch, and a couple of random people I talked to during class but nowhere else. I suspected Debbie, Allison, and Dan One were mostly interested in copying my English assignments, and Dan Two was a strange, manic guy I never quite understood. And while I liked Debbie, Allison, and the Dans, they didn't feel like my people.

A few weeks into the school year, I saw a flyer announcing that the drama club would be holding auditions for *Dracula* after school, and I decided that I absolutely had to go. I'd never acted before, but my older brother, Ryan, had spent most of his high school years in the theater, and he'd loved it, so I thought I might love it too. With an uncharacteristic burst of bravery, I showed up to the audition and signed in. Ms. C., the theater director, called my name and then handed me a photocopied page containing a monologue for a character named Renfield, who was the devoted and blood-bound disciple of Dracula.

I read one sentence before Ms. C. stopped me.

"Forget trying to read every single word the way it is on the page," she said. "Focus on the feeling."

I stood in the middle of Ms. C.'s classroom and scanned the block of text on the page she'd given me, unsure what she wanted me to do. After Kurt had knocked the book out of my hand, I'd made certain no one would bully me again, which I did by becoming a bully. I hadn't been able to change my outward appearance—my knobby knees and big nose and awkward everything—but I'd mastered hiding my weaknesses. I'd transformed myself from a quiet, shy, bookish boy into a young man who wielded words like knives, struck first, and kept striking until his enemy surrendered. Surely I could handle becoming Dracula's bloodthirsty bitch for thirty seconds.

As I faced Ms. C. and began to read, I morphed into the funny freak Renfield. I craved blood and the approval of my master more than anything in life or beyond. I saw the world through a lens of miserable madness. I felt a bottomless hunger etched on my bones that I couldn't sate. I understood in my soul that my master would never give me what I desired, but I strived to please him anyway.

And then I finished and transformed into the unfunny freak Shaun again.

"You're not psychic. You can't see the flies unless you're looking at them with your actual eyes." Ms. C. stood at the edge of the stage while I clawed at the air to my left for invisible flies that I looked for to my right.

I'd been cast as Renfield. Sure, it was on the B team, but I was a freshman who spent his afternoons with juniors and seniors who treated me like a weird little brother, so I'd hit the jackpot. Ms. C., however, was beginning to show signs that she was regretting giving me a shot.

We'd been rehearsing for weeks and I hadn't been able to transform into Renfield the way I had during my audition. Likely because I was a terrible actor. Ms. C. knew it; Phil, our Dracula, who moaned inappropriately during his death scene, knew it; the A team *definitely* knew it. Still, I kept trying. I willed myself to worship our Dracula, to imagine living and breathing only for him, but it was Alex, our Harker, whom I really worshiped.

Alex had wavy dirty blond hair that parted effortlessly down the middle, blue eyes, and a long nose. He reminded me of the Clown Dog boy from *Don't Tell Mom the Babysitter's Dead*. I followed Alex around like *I* was a clown dog, and I was ridiculously transparent about it.

I couldn't help myself. Alex talked to me, not when we were outside of rehearsals, obviously, but while we were waiting for the A team to finish so that we could get some stage time. All of us on the B team hung out. Ally, Maria, Alex, Phil. And me. I felt special. Like I'd dragged myself out of the water onto the shore of the Island of Misfit Toys, and they'd invited me to stay.

I don't know what any of those people actually thought of me. Maybe they genuinely liked me; maybe they only tolerated me because they could see I was a hot mess in danger of falling to pieces if they looked at me sideways. Either way, for a while, I felt like I belonged.

During one rehearsal, we were sprawled on the landing at the top of the steps in front of the auditorium doors. I sat with my pale, hairless legs stretched out in front of me. Ally was on one side, Maria on the other. Phil and Alex were whispering between themselves.

"Nice shorts," Maria said.

"My mom bought them for me."

She looked at Ally and laughed. "I figured."

My mom meant well. She was, after all, trying to clothe and feed four teenage boys on a budget. When it came to clothes, my mother had decided that Duncan was the undisputed arbiter of cool. Duncan was a sweet ex-Mormon who worked at the Gap and couldn't have found "cool" if it'd been clinging to his back, giving him a reach-around. The clothes he convinced my mom to buy were so uncool that they almost circled back around to cool again. Almost.

I'd once tried to discuss the situation with my mom.

Once.

Mom: What do you think of this shirt?

Shaun: It's kind of orange, yeah?

Mom: You don't like it?

Shaun: I didn't say that; it's just that it's so . . .

Mom: Orange. Yes, Shaun, I heard you the first time.

Shaun: Do they have it in another color? Or with fewer stripes?

Mom: I spend all week driving from store to store to find the best sales so that I can buy clothes for you boys and this is how you thank me?

Shaun: I'm only saying—

Mom: No, forget it.

Shaun: You know what? I bet this shade

```
of orange will go really well with those
turquoise plaid shorts you bought me
last week.
```

I wasn't wearing the plaid shorts that day in front of the auditorium. Instead, I was wearing denim shorts that were black on the legs, violet on the front pockets, red around the waist, and had emerald-green back pockets. I didn't own a shirt long enough to cover them.

"You're a virgin, right, Shaun?"

The question caught me completely off guard; I wasn't even sure who'd asked, Alex or Phil, or why they wanted my input on the subject. Both Alex and Phil were seniors, so I assumed they'd had lots of sex with many different girls, and how the hell was I supposed to answer? Would they make fun of me if I told them the truth? Would they believe me if I lied? Either way, I needed to answer quickly or they'd assume whatever I said was a lie, so "no" slipped out before I had the opportunity to think through the repercussions.

The girls didn't say anything, but Phil laughed. It was Alex's response that really surprised me, though. His eyes grew wide and he leaned forward, staring at me, and said, "For real?"

Backing down would have been a disaster. Admitting I'd lied would have been worse than if I'd told them I was a virgin in the first place. Besides, I wasn't lying; I was acting. I'd become another version of myself. One who'd had sex.

"What was it like?" Alex asked. Phil who? Ally who? Maria

who? As far as Alex was concerned, the others might as well have been abducted by aliens.

I was in trouble. Everything I knew about sex I'd learned from a book called *The Devil's Cat*, which I'd read when I was nine on a train ride from Florida to Washington, DC, with my mom and older brother. There was a scene in a cemetery with a woman and a cat and a couple of people possessed by the cat. I didn't understand any of what they were doing or why the cat needed to watch. It was an incredibly confusing and poorly written book, and I would not recommend that anyone read it. For leisure *or* sex education.

I'd also read *Then Again, Maybe I Won't* by Judy Blume, but I doubted sex was anything like waking up confused and ashamed in sticky underwear. And, of course, I knew how to masturbate, but I held firmly to the hope that sex had to be better than ten seconds of frantic activity in the shower while one of my brothers banged on the door, yelling at me to hurry up.

I'd had a girlfriend in eighth grade, but our relationship, which had spanned two weeks, involved writing notes during class and had felt more like homework than a relationship. We'd never even held hands or kissed.

Either way, I didn't know what to say to Alex. I didn't know what to say to any of them. I figured someone would see through my lie, but it wasn't just Alex waiting for my answer. They were all paying attention. Even Phil, though he was leaning back on his hands and only looking at me out of the corner of his eyes. I think they were all virgins. The people I'd spent the last few weeks idolizing didn't know any more about sex than I did. Hell, I could've told them that it felt like the chest-burster scene from *Alien*, only in reverse, and they probably would've believed me.

"Wet," I said. "But in a good way. And warm." It sounded like I was describing a bubble bath.

Alex leaned so far forward he looked like he was going to fall over. "But what was it *like*?"

Why was knowing so important to him? Was Alex trying to live vicariously through my experiences? More importantly, did I want to impress him so desperately that I was willing to fabricate my first sexual encounter?

Yes. Yes, I was.

"It was amazing," I said. "There's nothing like it. It was like we were this single person and . . . You just have to experience it." I shook my head condescendingly like I couldn't believe none of them had ever done it. "It was over fast, though." I added the last bit because they might have believed I'd had sex, but there was no way they'd believe I wasn't awful at it.

Phil left for the restroom and the girls went into the auditorium, but Alex stuck around. He kept staring at me like I was the end boss in a game he just couldn't figure out how to kill. Like he couldn't understand how someone as awkward and gangly and badly dressed as me had gotten laid while he hadn't. I get it. If our positions had been reversed, I also would have been confused.

Eventually Ms. C. called us back inside, and we finished rehearsals.

It was only a story, but after, when Alex looked at me, he no longer saw a spindly freshman who tried to catch flies without looking at them. He saw someone who'd done the one thing he hadn't. He looked at me with respect. He said hi to me outside of the auditorium, though still not when other people might see.

But he also asked me about sex whenever he had the chance.

"What was it like? Did you use a condom? Did she kiss you? Did you go down on her?"

Alex turned into an annoying sex detective, persistently digging out every excruciating detail of my fictional sexual encounter. The pressure was too much, and I began avoiding him. Not because of the lie. I had a good memory, and I improvised well enough that he didn't suspect I hadn't told him the truth. It was that I had to be this person all the time. I had to be this freshman who'd had sex. I wanted a friend; he wanted a story. My story. And it wasn't even true.

We made it through *Dracula*. The hastily constructed bookshelf fell on top of Harker, I knocked over a table I was supposed to be hiding under, and of course, our Dracula did his best sexy death moan on closing night and caused us to lose it onstage. I was relieved, in a way. Not having to see Alex every day meant I didn't have to be the person he thought I was anymore.

Except the story got around to a few people I knew outside of theater. Kids in my class. Mostly boys. They asked if I was a virgin and I had to say no. I didn't think it was that big a deal, because I imagined there'd be a day in the near future where I would have sex with a girl and it would probably be awful and short, and my lie wouldn't be a lie anymore. But when that day came, I wouldn't be able to call my best friends, which at that moment were the Dans, and tell them that I totally had sex! They both thought I'd already done it. I'd robbed myself of the opportunity to share that experience with anyone.

A couple of months after *Dracula*, I was in the auditorium to help run the lights for a choir show. I'd only done the one play, but the theater already felt like home. Watching the rehearsals was boring, so I climbed the catwalks to the spot booth where one of the spotlights was located. Maria was sitting on the floor with her knees pulled up to her chest. She had a kind of peasant-girl vibe to her that I thought was cool, and she was wearing headphones.

"Hey," she said.

"Hey," I said back. "What're you listening to?"

Maria had these piercing brown eyes that looked like she was boring through my skull into my memories. Then she said, "You never had sex, did you?"

Was she going to tell Alex? Was I completely screwed? If everyone learned I was a liar, my reputation would never recover. But Maria already knew, and I was actually relieved. Even if she didn't tell anyone, at least there would be one person I wouldn't need to wear the mask around.

I shook my head.

Maria pulled her headphones down and popped one side off the headband. "It's 10,000 Maniacs," she said. "Natalie Merchant is a fucking goddess."

I rushed to sit down beside her, and I pressed the speaker to my ear as "Stockton Gala Days" began to play. I'd never heard anything like it before. I was still listening to Phil Collins and Def Leppard and Guns N' Roses because that's what my brothers listened to, but this, this was music. This sang to my soul.

Natalie's voice rose near the end, the tempo picked up, and she was joined by a chorus of strings that sounded like summer and sunlight. I felt the crown of garlands on my head and smelled the wild apple blossoms in the air.

"Are those violins?"

Maria looked at me and grinned. "What did I tell you? She's a fucking goddess."

We sat and listened to the rest of the tape, and all Maria asked in return for sharing it with me was my company and the truth.

A WHOLE NEW WORLD

Winter 1992

MY FIRST JOB WAS BAGGING GROCERIES AT PUBLIX WHEN I was fourteen. Actually, that's not true. My first job was washing dishes and bussing tables at a diner where my stepbrother worked. The woman who ran the joint chased me around while yelling at me to run faster, scrub harder, move my scrawny little legs. I left at the end of that day and never returned. Bagging and carting groceries for old people turned out to be more my speed. I worked with a guy named Ben, who went to the same high school as me. We didn't have much in common, but I always had more fun when he was around.

He and I were working together the day before Thanksgiving, and I'd never seen the store so busy. The lines of customers seemed endless. There were always more groceries to bag and more people to help out to their cars. The only break we got was the short walk from the parking lot back into the store.

"So, you and Ashley, huh?" Ben and I walked our carts in from the far end of the parking lot. Every space was filled, and drivers prowled along behind us in the hopes of snagging an open spot so they could grab stuffing or cranberry sauce or whatever they'd forgotten that their Thanksgiving dinner would just be ruined without.

Ben nodded, a grin spreading across his face. "For a couple of weeks. When're *you* gonna find a girlfriend?"

No one other than Maria had questioned the story that I'd had sex, but the longer I went without a girlfriend, the more they began to see the gaping holes in it.

"What about that girl ringing the bell?" Ben asked.

"For real?"

"She was okay."

The girl ringing the bell was a young woman collecting money for the Salvation Army. I hadn't paid attention to her except to notice how annoying that damn bell was. Every time I wheeled a cart in or out of the store, she was there ding-a-ling-a-linging for everyone to hear.

"Yeah, I don't know."

"You got someone else in mind?"

"No, but—"

"Are you still upset about Stephanie?"

Stephanie was the first girl I asked out in high school. She sat in front of me in algebra, and often nudged me awake when Mrs. Kurtz called on me. I caught up to her at the end of class and asked her if she wanted to go to the homecoming dance with me while sweat rolled down my back and my stomach felt like it was turning inside out.

"Do you have a car?" she asked.

"I'm only fourteen."

It took a moment, with her staring down at me, to realize she hadn't been asking a question, she'd been giving me her answer.

Thankfully, no one had been around to hear our conversation, and I'd only told the Dans and Ben.

"No," I said, a little more emphatically than I meant to. As Ben and I returned inside, prepared to slog back into the hellish pre-Thanksgiving battle for another six hours, we passed by the bell-ringing girl, and I couldn't help noticing that she was watching us and smiling.

The rest of my shift passed in a blur of turkeys and "double bag those" and green beans. I didn't like working, but I noticed that if I kept my head down and focused on what I was doing, the hours passed more quickly, so I didn't see much of the bell ringer until later.

I finished loading a customer's bags into the trunk of her car, and she handed me two dollars. We weren't supposed to take tips, but my personal policy was to refuse once and then accept the money graciously so that I could buy a soda on my break. This time I didn't even bother with the refusal. I was parched, and nothing sounded better than a cold root beer.

I heard the bell ringing as I neared the front of the store. The girl caught my eye long before I reached the door and had a chance to pretend I wasn't paying attention. She had sun-bleached, curly blond hair and blue eyes. She smiled at me, revealing a pair of dimples.

Without thinking, I took the two dollars and slid it into the opening in her cash bucket.

"Thank you," she said. "I'm Tonia."

"Shaun."

Tonia giggled and pointed at my name tag. "I can read."

"Me too."

She laughed again. "Good to know."

"I should get back to work."

Tonia pulled a scrap of paper from her pocket, wrote her number and name on it, and handed it to me. "We should go out."

I took her number and practically ran into the store, nearly crashing into Ben, before more embarrassing words could fall out of my clumsy mouth.

Tonia was sixteen, had a car, and went to a private school. Our first date was to see *Aladdin* at the local movie theater. I rode my bike and met her there because my mom wouldn't let me ride with anyone she hadn't met, and there was *no way* I was going to introduce her to the first girl I was going on a real date with.

I'd scraped together every last quarter I had to pay for the movie and the snacks. My job at Publix paid a whopping $4.25 an hour, and I deposited all my checks into a savings account so I could buy a car when I turned sixteen. But I'd managed to skim a few bucks off my last paycheck and had saved my tips, which were always generous during the holiday season.

No one other than Ben knew about my date. I hadn't told my brothers or Debbie or the Dans. I wouldn't have even told Ben, but he'd been there for the initial awkward ritual. The reason I couldn't talk to anyone was because they would assume I had no reason to be nervous. That since I'd already had sex with a girl, going on a date should be no big deal. But the truth was that I was terrified. My palms were sweaty, my forehead was clammy. It was early December, but I was sweating like it was the middle of summer, because I had no idea what was going to happen on this date. I had no idea what I would be expected to do or what Tonia might try to do to me. The stories of H. P. Lovecraft, with which I'd recently become obsessed, lurked in my mind, presenting countless horrifying possibilities.

I imagined that during the movie Tonia would hold my hand. That I'd try to slip free so I could eat some popcorn but that her grip would be unshakeable. That she'd turn to kiss me, her mouth would open wide, and tentacles would spill out and shoot into *my* mouth. They'd squirm down my esophagus and into my stomach where they'd lay the eggs of an Ancient One who'd eventually hatch and consume my body from the inside out. And all of this would occur while the Robin Williams–voiced Genie manically danced through his dialogue.

And yet, I was still turned on.

Before settling on a movie, Tonia and I had spent a week talking on the phone. Okay, mostly I spent a week listening while *she* talked on the phone. I knew everything about her, her friends, and her family. Tonia didn't seem to care whether I added anything to the conversation, only that I was paying attention. She even quizzed me, though she didn't think I knew she was doing it.

In the middle of telling me about the fight she was having with her best friend, Casey, I'd interrupt and say, "I thought your best friend was Sarah," and she'd say, "Right, Sarah," with a triumphant note in her voice.

It was no accident I'd suggested we see a movie. Not only were there few options near enough that I could ride my bike to, but the theater was a place where talking was discouraged. So on the appointed evening, I told my parents I was going to see a movie with friends (not exactly a lie), hopped on my bike, met Tonia in front of the theater, bought our tickets and some snacks, and let Tonia choose a pair of seats near the back.

The lights went down.

My fingers were buttery and salty.

The previews played. The theater was packed with a mixture of high school students and younger kids with their parents. Slowly, while boxes of candy, cups of soda, and tubs of popcorn danced across the screen, Tonia slipped her hand into mine. She didn't even seem to mind the butter.

Throughout the movie, Tonia kept inching closer to me, but I wasn't exactly paying attention to her because I was more interested in what was on the screen. And who could blame me? Robin Williams was a comic genius. I might not have noticed

Tonia at all, except she wasn't the kind of girl who allowed anyone to ignore her. She squeezed my hand so hard my knuckles cracked, and as I turned to her to ask her what was wrong, she leaped at my face and shoved her tongue down my throat.

I was right! Kissing really was like an H. P. Lovecraft story, but with less xenophobia and racism.

I didn't know what to do, so I kissed her back. I think. I'm not sure if I'd call what I did "kissing." It felt more like a moist game of Hungry Hungry Hippos that I desperately wanted to end and was willing to forfeit so that I could finish watching the movie, but Tonia had her tentacles wrapped tightly around me and she refused to let me go.

So this was kissing. I felt a kind of detachment as it was happening. I wondered if I should have brushed my teeth better. I wondered how I could ask Tonia not to drink diet soda next time because the taste of aspartame made me a little sick. I wondered what the people behind us were thinking and whether they might complain to management. I wondered what I was supposed to be doing with my hands and whether it was normal to feel feverish and sick to my stomach.

Mostly, though, I was bored. I figured at least part of me was enjoying kissing Tonia because I had a hard-on, but I was also fourteen and everything gave me a hard-on. I couldn't turn around in tight jean shorts without getting excited. While Tonia clutched and grabbed at my skinny ass, I tried to think of a way to distract her, but she was determined, and eventually I gave in and let it happen.

I didn't like Tonia, and I didn't want to go out with her again. But I did anyway. A few times. We went to *Aladdin* a second time, though it wasn't until it came out on video a year later that I actually saw the entire movie. Another day, I met her at Publix, and she drove me to her house where she groped me on the couch while *The Little Mermaid* played in the background, forever ruining my ability to enjoy Disney movies.

"What's wrong?" Tonia asked as she lay on top of me, gyrating against me.

"I mean, I'm kind of into the movie." And why wouldn't I be? Ursula was an icon.

Tonia grabbed my crotch in a way that I think she thought was sexy but actually just hurt. "This says otherwise."

"Sorry. I need to pee." I crawled out from under Tonia, ran to the bathroom, and locked myself in. I turned on the sink faucet and sat on the edge of the tub.

This was happening way too fast. I'd only known Tonia a couple of weeks and she seemed like she was insinuating that she was ready to have sex with me. On the one hand, it was tempting because then I wouldn't be lying anymore. I could do it with Tonia, and then I'd know what I was talking about for real.

Everyone laughs at boners or thinks they're gross and wishes no one would ever discuss them, but they were the bane of my existence. They were hormonal and uncontrollable, and were viewed as a barometer of my sexual interest in whomever was closest, which was, for the most part, just not accurate. I was *not* sexually attracted to Tonia, but this fleshy protrusion hanging off of me was determined to tell her I was. My body and biology had betrayed me, and there was nothing funny about it.

I didn't want to do it with Tonia. Regardless of what my dick said, I was more interested in singing along to "Poor Unfortunate Souls" with Ursula than having sex.

"Are you all right in there?"

I flushed the toilet out of panic and shouted, "Just finishing up!"

When I got out of the bathroom, I made up an excuse to get Tonia to take me home and then I dodged her calls for the next week. I kept hoping that she'd give up and I wouldn't actually have to break up with her, but I don't think Tonia had ever given up on anything in her life. So I finally answered the phone and told her I didn't want to go out with her again. I stayed on the phone while she cried, I stayed on the phone while she cussed me out and told me I was cruel, I stayed on the phone while she asked me to reconsider, and then, when Tonia finally ran out of things to say, I hung up.

Ben caught up with me while I was collecting errant carts in the parking lot. Christmas was in a couple of days, and I'd been working as much as I was allowed while I was off from school. Every time I heard a bell ring, I flinched, but Tonia didn't ring the bell at my store anymore.

"What's up?" Ben called.

"Nothing much. Just slacking off."

"Hey, you and your girlfriend want to hang out with me and Ashley?"

"She's not my girlfriend anymore."

Ben's eyes widened. "What happened?"

I shrugged.

"Did you guys . . ." He left the thought unfinished, but I knew what he was asking.

"No," I said. "But she wanted to."

"And you didn't?"

The way he said it felt less like a question and more like an accusation. Like by admitting I'd had the chance to have sex with an actual girl and turned it down, I'd betrayed not only myself, but every guy who had, did, or ever would live.

"You know?" I said. "I just think I could do better."

And then I waited for Ben's reaction. After a second, a smile split his face and he clapped me on the back. "We'll find you a girl."

"Can't wait."

I WANNA MARRY THE PRINCESS

Fall to Winter 1993

I SURVIVED THE REST OF MY FRESHMAN YEAR BY KEEPING my head down, but I was lonely.

The drama club put on *Little Women* in the spring, but there were no roles in it for me. However, I was so determined to be a part of the group that I volunteered to be the stage manager. It wasn't the same as it had been during *Dracula*, and I was happy when the show closed and my freshman year of high school ended.

I spent the summer working and riding my bike around town with Ben. We didn't have anything in common, but he was someone to waste the endless days with, and I guess I was grateful for that. I also spent a lot of time reading. It seemed like overnight my parents and stepbrothers had become unbearable, and reading was the easiest way to escape them. It wasn't just my family that had become annoying, it was the entire damn world. It was existing. Every sound was too loud, every light too bright. I couldn't even put on my socks without the seams on the inside irritating my toes to the point that I'd tear them off and sit on the edge of my bed shaking and crying from frustration.

My entire day could be quickly ruined by something as simple as there not being enough milk for my cereal or by having to do chores when all I wanted was to read a book.

Most of the time, I swallowed my anger. I drove it to the pit of my stomach and tried to bury it, until it would erupt from within me in a fiery plume of angry words or tears or blind rage that I directed at whatever inanimate object was closest. I kept my meltdowns to myself, because when they passed I was overcome with shame. I was confused. Then I turned *that* inside and began the whole process over again.

By the time the summer ended and sophomore year began, I was ready. I'd even go so far as to say I was excited. And this time there was no hurricane to prevent me from going.

On a whim I'd decided to take journalism, which was where I met Alan. He sat beside me but ignored me until the day he saw a copy of *The Sword of Shannara* in my backpack. From there we talked about Robert Jordan, the Dragonlance Chronicles, and other fantasy authors and series we were obsessed with. Alan was a year older than me and worked for a local bookstore, which I thought was probably the coolest job in the world. Eventually he invited me to join his Dungeons & Dragons group. Alan was loyal but arrogant, kind but demanding. He acted like he believed relationships with girls were transactional, and seemed to have no idea how to view women as anything other than the objects of his sexual and romantic desire. He was, however, one of my few good friends, and I was willing to ignore many of his most problematic qualities to keep him around.

Shortly after I started tenth grade, Ms. C. announced auditions for *Aladdin*. Despite how I'd been traumatized during my first date with Tonia, I tried out for the show. I desperately missed performing, and I was eager to slip out of my skin and into someone else's. Ms. C. gave me the role of the Vizier's bratty son, whose only memorable line was "But *I* wanna marry the princess!" which I whined to perfection.

Playing the role of my father, the Vizier, was Madelyne. Maddie and I had met on the bus during freshman year, "dated" for a week until she broke up with me, and then sat as far from each other on the bus as was necessary to ensure we didn't have to talk. I'm not really sure if she'd qualified as a girlfriend, and our relationship had been so short that I hadn't bothered to tell any of my friends.

I'd never expected to have anything to do with her again, and she was the last person I wanted to spend my afternoons with, but despite my misgivings, Maddie and I were radiant onstage together. She was sly and arrogant, I was obsequious and demanding, and we played off of each other's energy better than anyone else in the cast, nearly stealing the show.

Off stage, we remained somewhat cautious of each other. I was weird and she was nerdy, but I felt like, in spite of our rocky beginning, Madelyne was someone I *wanted* to know, even though I couldn't have said exactly why. Like with Alan, Madelyne simply felt like one of my people.

It was also during *Aladdin* that I met Leigh. We flirted awkwardly throughout the show, and I eventually asked her out.

I held the phone to my ear while I sat in the den watching TV. "And you like this show?" I'd heard of *Power Rangers* before, but I'd never sat through an entire episode, and now I knew why.

"The kids like it," Leigh said. She was babysitting, a job she did most days after school, meaning I rarely got to see her. We'd been dating for a couple of months. *Aladdin* was over, and we were crawling toward holiday break. "What's your favorite show?"

"Probably *Star Trek: The Next Generation*."

"But you're making fun of *Power Rangers*?" Leigh had a loud, high-pitched laugh that made me both wince and smile.

"Hey! *Star Trek*'s nowhere near as cheap looking as this." So far every villain resembled a shaved Muppet, except for Rita Repulsa, who looked like she was wearing the cone-shaped bra on her head that Madonna had worn on the first stop of her Blond Ambition tour.

"I'm not making fun of it."

"You sure? Because I'm not sure I can have a girlfriend who hates *Star Trek*."

Leigh hesitated. "So I'm your girlfriend?"

"Of course!"

"And you don't like someone else better?"

"Uh, who?"

"I don't know."

I racked my brain trying to think of what Leigh was getting at. As far as girlfriends went, Leigh was pretty cool. People had made fun of her because her eyes were a little buggy, but I didn't care. I'd spent years with buck teeth and an overbite that had caused me to drool so badly when I slept that I frequently had a rash where my face had touched the pillow, and even though everyone kept promising I'd grow into my nose, it still took up a massive amount of real estate on my face, so I was never going to judge Leigh for something totally outside of her control. I'd met her parents, who seemed to like me. They kept turkeys, which I found odd and fascinating. Leigh was easygoing and kind, and she let me watch movies without trying to devour my face or hump my leg.

"Just you, Leigh," I said.

"Not Madelyne?"

I didn't mean to bust out laughing, but I couldn't help myself. "Madelyne? Seriously?"

"You spend a lot of time together."

"When?"

"Lunch," Leigh said. "And class."

Madelyne and I had exactly one class together, English, which I was kind of in danger of failing, unlike geometry, which I was definitely failing. "I'd sit with you at lunch if we had it the same period. I only sit with Maddie because I don't have anyone else to sit with." Which wasn't true. I sat with Maddie because I liked spending time with her. Just not in the way that Leigh suspected. Our time playing father and son together during *Aladdin* had cemented our friendship, and I had no interest in her beyond that.

"I know," she said. "It's just . . . I love you."

Oh shit. "Thanks?"

Alan picked me up after I finished working at Publix, and we slow-drove back to his house for our weekly D&D game with Chris, Bill, and Greg. I was the youngest in the group and the only one without a car, but they didn't seem to mind. We were all weird and outcast in our own way, and I was just happy that we could all be outcasts together.

"Leigh told me she loves me," I said as we drove.

The more Alan and I hung out, the more we found we had in common. We were both seriously into computers and computer games—he was the only other person I knew who actually had e-mail—and we filled in the gaps in each other's knowledge of fantasy literature. He introduced me to Michael Moorcock, I introduced him to David Eddings. He was someone I felt comfortable talking to, especially about girls, even though he'd never had a girlfriend.

"Whoa! Look at you, Mr. Suave. You gonna go for it?"

"Go for it?"

"Say it back? Make the next move?"

"You mean sex?"

"That's not exactly where I was going, but it sounds like that's what she wants."

"You think?"

"A girl doesn't say she loves you if she's not looking for something more."

Just because I could talk to Alan didn't mean I thought he was right. In fact, I wasn't surprised he'd never had a girlfriend. To him, girls were puzzles to be solved, prizes to be won, foes to overcome. He dissected every conversation he had with every girl to determine their nefarious intentions, even when all they'd said to him was "hi."

But I worried he was right about Leigh. I worried she was pushing me to level up our relationship, and that thought terrified me.

"All we've really done is make out."

We'd spent a lot of time making out, actually. Leigh might have been shy in public, but she really seemed to love kissing, and she was better at it that Tonia had been, though kissing still gave me that sweaty/nauseated/horny feeling that made me unsure whether I was going to puke or have a spontaneous orgasm. The possibility of both happening at the same time was frequently a concern.

Alan pulled into the driveway. His house sat at the end of a cul-de-sac in a typical South Florida neighborhood. All the lawns were green and neatly cut, all the houses were some shade of white or off-white. Greg's and Bill's cars were parked on the street, and I assumed Chris had gotten a ride with one of them.

"Well?" he asked. "What did you say?"

"I thanked her."

"Ouch, compadre. And she didn't break up with you?"

I shook my head. "She said she understood and that I could say it when I was ready."

"You know she didn't mean that, right?"

"What'd she mean?"

"That you'd probably better call her and tell that girl you love her unless you want to be single again."

"Right now?"

Alan laughed. He had an arrogant laugh that was all sharp edges and slick, smooth surfaces. "After the game."

We got out of the car and walked toward the house, where the others were probably waiting at the dining room table, eating all the good snacks Alan's mom usually prepared for us.

"What if I don't?" I asked Alan before he opened the door.

"Don't love her?"

"Don't want to have sex with her?"

Alan laughed again and slapped me on the back. "Well, now you're just being foolish. Of course you want to have sex with her, so just tell her you love her and go for it."

I usually slept through geometry. I'd done poorly in algebra, not because I didn't understand it, but because I never turned in homework or solved the equations the way I was supposed to. I was failing geometry for an entirely different reason. I couldn't visualize the shapes in my brain the way others seemed able to. I thought in words, not pictures, and so when it came to figuring out angles and sides, I was utterly lost.

My only friend in geometry was Kaylee, a junior with a thick Southern accent who was also failing the class, even though it was her second time taking it. It didn't help that Mrs. Sutherland was awful, constantly jumping from one topic to the next in an unenthusiastic voice that drove me instantly to sleep. Occasionally Kaylee and I would skip class and go to Wendy's for lunch.

"You ever been in love?" I asked her as we sat in her car eating cheeseburgers.

"Leon," she said with her mouth full.

Leon was one of our school's star football players, and I'd never seen him and Kaylee together. "Does he know?"

Kaylee shrugged. "Who cares? That boy's gonna be mine one of these days."

"Okay," I said. "So then have you ever been in love with someone you were actually dating?"

"Sure."

Now we were getting somewhere. "How do you know if you're really in love?"

"Same way you know you're hungry," she said.

"But don't you sometimes mistake being bored for being hungry? Like, you think you want to eat, but really you just need something to do during commercials?"

Kaylee slurped her soda and then turned to face me. "Are you asking me the difference between being in love and being horny?"

"Maybe? I don't know."

"Spit it out, Shaun. What's this about?"

This was why I liked Kaylee. She knew shit and she didn't screw around. "My girlfriend told me she loves me, and I eventually said it back because I felt bad for not saying it right away, but I'm not sure if I actually do love her."

"You having sex?"

"No."

"You want to?"

"I don't know."

Kaylee ate a couple of fries while I sat quietly waiting for her sage wisdom. "You'd know if you were in love with her already, so you've got two choices. Fake it until you feel it, or fake it until you get what you want and then break up with her."

"What if I don't want anything from her?"

"Then you take the third option and just break up with her."

I didn't know what to do. Being with Leigh or a girl like her, wanting to be in love with her, wanting to have sex with her, was what I was supposed to want. Westley died and came back for Buttercup, Johnny bravely declared that nobody puts Baby in the corner. I had what books and movies told me I was supposed to want. I was able to envision a future with Leigh in it, and yet I still wasn't happy.

So when I got home from school, I called Leigh, watched a few minutes of *Power Rangers* with her, and then told her I thought we should break up.

TO BE OR NOT TO BE, GIRL

Spring 1994

THE REST OF MY SOPHOMORE YEAR WAS MOSTLY UNEVENTFUL. In expectation of getting my license on my sixteenth birthday, my parents and I went car shopping. We found a white 1990 Mustang hatchback that had been owned by a little old woman who'd sold it when her husband died. It only had a few thousand miles on it, but it cost twice the amount of money that I had saved working at Publix. It turned out my mother had also been saving money, and she matched what I had, allowing me to buy the car. I couldn't even test-drive it, but I was still excited.

Leigh and I remained friends, but I spent the majority of my time with Alan and Madelyne. Alan and I continued gaming on weekends with the group, but he and I also hung out and talked computers and rented movies. I spent my lunches with Madelyne, and we grew even closer. Where Alan and I talked about specific things—books, computer games, D&D campaigns—Madelyne and I talked about *everything*. We discussed our hopes and dreams, our plans for the future, whether it was possible to make a living as a sex worker who traded sixty-second blow jobs for nickels. Our lunchtime conversations spanned the universe.

My life at home wasn't going as smoothly. Noises and voices always seemed too loud, like everyone was shouting through a megaphone. Every time my mom asked me to do something, I felt like she was dropping the weight of the world on my back while I was already carrying twice that amount. Her criticisms stung like insults, and the only way I knew how to respond was by yelling, but I didn't know why. It was like there was a short circuit in my brain somewhere. The same thorny knot in my brain that made it difficult for me to put on socks in the morning without having a meltdown made it impossible for me to interact with my family without wanting to lock myself in a room and burn it to the ground.

The only things I looked forward to were weekends with Alan, lunches with Maddie, and the spring play.

I had no idea what Ms. C. had in store for the second show of my sophomore year, but I was eager to find out. I may not have been getting along with the family I was born into at the moment, but I loved the drama club because they were the family I'd chosen.

Instead of an actual show, Ms. C. announced that we were going to perform a night of one-act plays and monologues. Part of me was thrilled by the idea of having the stage to myself, of having every eye in the audience on me, even if only for a few minutes. But part of me was also disappointed that I wouldn't be playing off of Madelyne the way I had during *Aladdin* or that I wouldn't be sharing rehearsals with my found family the way I had during *Dracula*. Instead of feeding off of the energy of my fellow actors, I was going to have to find a way to perform on my own.

I chose a monologue from a play called *I Hate Hamlet* by Paul Rudnick. In the scene, the character, Andrew, is recalling his turn as Hamlet from the previous night. Explaining how he'd been so ridiculously awful throughout the majority of the show that he'd noticed a kid falling asleep in his seat. How, for one brief, shining moment, he *became* Hamlet and fully embodied the character. And then how he lost it and spent the rest of the performance wallowing in uninspired mediocrity.

I was drawn to the monologue, mostly, because I also hated Hamlet. We rehearsed primarily on our own, and I prepared to recite my monologue the way I prepared for everything else: by waiting until the last minute.

"You should have this memorized by now!" Ms. C. yelled at me. Having performed in two shows and stage-managed one, I knew exactly what phase of performance anxiety Ms. C. was in. The eye rolls began a few weeks before opening night. With less than three weeks to go, we got the "I don't have to be here if you're not going to take this seriously" lecture. The frustrated yelling usually began around dress rehearsals.

"Sorry," I said. "I do. Kind of."

This was our one and only dress rehearsal, and it was not going well.

"Then put down that paper!"

Because my character was supposed to be performing this monologue in his apartment, I'd decided I could get away with wearing jeans and a Polo. I folded the printed monologue and shoved it into my back pocket, cleared my throat, and looked down at my feet as the lights went dark.

There were three of us onstage, and I was the last to perform. I kept mentally reciting my lines while the others did their thing. The entire monologue was only 266 words long, so it was laziness that had kept me from memorizing it completely, but I figured I could fake my way through rehearsal and then get it perfect before opening night. Compared to the original thirteen colonies, this was cake.

And then the spotlight hit me. Sweat beaded on my lip and forehead immediately. Seated in the audience were a dozen or so other students who were waiting for their turns to rehearse, a few parents, and a couple of teachers who'd dropped by to watch.

I got through the monologue, stumbling in only a few places, but no one would have called what I'd done "acting." Under normal circumstances, I wouldn't have been able to see the audience, but the house lights were up, so I could see every bored face, every yawn, every minute facial tic indicating that they were wishing for me to spontaneously combust or something. Anything to get me off the stage.

"Good," Ms. C. said. "That was fine. Just do that again tomorrow night."

"Sure, okay." But if I gave the same performance on opening night, it'd be a disaster because I believed it was worse to give a boring, forgettable performance than a bad one.

I stayed up late trying to understand the character. It might have helped if I'd read the entire play the monologue had come from, but I didn't have the play, nor the time to find it, so the best I could do was try to interpret what I had. Eventually, frustrated and exhausted, I went to bed.

The next morning during breakfast, I had an epiphany.

"Why do you have Mom's flip-flops?" my stepbrother asked.

"Don't worry about it," I told him. "And don't tell anyone." I also grabbed a white T-shirt and a pair of denim shorts and stuffed them into my backpack.

All during school, my plan continued to solidify. I skipped lunch to memorize the monologue, and made sure I could recite it without stumbling, because I was going to be too focused on other aspects of my performance to worry about remembering the words.

A single night of one-acts and monologues meant no do-overs, no room for error. But if I nailed it, I'd pull off the performance of my high school career. My stomach was a jittery mess while I sat in the boys' dressing room and put on my makeup. As the only guy in the show, I had the dressing room to myself, which was lonely but also lucky. During *Dracula* and *Aladdin*, my castmates had shown me how to apply my own makeup, and I'd gotten pretty good at it. I could put on eyeliner and mascara without flinching, and I could even shade my nose to make it look a little smaller.

Kara popped her head in. "We're on in ten." She stopped and stared. "You're not even dressed! And your makeup's a little heavy, don't you think?"

"It's fine," I said. "I'm getting dressed now."

I wasn't sure until the moment I got onto that stage that I was going to go through with my plan. It was risky, which was why I hadn't told anyone, not even Ms. C. If this ended in disaster, I wanted everyone else to have full deniability.

It was time. I finished getting dressed and headed toward the stage. Sonia, a freshman who was our stage manager, gawked as I scurried past her and took my place in the dark. But she couldn't stop me or ask me what the hell I thought I was doing because the curtain was rising. It was too late to turn back now.

I kept my head down while the others gave their performances, trying to make sure I didn't draw any attention away from them, though I could already hear some giggles from the people in the front row. I wondered what they were thinking. I wondered what my parents were going to think, how other peoples' parents and my teachers were going to react.

Finally, the spotlight hit me, not with the slow light of a dawning sun, but with the flare and heat of a goddamn flamethrower.

"Last night, right from the start, I knew I was bombing."

There I was, wearing denim shorts I'd rolled up higher than midthigh, a white T-shirt with the hem pulled through the collar so that it was a midriff, and my mom's pink flip-flops. My makeup was bold, my eyes heavily lined, and my lips bright ruby red.

Everything clicked in that moment. My outfit, my makeup, my accent. I wasn't Andrew the way Paul Rudnick had likely envisioned him, but I wasn't Shaun either. I was someone unforgettable.

Feeling confident, I recited the first part of the monologue, the part where Andrew is recounting what a phony he is. How he's ridiculously out of his league playing Hamlet, and how there's a kid in the audience on the verge of falling asleep. I stood onstage with my pale stomach and pasty legs exposed. With my hip jutting out to the side and my limp-wristed hands flailing about like I was back in *Dracula* trying to catch those invisible flies.

I connected to the words in the monologue, the feeling Andrew experienced of failing hard, and his need to prove to the audience that he was capable of more than anyone believed he was. And like Andrew, I dug deep, preparing for the big moment, and poured my soul into it.

I'd dredged up my Southern accent, the one that only came out at family reunions, and cranked the volume way up. I gave the audience Dolly Parton in *Steel Magnolias*, I gave them Hollywood in *Mannequin*. I served up Tito, and I was fierce.

"'To be or not to be, girl, *that* is the question;
Whether 'tis nobler in the mind to suffer
The slings and arrows of *outrageous* fortune,

> Or to take arms against a sea of troubles
>
> And by opposing end them.'"

I didn't need a cast to play off of, I didn't need Madelyne's energy. I fed directly from the audience. Their laughter, their giggles, their mortified, open-mouthed stares. I devoured their reactions like I was at a free buffet. For 266 words, I *owned* the audience, and they owned me.

And then it was over. Applause.

Fade to black.

"I hope I didn't stretch your flip-flops."

My mom and dad didn't say anything on the drive home. Ms. C. hadn't been pleased that I'd kept my plan from her, but she hadn't yelled at me either. Everyone seemed to have liked what I'd done. Dr. Truman, my high school's debate coach, had even invited me to join the team. They had an event called dramatic interpretation that he thought I'd be perfect for.

"What was that?" my mom asked when we got inside.

"I was playing it gay," I said.

"But why?"

I shrugged. "Because the monologue was boring, and I wanted people to laugh."

"You know that's not how gay people really act, though."

"Whatever," I said. "It was just a play." I ran upstairs.

My mom was wrong. Of course that's how gay people acted. I'd modeled my performance on every fag I'd seen on TV and in movies and in life. Being gay and being a fag were one in the same to me, and all I'd done was play the stereotypes I'd absorbed.

But as I stood in the shower and scrubbed off my makeup, I felt less like I was getting out of character and more like I was slipping back into one.

COMPETITIVE BULLSHITTING

Summer 1994 to Winter 1995

THE DAY I TURNED SIXTEEN, MY MOM AND I DROVE TO THE DMV, and I took my driver's test. I passed on the first try, but I was so amped up afterward that I had to ask my mom to drive home. A couple of days after passing my test, I drove to the mall and applied for a job at the Gap so that I could have some say over the clothes I wore. Never again would I be forced to abide wearing a shirt with horizontal green and purple stripes.

After being chased around long enough by Dr. Truman, I finally agreed to join the debate team for dramatic interpretation, an event where I'd perform a scene for the judges, playing every character myself.

I tanked all of my initial competitions and began to wonder about trying some other events. I convinced Dr. Truman to let me try extemporaneous speaking, which is basically competitive bullshitting. In extemp I was given a topic on either domestic or foreign politics—something like, "Should the United States expand Medicare to include all citizens?"—and then I'd have thirty minutes to prepare a seven- to nine-minute speech using only the materials I'd brought with me. Those materials were plastic tubs full of clippings from the *New York Times*, the *Wall Street Journal*, or any newspaper or magazine I thought might be helpful. After school, those of us who competed in extemp spent hours cutting and organizing articles.

At the end of the thirty-minute prep period, I'd go to my assigned room and give the speech I'd prepared without using any notes. All facts, figures, quotes, and sources had to be memorized. It wasn't against the rules to use a single notecard, but it was frowned upon, and I'd never done so.

I excelled immediately at extemp. It exploited all of my strengths. My ability to quickly memorize massive amounts of information for a short period of time, my ability to pull together many disparate threads into a single cohesive narrative, my improvisational skills, and, if all else failed, my ability to make shit up on the fly. If the audience was beginning to look bored, I'd toss out what I'd planned to say and launch into a personal story to rope them back in.

Instead of placing consistently last like I had when I'd competed in dramatic interpretation, I scored top marks in extemp.

In debate, I'd found another family.

And then school ended. I spent that summer working at the

Gap, gaming with Alan, and attending summer school to make up the F I'd earned in geometry.

My life began to change when I started my junior year of high school. Ms. C. had handed the drama club over to a new teacher, Mr. Higgins, who looked like he played Santa Claus during the holidays; I gave up dramatic interpretation in debate and went full time into extemp; Alan was starting his senior year; and it was nearing time for me to decide what I wanted to do with the rest of my life.

"I think I want to be an actor." I was working in the fitting rooms at the Gap, folding the massive pile of clothes left behind by customers, while Wendy hid from Ginny, our manager.

"Really?" Wendy was older than me, in community college, and easy to talk to.

"I used to think I wanted to be a lawyer, and maybe I still do, but I also really want to act. Go to New York City and perform on Broadway or something."

Wendy leaned against the wall around the corner. "I wanted to be a vet. Life doesn't always work out like you want."

I shook my head. "No way. I'm not getting stuck in Florida for the rest of my life. This place is death."

The idea that I wanted to get out of Florida had been growing in my mind since I started eleventh grade. Something, I felt, was missing from my life, but I didn't have a clue what it was. I had good friends. Maddie and I still ate lunch together, and we'd added a new friend, Jane, who'd moved from Arizona, to the table. Jane was wild and exuberant where Maddie and I were both fairly subdued, but instead of clashing, Jane complemented us. And even though Alan was leaving at the end of the school year to attend college, we hung out more than ever. Alan had even tried out for and been cast as the Sheriff of Nottingham in the school's production of *Robin Hood*, while I had been cast as Robin. And I was doing well enough in debate that I'd been invited to compete in tournaments at universities like Harvard, Wake Forest, and Emory.

My life at home had even mellowed some. I was too busy to be mad at my mom all the time, and she'd begun giving me some much needed space. As a result, we rarely fought anymore.

Despite that, I still felt wrong, somehow. One moment I'd be fine and the next I'd be overwhelmed with *feelings*. Not one particular feeling—all of them at once. It was like every person I came into contact with was plugging themselves into me, and occasionally I'd overload and short out. Sometimes that meant disappearing for a couple of days, sometimes that meant sitting on the floor of my bedroom crying, sometimes it meant screaming down I-95 in my car, blasting Smashing Pumpkins and yelling until my throat felt like I'd swallowed a cactus.

If I'd had to point to one thing that was wrong with my life, I would have pointed at me, but I'd have been damned if I'd been able to explain why.

SO. MANY. DICKS.

March 1995

LESS THAN A YEAR AFTER TAKING THE JOB AT THE GAP, Madelyne convinced me to come work with her at Waldenbooks. We got a great discount, the managers were cool, I wouldn't have to handle clothes from fitting rooms anymore, and I got to work with my best friend. What could go wrong?

The job was, for the most part, not terrible, though I came to loathe shelving books. The addition of one new book required snaking entire shelves around to make it fit. I spent hours and hours sticking books back in shelves and then glowering at the customers who inevitably came along and ruined all my effort. Shelving books in a bookstore is a ridiculously Sisyphean task that's probably also used as a punishment in one of the outer rings of hell.

The other part of the job I hated was peddling the reward cards.

"I just renewed someone into 2000," Madelyne said. She was grinning because she was good at the game. We were required to sell a certain ratio of reward cards to transactions, and since renewals counted, the best way to keep our numbers up was to renew someone ahead of time.

"What if Waldenbooks isn't around in 2000?" I asked.

Madelyne shrugged. "It's a bookstore. Where's it going to go?"

"Yeah. You're probably right."

It was a slow day, and we were hanging out behind the registers. The cash wrap stood on a platform, and it was a mess of supplies, special orders, books that needed to be put away, and pornographic magazines. The basics: *Playboy*, *Hustler*, *Playgirl*. I'd worked there a couple of months and had never sold one.

"Any plans this weekend?" Maddie asked.

"Gaming with Alan and the gang."

"Oh. Have fun!" She headed onto the floor to shelve books, leaving me at the cash wrap alone.

I felt bad not inviting her, but Alan had a crush on her, and that was some drama I didn't want to deal with. Not only did I worry about the fallout of them dating and breaking up and forcing me to choose between them, but as I've already said: Alan was a creep when it came to girls, and I didn't want to expose Maddie to his "nice guy" behavior. It might have been easier if I'd told her why I didn't want them to go out, but my loyalty to Alan kept me from being honest with Maddie about his shortcomings.

After Maddie took off, I started cleaning around the cash

wrap, and the porn mags caught my eye. I'd downloaded some porn from local bulletin boards (called BBSs), which were kind of like websites that you had to dial into individually, but it took ten minutes to download a single pixelated picture, and none of them had done much for me. But the *Playgirl* was something I hadn't seen before. Maddie was on the other side of the store, obscured but for the top of her red hair by the shelves, so I plucked the *Playgirl* from the slot to take a peek. A man with muscles, a smooth chest, and a wide, suggestive smile beamed at me from the glossy cover. I wasn't sure what he was suggesting, but I was definitely curious to find out.

Huh. I wonder what he looks like naked.

Strangely, I was sixteen and I'd never really seen another man naked before. I'd escaped the horrors of being forced to shower in front of my peers during both middle and high school. In middle school we didn't even have locker rooms, so after PE we had to change back into our uniforms and quietly stew in our own sweat for the rest of the day. In high school, I'd continued the tradition of not showering, and no one bothered me about it.

There was a picture of a man's naked crotch in the sex ed book my mom had stealthily left on my bookshelf when I was ten, but the book had been written in the 1970s and the crotch was 90 percent pubic hair and looked like a mole rat hiding in a Brillo pad. It was neither sexual nor educational.

Of course, I'd seen myself naked. Hair was growing where it was supposed to and I had all the requisite parts, but I had no way of knowing if the parts were deformed or normal, though I assumed the worst.

Most of the time, I didn't feel normal. Too skinny, too awkward. Every time I got an erection during class, I firmly believed at least half the of people around me knew, like they had finely tuned boner detectors that went off every time I did. Compared to some of the guys on the football team, I still felt like a little boy. I still looked like a little boy.

But I was a man, right? I should know what men looked like naked, right? It was only normal for me to want to know what other men look like naked so that I could compare myself to them. Right?

Right!

I needed that *Playgirl*.

But there was no way in hell I was going to buy it. Which meant I was going to have to steal it.

I couldn't do it that night, though. So I waited. It was a couple of weeks before the right opportunity presented itself. I was closing alone with Kim. Each time I rang up a customer, I felt the man on the cover of the magazine judging me. It didn't help that he was wearing a police uniform and kept telling me I should just cough up the cash and buy him. But I didn't. I couldn't.

When we finally closed for the night, I counted my register as quickly as possible. Then, when Kim took the money into the back to put it in the safe, I raced behind the register, grabbed the *Playgirl*, and stuffed it down the front of my pants.

My heart was trembling. Sweat broke out on my forehead and upper lip. What if Kim had X-ray vision? What if she saw the magazine through my shirt? What would she think of me stealing a *Playgirl*?

It was the longest closing shift of my life. Each time I moved, I felt the magazine squirming around in my pants, and I wondered if Kim heard the plastic wrapping around it crinkle.

Finally, we finished and left. We walked to our cars. I climbed into my Mustang and turned on the engine. Then I waited. I watched Kim get to her car. Fumble with her keys. Sit in the seat doing whatever she was doing. It felt like an hour passed before she finally put her car in drive and took off. The moment she did, I yanked the *Playgirl* out from the front of my pants and set it on the seat beside me.

I wanted to open it immediately. But I didn't. I had to get home.

My mom was still up, sitting on the couch when I walked in. I had my backpack slung over my shoulder and the magazine inside, but I felt like there was a sign over my head announcing that not only was I a thief, but that I was a pervert in possession of a magazine full of naked men.

I raced up the stairs to my bedroom, locked the doors, and waited. I waited for my stepbrothers to go to bed. I waited for my parents to go to bed. I waited until everyone in the house was asleep and snoring so that there wasn't even a sliver of a chance that one of them might see my light on and check to see what I was doing. And only when I was certain that no one would disturb me did I pull out the magazine and tear off the plastic wrap.

Inside were men. And they were naked. Like, totally naked. It was an oasis and I hadn't even realized I was thirsty.

I turned each page slowly and carefully with my thumb and first finger like I was handling the *Book of Kells*, and there were so many different types of men. Some were beefy and muscular, others were lean and toned. There were men with hairy chests and men who were smooth and oiled. There were pretty men and rugged men and men whose smiles leaped off the page.

And then there were the dicks.

So. Many. Dicks.

I had no idea penises could look so different. The photo spread of the cop started off with him wearing a policeman's uniform but ended with him naked like everyone else. His dick was curved like a banana, which was something I didn't know was possible. Before I'd paged through the entire magazine, I took off my clothes and stood in front of the mirror in my bathroom. I compared myself to one of the men—a guy with wavy blond hair. I looked nothing like him. Not even close. Not from the waist up and certainly not from the waist down.

Playgirl had answered my question. I was definitely abnormal.

I closed the magazine and hid it inside a shoebox at the top of my closet under a stack of books. My mother was nosy and often went through my things, but she wasn't tall enough to reach the top shelf, so my secret was safe.

Stealing the magazine had been reckless, and I swore I was

going to throw it out at the first opportunity. Spoiler alert: I didn't get rid of it.

A couple of nights later, I dug it out of my closet. I paged through it, picking up where I'd left off. I reached a section of photos of men submitted by their wives or girlfriends. Average men; not models. None of them looked like me either. They weren't as muscular or as fit as the models, but they were still more muscular and more fit than me. They were still better than me.

Each night for weeks, I took the *Playgirl* out after everyone had gone to bed, and I stared at the men. I wondered how my life would change if I looked like one of them—if I would find someone I cared about and who cared about me and if I'd finally feel the way about a girl I was supposed to—knowing that I didn't look like those men and never would. Knowing that I was ugly. Knowing that the only way I would ever find someone who cared about me was to look like one of the men in the magazine.

And each night, after I'd looked at the magazine and then stared at myself naked in the mirror, I returned it to my closet and swore never to look at it again.

A month after I stole the magazine, a man who worked for the Waldenbooks corporate office came to the store and met with Kim in the stockroom. Maddie and Anna were working when I arrived, and they were whispering about the man.

"Some Dungeons & Dragons art book is missing," Anna said. "It cost, like, a hundred and fifty bucks."

I believed that. The cost, not that it was missing. Me and Alan and Bill loved going over the artwork in some of the modules, especially the stuff by Tony DiTerlizzi.

Maddie and Anna were both looking at me. "What?"

"Do you know anything?" Maddie asked.

"No."

I'm not sure if she believed me. I never had the courage to ask. For the record, I didn't steal anything from Waldenbooks other than the *Playgirl*.

An hour later I was called into the office. The man's name was Oscar. He was older than me but younger than my mom. He seemed okay. He told me to sit at the desk while he perched on a stool beside me.

"Do you know why I'm here?"

I shook my head, even though I was pretty sure he knew that the gossip had gotten around to me by now.

Oscar explained that an expensive book had gone missing, that he was from Loss Prevention and his job was to find it. He asked me a lot of questions about gift cards and whether I'd ever rung up another employee without my manager signing off on it. I didn't know anything about the D&D art book and I'd never done anything wrong at the register.

But I'd stolen the *Playgirl*. And I was sure Oscar knew.

"There are cameras in the store," he said. "Did you know that, Shaun?"

I couldn't speak, so I shook my head.

"We've suspected problems in this store for a while, so we had tiny cameras inserted through the ceiling tiles. I've seen everything that's happened in this store for the last couple of months." Oscar paused. "Additionally, I've had my own agents posing as customers."

Quietly, I said, "Seriously?" My stomach was hurting and I felt like I was going to puke and my ears were hot and I was sure that I was sweating through my black Polo shirt. I'd gone through a bit of a klepto phase when I was in elementary school. Mostly pens. I was obsessed with stealing pens. I once hid under my desk in the third grade at the end of the day, waited for my teacher to leave, and then ransacked her desk for interesting pens. I was weird. Whatever. I grew out of it. But I'd never stolen anything of value. I'd never stolen anything I was so terrified of being caught in possession of.

Oscar nodded. "Look, Shaun. We already know everything, but you'll save yourself some trouble if I hear it from you. Okay?"

"A magazine," I said.

"What?"

"I took a magazine."

Oscar pursed his lips. "What magazine?"

"One of the ones behind the counter."

"The *Playboy*?"

I shook my head. I looked at my shoes because there was no way I could look him in the eyes.

"If you want me to help you, I need you to tell me what you stole."

"*Playgirl*."

"What?"

"A *Playgirl*," I said louder. A shiver tore through me and my eyes watered and I started heaving and crying and snot was running out of my nose. I was so ashamed. He obviously now thought I was a faggot. That I was disgusting and had AIDS, and he couldn't wait to get out of the same room as me.

Oscar didn't say anything for a few minutes. He handed me a tissue and sat across from me in his blue button-down shirt and khaki pants and watched me with his hands on his thighs.

"Is that the only thing you took without paying, Shaun?" His voice was softer now, more sympathetic.

Through a nose full of snot, I said, "Do you really think I'd admit to that but not the D&D book?"

"No, I don't think you would." He paused and then said, "I've got a cousin who's gay—"

"I'm not gay!"

Oscar held up his hands. "I'm not saying you are."

I grabbed a couple more tissues and blew my nose. When I'd composed myself, Oscar slid a legal pad and pen in front of me.

"I need you to write down what you took and when. Just keep it simple, but list everything like you told me."

The color drained from my face, and I shook my head. "Do I have to?"

"Don't worry," he said. "This, what you told me, stays between you and me. It'll have to go in your company record, but I won't tell your manager or coworkers, so they'll never have to know."

"Are you sure?"

Oscar clapped his hand on my shoulder. "I promise." He

stood. "I'll give you some time to write." And then he left the office.

It took me twenty minutes to write my version of what I'd done, though I wasn't sure why I needed to since they obviously had the whole thing on video. Unless that had been a lie to get me to confess. Yeah. It had most likely been a lie, and I'd fallen for it. I started crying again. Tears smudged the ink and I had to start over.

Oscar returned as I was finishing up.

"All done?"

I nodded.

"You know this means we're going to have to fire you, right?"

"I figured." Not that I would have stayed anyway. I couldn't bear to continue working at Waldenbooks thinking at any time someone might find out what I'd done.

"All right then." Oscar shook my hand when I stood, and there was something in his eyes. Something like regret. But before he opened the door, he rested his hand on my back and said, "Hey, you're going to be okay."

I wish I could've believed him, but it made me feel a little better knowing that even if it wasn't true, he wanted it to be.

VOCABULARY LESSON, PART 2

March 1995

I WASN'T GAY. I *COULDN'T* BE GAY. BEING GAY, BEING A fag, was a role I'd played for laughs. Because that's all the life of a gay person was good for. There was no future in being gay. There was no future in it for me.

I wanted to be a lawyer or an actor or maybe even a journalist. I'd taken a staff writer position on my school's newspaper, and I'd already gotten in trouble with the principal for writing an article exposing the number of teachers at the school who weren't properly certified. So maybe I had a future in journalism. I was going to go to college, get a degree, marry a girl like Madelyne or Leigh or Bella—a friend from drama and debate who'd turned me on to Belly and the Smashing Pumpkins. I was going to buy a house and have some kids and live the American Fucking Dream.

None of which was possible for a fag.

Don't believe me? Here's what I knew:

In the movie *Philadelphia*, which came out in 1993, Tom Hanks played a lawyer dying of AIDS, represented in a wrongful termination lawsuit by a character played by Denzel Washington, who was revolted by the mere idea of being near a gay man with AIDS. We were meant to sympathize with Washington's character, and to cheer when, by the end, he inched toward seeing his client, one individual, as an actual human being. But that didn't change the number of people who walked into the movie believing that gay men weren't people to begin with.

On February 28, 1994, the Clinton administration instituted the Department of Defense Directive 1304.26, otherwise known as "Don't ask, don't tell," which allowed homosexual soldiers to continue serving in the military so long as they kept their sexuality hidden.

On March 6, 1995, Scott Amedure taped an episode of *The Jenny Jones Show* on which he told his friend Jonathan Schmitz that he was gay and attracted to him. Three days after the taping of the episode, Schmitz shot and killed Amedure.

Those events were my real vocabulary lesson.

Movies like *Mannequin* defined gay men as flamboyant comedic reliefs whose sole purpose was to help satisfy the needs of straight people. Movies like *Philadelphia* defined fags as something less than human. Not as victims of AIDS but as a group that deserved it. The United States government defined being gay as something so awful, so shameful, that gay men and women had to hide for fear of having their lives ruined. The lack of sympathetic coverage surrounding the death of Scott Amedure defined fags as a group of people so worthless that they didn't even deserve to live. Gay people, especially gay men, were so often portrayed as promiscuous sexual deviants and drug abusers that, even in spite of my own limited personal experience, it's how I saw them too.

By society's definition, any gay man was going to live a lonely life of constant lies, die of AIDS, become the victim of someone who didn't even see him as a human being, or worse. There was no future to being gay.

Therefore, I couldn't be gay. I had a future. I'd spent a lifetime building the vision of who I wanted to be, and that person was not a fag.

HIDDEN TRUTH

Summer 1995

THE SUMMER AFTER I TURNED TEN, MY MOM AND DAD sent me and my younger stepbrother to stay with our aunt and uncle in Philadelphia.

Just to clarify, most of the time when I refer to "dad," I'm talking about my stepdad. He and my mom married right before I turned ten, and I only saw my biological father every other weekend. I don't talk about him in this memoir because, for good or ill, he didn't play a role in this part of my story.

Moving on.

At my aunt and uncle's house, my uncle had his own bathroom, complete with a television, a phone, and a stack of *Playboy* magazines that were casually hidden under a couple of other magazines. The first time I found them, I was intrigued, but after flipping through the pages for a couple of minutes, I returned the magazine to where I'd found it and had no desire to look at it again.

During the summer of 1995, the Internet was growing into . . . *something*. None of us were sure what it might become, but we were all excited to be in on the ground floor. I was one of the few people I knew who had his own e-mail account. I also built my first website over that summer, though it was a monstrosity of terrible graphics and badly written HTML. I also became aware that it was possible to find porn on the Internet but, much like with my uncle's magazines, I had no interest in downloading pictures of naked women.

But I did occasionally sneak out the *Playgirl* I'd stolen and flip through its pages.

I'd gone with the debate team to a tournament held in Atlanta the previous school year. While we were there, we visited the Underground mall in Five Points. There was a kiosk selling these Magic Eye books filled with abstract pictures from which, if you looked just the right way, a 3-D image would emerge. While everyone else was buying candy and CDs, I became obsessed with those Magic Eye pictures. I'd stare at one, confused and frustrated until suddenly the picture emerged. Finally seeing the 3-D picture resolve felt like dunking my head in a cool pool on the hottest summer's day. It was like everything slid into place and I was seeing the world the way it ought to be.

Which is how looking at the naked men in my *Playgirl* felt. I didn't jerk off to them, but when the world stopped making sense and I couldn't see how anything was worth living for, I'd pull the *Playgirl* from the top corner of my closet, peel back the cover, and the world just felt right.

But I didn't know why, and I did everything in my power to avoid thinking about it.

Alan graduated high school and was bound for college. Our gaming group took on a manic vibe that summer because Chris, Bill, and Greg had all graduated too. While I knew I was going to miss our weekly campaigns, none of which we ever actually seemed to finish, I was going to miss Alan's friendship most.

I'd made sure to spend as much time as I could hanging out with Alan when I wasn't at the Gap. I'd begged Ginny for my job back, though I'd left out that I'd been fired from Waldenbooks and what I'd been fired for, and she'd set me right to work folding denim.

Alan and I tinkered with computers, we played Magic: The Gathering, we went to movies, we watched movies at his place, we shared short stories we'd written. We were even working on our own RPG based off of a series of fantasy books we both loved.

We were in Alan's car, an older Cadillac that he was immensely proud of, on our way to the mall. He was blasting Live, one of the many rock bands Alan loved that I endured when he drove. Alan might have had great taste in books and computer games, but he had awful taste in music.

"So what's the deal with you and Bella?" Alan asked.

Bella and I had grown close during junior year, not only because she'd played Maid Marian to my Robin in *Robin Hood*, but also because we'd gone on all the same debate trips together. Unlike Alan, she had excellent taste in music.

I shrugged. "She's kind of hung up on her ex-boyfriend, but we've been e-mailing a lot."

"You want some advice?"

I didn't, but I couldn't say so without hurting Alan's feelings. "Sure."

"Try not to care. Take this as easy as it comes. Call her on occasion, but pretend you aren't interested."

"Honestly, I don't even know if I am."

"C'mon, man! You can't fool me!" Alan glanced at me as he drove. "You've been talking about this girl for a year."

Alan wasn't wrong. Bella and I spent a lot of time together—not as much as Maddie and I did—and there was a density to our conversations. There was no small talk, no discussion of inconsequential things. We talked in layers, cramming ten conversations into the space of one.

"Besides, she's probably not even interested in me like that."

"A girl doesn't spend that much time with a guy if she isn't interested."

"But she's hung up on her ex."

"Or," Alan said, "she wants you to think that so that it'll make you jealous." He slapped the steering wheel and laughed. "She's messing with you, man! Girls play games, it's what they do. If you want to win, you've got to make your own move instead of waiting for her to do it."

Seeing as Alan had graduated high school without having a girlfriend, I wasn't sure how much his advice was worth. Many of the guys I knew thought of women the way Alan did. That men and women could never be "just friends," that women played games with men, that they said one thing and meant another. But that's not how my mom raised me to think. And my friendship with Madelyne certainly defied Alan's "wisdom."

"So you ready for college?"

"I can't wait to get out of here," Alan said. "To finally get away from the idiocy of high school."

"I bet."

"Don't look so glum! You've only got one year left, and then you'll be out too."

"It's the last year I'm worried about."

"Have you decided where you're applying to?"

"I'm thinking NYU," I said. "For acting."

Alan whistled. "Whoa. The big city, huh?"

"I don't know."

"I hope you're not giving up on writing."

Alan and I had both experienced some rejection after submitting stories we'd written to different fantasy magazines, and I'd been somewhat disillusioned with the creative writing class I'd taken junior year. "Not giving up, no. But I don't think it's something I can really make a living doing."

"You're as good a writer as you are an actor," Alan said.

He probably meant to imply that my writing was at the same high level I believed my acting was, but instead what I heard was him say that my acting was as awful as my writing.

"I'm just not sure about anything," I said.

Alan clapped me on the shoulder. "Buck up, Shaun. You'll get into NYU and become some hotshot movie star who won't have time for his friends. You'll get rich, you'll get famous, and you'll get the girl. Trust me.

"Now, let's talk about how you're going to handle Bella."

But no amount of discussing Bella, or any other girl, could ease the feeling that I was missing something. That there was some hidden truth lurking at the edge of my sight, and that if I could look at my life the right way, it would emerge and change everything. After stealing a magazine filled with naked men, it might seem implausible that I hadn't at least considered the possibility that I was gay, but the idea simply hadn't occurred to me. In my mind, I had better odds of discovering latent magical abilities than I did of being gay.

Ever hear of the allegory of the cave? No? Well, here's the short version. Google the long version later. It's worth it.

A group of people are chained in a cave. They were born that way, grew up that way, and have never known any other existence. They can only face forward. On the wall in front of them are shadows moving back and forth. The shadows are cast by people walking through the cave, but the prisoners don't know that. They think the shadows are real beings. One of the prisoners escapes the chains, sees that the shadows aren't actually real and that there's more to their lives than just what's in front of them. But when the escapee tells the others, they don't believe him because they still can't turn their heads. Their reality is shaped entirely by what they can see. Get it?

At that point in my life, it wouldn't have mattered if my future self had appeared in front of me and told me I was gay, because all I could see were the shadows on the wall.

PART 2

I WROTE MY WAY OUT

DEPRESSION SCREAMS

Fall 1995

SUMMER ENDED. I LET MY HAIR GROW LONG, DOWN PAST my eyes. With the fashion freedom my job at the Gap gave me, I chose to wear sandals with a rotating array of argyle socks. Alan moved away to attend college, and though we kept in touch through e-mail, I felt like I'd lost my best friend. Thankfully, my friendship with Madelyne grew to fill its place.

With a mixture of relief, trepidation, and a sense of "Can we just get this over with already?" I began my senior year of high school.

When I envisioned my senior year, I imagined I'd sleep through most of my classes, go to parties with my friends, find a girlfriend and take her to prom, kick ass in debate, land the lead in whatever shows Mr. Higgins had planned for us to perform, audition and get into NYU, and leave high school behind on a wave of happy memories.

I definitely slept through a lot of my classes, but I wasn't happy.

August 14, 1995, 12:30 a.m.
I am beginning to get scared that I am going to end up alone.

August 23, 1995, 10:25 p.m.
I think that this is going to be a shitty year.

August 27, 1995, 10 p.m.
I just think that I will not have many happy memories of this year :(

September 12, 1995, 9:35 p.m.
Things should be going better than they are and I really don't know how to fix them.

September 22, 1995, 11:10 p.m.
I don't really know why I am writing tonight other than I have nearly slit my wrists a few times in the last few days. I don't know why, I am not getting beat, I am not in trouble with the law or anything, it's just that for some reason I am in this depression from which I am finding it

very difficult to escape. I just can't seem to make my self commit to any action, it is like I have no passion or fire. I am really scared.

September 28, 1995, 10:20 p.m.
Where is that exacto Knife.

November 5, 1995, 9:50 p.m.
I swear, that had I been near a knife I would probably be dead.

November 25, 1995, 11:45 p.m.
I wonder if it [love] is something that I am capable of?

Depression speaks. It screams. It's not like actually hearing voices. I know the voice in my head isn't real and I know that it's lying, but knowing those things doesn't make it go away. I still hear it, and it dredges up my worst fears and yells them at me until it drowns out everything else. I eventually learned how to mute that voice, but back then I had no idea how to lower the volume.

No matter what I accomplished, no matter how hard I worked, I felt like a failure. Nothing I did seemed good enough. I felt ugly, I felt stupid, I felt talentless. And those were the good days. On the bad days I prayed for the pain to stop. On the worst days I'd drive fast and reckless, hoping to spin out and crash and die.

I had a vision of who I wanted to be in the future, of the person I wanted to become, but I knew something was wrong, and that threw my vision of the future into doubt. Which I might have been able to work through because the future is constantly changing. *We're* constantly changing. We adapt. But instead, depression slithered into that space where my future self should have been and whispered, *Let me show you how fucked up your future's really gonna be.*

MOODY LITTLE BITCH

November 1995

"HEY, COME ON AND GO FOR A RIDE WITH ME." MY BROTHER stood by the garage door with his hands in his pockets. It was near Thanksgiving, and I'd just gotten home from the Gap, where I'd spent eight hours folding jeans and trying to convince strangers that they absolutely *had* to have a pair. No, three pairs. Everyone needs at least *three* pairs of jeans. As a result, I wasn't in the mood to get into a car with Ryan, who was an objectively terrible driver.

"Come on," he said, as if he could read my thoughts. "Just run up to the store with me."

He was going to keep at me until I agreed, so it seemed easier to get it over with. Ryan drove a little blue Suzuki Samurai with brakes so badly in need of being replaced that the whole car shuddered when he pumped them. He backed out of the cul-de-sac and headed toward the beach.

I hadn't really seen Ryan in a while because he'd been off at college, and we hadn't had much of a relationship before that either. He'd gone to live with our biological father when he was fourteen, so I'd only seen him on the weekends. With five years separating us, and living in different houses and going to different schools, we'd drifted apart. I hardly knew my brother, and I'd gotten so busy with my own life that, I'm ashamed to say, I didn't think about him often.

"How have you been?"

I shrugged. "School, work. You know how it goes."

"It's your senior year. You don't seem too excited."

"I'm excited." I plastered on a Joker grin and pointed at it. "See. Super excited."

Ryan and I may not have known the details of each other's lives, but he still knew me well enough to recognize that I was lying. "Is everything okay? School problems? Girl problems? You can tell me, you know?"

"I'm fine."

"You sure? Mom says you've been a moody little bitch lately."

"I said I'm fine!"

"Calm down," he said. "I'm just . . . forget it."

There was something in his voice, in the way he was looking at me. He was really trying, really being serious. After all these years, he wanted to be my brother. It was sweet, but a few years too late. I didn't need him. I didn't need *anyone*. Whatever my problems were, I could handle them on my own.

"I really am fine," I said. "Seriously."

Ryan paused and frowned like he didn't believe me. "So Mom says you're going to NYU."

"I'm applying," I said. "My audition's in a couple of weeks. Mom got us tickets to see *Miss Saigon* and *Cats*."

"Well, she has always wanted to see *Cats*."

"Right?"

"Remember when she took us to see *Little Shop of Horrors*?"

It was the same trip where I'd read *The Devil's Cat* on the train. We'd gone to Washington, DC, Philadelphia, Boston, and New York. While we were in New York, we saw *Little Shop* with the original off-Broadway cast and even got to meet them.

"I remember having to hang your nasty-ass sneakers out the window because they smelled so bad."

Ryan laughed. "That was a fun trip."

"It was."

"You're gonna do all right in New York," he said. "Just remember to be yourself."

We got to the store and picked up the stuff Dad had forgotten when Mom had sent him earlier. Publix was a madhouse, with everyone fighting for the last jar of gravy and the last can of cranberry sauce. I was glad I didn't have to work there anymore, though the Gap wasn't much better.

Ryan stopped along the beach road on the way back to the house. "I have something I want to tell you, and I don't want you to be upset."

"Why would I be upset?"

He was trembling. I couldn't remember the last time I'd seen him so nervous. My brother didn't get nervous about anything, but he was terrified by how I was going to react to what he wanted to tell me.

"I'm gay."

"Oh."

"You know what that means, right?"

"I own a dictionary," I said.

"I guess I've known for a while, but—"

"Why are you telling me?"

I'm certain that Ryan had played out how the conversation would go between us a thousand times in his mind, but he hadn't imagined this. That I wouldn't care. That I was so far removed from his life that this news, this monumental event in *his* life, meant nothing to me.

It's not that I didn't care, it's that I hardly knew my brother. I didn't know how huge this was to him. I didn't understand how vulnerable he'd made himself by telling me. I didn't realize he needed at least one person in our screwed-up family to understand and tell him that he was still loved and still the same person. All I saw was that my brother had shown up out of the blue and told me something very personal about himself after having spent the last few years showing exactly zero interest in my life. I didn't know how to react, so I reacted like an asshole.

"I wanted you to know," he said.

"Cool."

"That's it?"

"You're not gonna start wearing dresses and shit, are you?"

"I hadn't planned on it."

"I don't hate you or anything, if that's what you think."

Ryan sighed. "I never thought you did. I was just hoping we could be friends, I guess."

This was not how I'd planned to spend my evening, and the annoyance crept into my voice. "We don't have anything in common. You've been off doing your thing since high school. You didn't have time for me then, why's it different now?"

His shoulders fell. "You're right, forget it. Let's head home."

I think Ryan expected that telling me the truth would bring us closer together, but in my mind it pushed us further apart. I loved my brother so much, and I didn't hate him for being gay, but after he came out to me, I assumed that he was going to wind up the way I believed every gay man wound up. Lonely, sick, addicted to drugs, or dead.

THE AMERICAN DREAM

December 1995

I'D APPLIED TO NYU FOR EARLY DECISION, AND RECEIVED an audition and interview date of Monday, December 4, 1995, at 10 a.m.

My mom's philosophy when it came to me was best described as cautious encouragement. She'd been thrilled when I'd said I'd wanted to be a lawyer, and she'd been equally thrilled when I'd declared I wanted to attend NYU to become an actor, but she'd also made certain to let me know that acting was a difficult career path and I should have a backup plan. NYU might not accept me, we might not get the financial aid I'd need to pay for it, I might hate acting professionally and change my mind about going. There were a million possibilities, and she wanted me to be prepared for all of them.

But I didn't have a backup. I had to get into NYU. I *needed* to get in. I felt like my future and my life depended on it, though I couldn't explain why. It was like seeing the Magic Eye pictures and looking at the naked men in my *Playgirl*. NYU just felt *right*.

Acting was, for me, less about the mask I got to wear when I stepped onstage to inhabit a new role, and more about the masks I *didn't* have to wear. I was *not* a good actor, but I didn't know that because I was good compared to the other actors at my high school, and I thought if I worked hard enough, I could be even better.

My *I Hate Hamlet* monologue had been a success, and I'd earned applause for my turn as Robin in *Robin Hood*, though not necessarily for the reasons one might hope.

I'd been cast as Robin, Alan as the Sheriff of Nottingham, and Bella had played Maid Marian. There was a pivotal scene in the play where the Sheriff captured Marian and used her to lure Robin out so that he could fight, defeat, and capture him. Mr. Higgins had erected a large three-foot-tall platform on the stage for Marian to stand atop of. After the Sheriff paraded Marian around, I was to run in from the wings, leap onto the platform, and proudly declare, "Never fear, Robin's here!" After which, the Sheriff would reveal himself, and we would fight.

Alan and I spent hours upon hours of our own free time practicing the fight with real foils, and we were ridiculously proud of our choreography.

During every rehearsal, the scene went brilliantly. Leap, line, fight. Leap, line, fight. No mishaps at all. Not even during dress rehearsals when I was wearing little black slippers instead of my usual socks and sandals.

But on opening night, I showed up to the theater to find that Mr. Higgins had come up with the brilliant idea to surround the platform with potted plants to make it look more like a forest. It looked like the gardening department at Home Depot, but I wasn't going to tell him that, and I didn't think it would be a problem.

The play began. Everything was going well. I robbed the rich and gave to the poor. The Sheriff twirled his mustache, Maid Marian was captured. Finally, the moment arrived.

I stood in the wings. I took a deep breath. And then I raced across the stage, leaped through the air, and landed on the platform. Only, this time, I also landed on the leaves of one of the new plants. My feet flew out from under me. I hung in the air for what felt like an eternity, and then I slammed down on my back onto the platform and hit my head.

The audience fell completely silent. Bella was looking down at me. My head was throbbing, my ears were ringing, and everything hurt. And then I opened my mouth and said:

"Never fear, Robin's here!"

The audience laughed, Bella helped me up, Alan and I fought, and the show went on. Not that I actually remember any of it.

When the curtain finally closed, Mr. Higgins asked me if I needed to go to the hospital, but I told him I was fine. He then asked if I could slip and fall during every performance.

I politely declined.

Instead of seeing that as a reason why I *wasn't* a good actor, I used it as an example of why I was. I might have had a concussion, but I carried the show to the end. Nothing was going to deter me, not a head injury, not money, not doubt. NYU was my future, and nothing else mattered.

My mom, my dad, and I crowded into our nosebleed seats in the theater for *Miss Saigon*. I knew little about the show other than that it revolved around the Vietnam War. From the moment the curtain opened, I was enthralled. The way the actors owned the stage, the way their voices soared all the way up to where I was sitting like they were singing just for me, the costumes, the dancing. They inspired me. No, I didn't know how to dance, but I could learn, damn it. I *would* learn. I was going to get into NYU and study harder than I'd ever studied in my life, and then one day I was going to be on that stage. Some kid from Florida or Texas or North Dakota with dreams of escape was going to be watching me and deciding *their* future.

Seeing *Miss Saigon* that night was one of the most profound experiences of my life. The music and the songs lifted me up and drove away depression's whispers for a while. I could do anything, I could be anyone! The world belonged to me. At least for that night.

Sunday we toured the NYU campus, which was spread across the city, checked out the dorms, and then it was Monday at 10 a.m.

I was brought to a small, dark room in which a woman was seated and awaiting my arrival. I remember that she had a sympathetic face.

First, she had me perform my monologue. I actually have no

idea what monologue I performed, except that it wasn't *I Hate Hamlet*. I'm sure it was some uninspired choice from one of the monologue books Mr. Higgins kept in his classroom. Regardless, I thought it went well, and I settled down in a seat across from my interviewer, eager to continue.

I'd done some research and preparation for this part. The Tisch School of the Arts focused on different methods of acting, and I'd done my homework and was confident I understood the various styles well enough to discuss them or answer any questions thrown at me. I believed I was a method actor, a technique pioneered by Konstantin Stanislavski, which in retrospect was ironic given how little I understood myself.

I wasn't afraid of the interview, because not only did adults usually like me, but all those debate tournaments had finely honed my ability to bullshit my way through anything. Which is what I was doing well until the interviewer asked, "Who's your favorite actor?" At which point, I froze.

The question should have been an easy one, right? There were so many people I could have chosen from, but my brain went completely and totally blank. Flop sweat spread across my back and under my arms. How could I not think of a single name?

Except a name did pop into my head, and I blurted it out because any name was better than silence.

"Patrick Stewart," I said. And proceeded to launch into a desperate monologue describing the reasons why Patrick Stewart was my favorite actor. Never mind that the *only* program I knew him from was *Star Trek: The Next Generation*. I rhapsodized about the brilliance of his performance in the episode "Darmok," spent a good five minutes discussing the nuances of his character choices in "The Inner Light," made a list of every episode in which he'd shown range beyond that of any other Starfleet captain, and even did a quick compare and contrast between Stewart and William Shatner.

The interviewer listened patiently and didn't interrupt, though it might have been better for both of us if she had, and when I was done, she smiled and said some nice things about Patrick Stewart, and then asked, "But do you have any favorite *stage* actors?"

Oh, come on!

There's no way she didn't smell the fear drenching my shirt as I sat across from her and struggled to recall one name. I'd just seen *Miss Saigon*, and all I had to do was remember the names of any of the performers, any one would do, but I couldn't. The interviewer likely knew the name of every great thespian who'd ever lived, and there was no way I could make up one and hope she'd believe it was someone she'd never heard of.

So I smiled and shrugged and said, "Patrick Stewart?"

December 5, 1995
Well, everything went great. Based on the way the woman acted after my audition, I would say that she is going to recommend my acceptance.

CHINA

January 1996

MY LIFE AFTER I GOT HOME FROM NEW YORK REVOLVED around waiting for that letter. Waiting for someone on the other end of the country to decide whether or not I deserved to escape my town and my life and start again new. Waiting for my dreams to come true or for my nightmare to burst out of my head and consume reality.

I skipped so many classes during the first half of the school year that I was in danger of not graduating, and I sleepwalked through the classes I *did* attend. The only class I stuck around and stayed awake for was creative writing. I had a green Marvin the Martian notebook that I carried with me everywhere and filled with journal entries and poems. I'd been writing since third grade. I wrote fan fiction before the Internet existed, adding sequels to movies like *The Lost Boys* and *Adventures in*

Babysitting, I wrote short stories inspired by the fantasy novels I loved to read, and I even wrote an original speech about political correctness that I performed and won second place with in a state-level debate tournament. But I didn't consider myself a writer. I didn't consider writing to be a thing I could do. I didn't see a future where I spent my days sitting at a desk making up stories for a living.

For a couple of months, we had a student teacher named Michelle, a young woman close to graduating with a degree in education who came up with the lesson plans and taught us and graded our stories while Mrs. McCoy sat in the corner and pretended to care.

Michelle stood at the front of the classroom, leaning against the desk when I trudged in. "Hey, Shaun. We missed you Friday."

"Debate tournament," I said.

"Did you win?"

My desk was in the front row against the wall, and I tossed my notebook down before sitting. "I did okay."

Michelle nodded. She wore plastic glasses and long, flowing skirts that reminded me of the ones Natalie Merchant had worn when I'd seen her in concert a couple of months earlier. "We read your story."

I ducked my head, looking anywhere but at Michelle. "Oh."

"There were a lot of strong reactions to it."

For the Sole Sake of Living was the first nonfantasy story I'd ever written. It was about an older brother on trial for murdering his younger brother, who was slowly dying of a terminal illness.

"Sorry. I didn't mean—"

"That's a good thing," she said. "Every writer learns that inspiring powerful emotions, be they love or hate, is better than inspiring nothing."

Other students had started streaming in, and I didn't want to be the center of attention, so I tried to cut the conversation short. "Yeah, well, I'm not a real writer, so it doesn't matter."

Michelle took the hint and left me alone. The bell rang and class began. While the stragglers took their seats, Michelle set up a portable CD player on top of her desk.

"Today we're going to talk about poetry."

There were a few groans from the back, probably because we did just as much reading as writing, and they rightly assumed we'd be reading a lot of poetry before the term was up.

"But I want you to understand that poetry is more than rhyming couplets. Poetry is the way your soul speaks without your mouth in the middle to muck things up. It doesn't have to be romantic. Poetry can be rage, poetry can be sorrow. Poetry can be whatever you want it to be, just like *you* can be whatever you want to be.

"Now, I want you to close your eyes."

Half the students had closed their eyes the moment Michelle had said the word "poetry," so they were ahead of the game, and the rest of us followed along.

"I want you to listen to this song. I want you to listen to the words, listen to the words that aren't being said. Listen to the images created by the music."

Click.

Silence. A piano. And then a ghostly voice singing about China or china, depending on how you interpreted it, expanded throughout the classroom, driving out all other sounds. Tori Amos's voice filled my ears and nested in my brain. This *was* poetry. This *was* the soul speaking, beautiful and fierce. I know that I breathed during those five minutes the song played, but I felt like I didn't. I felt like I didn't need to. I was sustained by the power of Tori Amos. Her piano, her voice, and her words.

When the song came to an end, Michelle gave us the rest of the period to write our own poems or songs or whatever came from within us. Nothing came out of me. I stared at a blank sheet of paper, willing words to appear, digging deeply for just a tenth of the emotion Tori Amos had put into her music, but it remained empty until the bell rang.

"Bring your books tomorrow!" Michelle shouted over us as we got up to leave. On my way out the door, she handed me back my short story with its grade, but I stuffed it between two books without looking at it and took off.

I skipped sixth period and drove to the record store in the mall. I found two of Tori Amos's CDs, *Under the Pink* and *Little Earthquakes*, bought them, and went back to my car where I spent a few frustrating minutes tearing off the plastic wrap and then peeling back the ridiculous security tape. I slid the *Little Earthquakes* CD into my player first.

"Every finger in the room is pointing at me . . ."

Tori Amos wasn't just speaking from her soul, she was

speaking directly to mine. Like she'd stolen into my room and read my journals for inspiration. I don't know how many millions of copies of that album she'd sold, but I felt like I was the only audience.

I sat in the mall parking lot listening to the CD. Somewhere between "Leather" and "Mother," I pulled out the story Michelle had returned to me. The A was circled on the front, but my eyes went immediately to the mistakes. To the red ink pointing out a misused comma or a "their" that should have been a "they're." I flipped through the pages, marking each error in my mind as a personal failure, ignoring the places where she'd written, "Nice word choice!" or "Great imagery!"

And then I flipped to the last page and stopped. I'd expected Michelle to write in red ink a lengthy note about how horrible the story had been and how she'd only given me an A because I'd fulfilled the requirements of the assignment and *not* because I'd written something worthy of the grade. But no. That's not what she'd written.

Michelle's final note, written in blue ink, said:

Shaun,
You are a real writer. Please keep writing.

DOUBTFUL

February 1996

JOHN HUGHES HAD TAUGHT ME THAT GEEKS STUCK WITH geeks, jocks stuck with jocks, cheerleaders with cheerleaders, ad nauseam. There were certainly cliques at my high school, and there were definitely football players who thought they were too good to hang out with anyone they felt was beneath them, but I'd managed to find my people in many different groups. I was something of a social chameleon, turning into whoever I needed to be to fit in. But my core group of friends consisted of Madelyne and "the gang."

Madelyne was *in* "the gang," but she and I also had our own thing going on. The gang consisted of Debbie, Bella, Ben and Ashley (who were, indeed, still together), Dan (who wasn't one of the original Dans—one had moved away and the other had dropped out), James, Mike, Mike, Scott, and Heather. A few other people rotated in and out over the years, but they were the core of the group.

During the first part of senior year, Heather and I had gotten close because we both hated going to classes and loved skipping. I'd pick her up before first period, and we'd go to Brooklyn Bagels for breakfast or skip lunch and wind up missing the rest of the afternoon.

One day, we decided to take off after fifth period and hang out at my house. My dad was at work, and my mom was shopping like she did every Friday.

"What're we listening to?" Heather asked.

"Tori Amos?"

"It's . . . interesting."

Tori was all I'd been listening to since I bought the CDs, and I didn't care if Heather liked it.

We pulled into my neighborhood and drove down the hill toward my house.

"Shit!" I slammed on the breaks.

"What?"

"My grandma!"

After Nana's cancer had gone into remission, my mom had convinced her to move closer to us, into the same neighborhood, so that we could watch after her better. But Nana didn't leave the house often, preferring to spend her days reading. Only, there she was, shuffling down the sidewalk in the same direction we were going.

"What do we do?"

We crept along behind her as she shambled past my cul-de-sac. I couldn't let her see me or she might tell my mom, and I'd already promised I'd stop skipping so many classes. The pace was agonizing, but when Nana finally rounded the corner, I zipped into the driveway, opened the garage door, and parked my car inside.

"That was close," I said. "We probably should give her an hour to walk back to her house before we leave."

"Fine with me."

Heather and I went upstairs to my bedroom, and she sprawled across my bed while I dialed in to check my e-mail.

"So what's up with you and Nicole?"

Nicole was a girl I'd been friendly with on-and-off for a couple of years. She'd been kind of flirting with me, but not the kind of flirting I took seriously. "Nothing."

Heather pointed at a picture taped to the side of my desk of Nicole kneeling in front of a huge snowball that she'd carved my name into. "That doesn't look like nothing."

"We're just friends."

"Why?"

"What do you mean?"

"You should ask her out?"

I shrugged. "What if I don't want to?"

Heather was nosy and pushy, and I didn't take anything she said seriously. "She's beautiful and she clearly likes you. You should go for it unless there's someone else you like."

I hadn't said I liked Nicole, but I was sure Heather was going to tell *everyone* I did like her before the day was done if I didn't do something. "Maybe there is someone else I like."

Heather sat up and turned her full attention to me. "Who?"

"No one."

"You can tell me."

I laughed. "No, I really can't."

Heather fell quiet for a second. Then she said, "There's someone I like. I'll tell you who it is if you tell me."

"It's complicated."

"It's a name."

"What if it's you?"

Heather sat on the edge of my bed, leaned over, and kissed me. I kissed her back. I crawled onto the bed, and we made out. My lips and my tongue were doing their things, and all the blood had rushed *away* from my brain, but the truth was that I'd never actually considered dating Heather before. She was annoying and cruel and backstabbing.

But as we made out, I started to consider it. I'd have a girlfriend. I'd get into NYU. I'd go to prom with a girl I might grow to care about. I'd lose my virginity for real. I saw it all so clearly, so perfectly. My future. Right there waiting for me.

"Heather doesn't want to go out with you," Debbie said. "And I know you don't want to hear this, but you could do so much better than her." Debbie and Heather had never gotten along, so it was difficult to know whether Debbie was being honest or petty.

"She couldn't even tell me herself?" I leaned against my car where Debbie had ambushed me Monday morning before first period.

Debbie folded her arms over her chest and shook her head. "I don't even know why you like her."

I wasn't sure I ever had. We'd made out until it was safe to leave without running into Nana, and then we'd gone back to school. When she'd gotten out of the car, I'd asked her to go out with me. Instead of answering, she'd said it was complicated, and I'd said it was just an answer.

An answer I finally had.

Debbie wrapped her arm around my shoulders. "Forget about her, all right? You'll find someone better."

"Doubtful."

February 26, 1996
I have decided that I am through putting my feelings into anything because I am tired of being hurt. So I am going to be me as I have wanted to be. I will say what I want and who gives a fuck about the consequences.

THE ROUND TABLE

February to March 1996

The set for this scene consists of a small round table and four chairs.
—The Round Table

I liked writing for two reasons. The first being that I could use it to make people laugh with me instead of at me. I'd discovered the power in the third grade when I'd written a short story about the Kool-Aid Man busting into our classroom that I'd read aloud. But I also enjoyed writing because it allowed me to control the beginning, middle, and end of the story.

I felt so helpless in my life, especially when it came to the future. Somewhere in New York was a person or group of people who were going to open a file containing everything they knew about me, and they were going to use the information within it to determine whether I was allowed to escape Florida or whether I was doomed to rot there forever, and there was absolutely nothing I could do to change the eventual outcome.

Except in stories. When I wrote, I built the whole world. I was creator and destroyer, and that sense of control kept me from completely melting down.

While I was waiting to hear back from NYU, I began writing a play called *The Round Table*, which followed four characters—Alissa, Jordan, Christian, and Andrew—through some pivotal moments in their lives. It was not a good play, and I was not a good writer, but everyone starts somewhere, and it's usually at the bottom.

Alissa was an amalgam of girls I knew at the time. She was artistic, witty, strong, and had horrible taste in men. Of course, she only dated those awful boys because she was secretly in love with Christian.

Jordan was brash and fiercely loyal, but was also self-destructive. When the play began, he was spending the majority of his time drinking heavily and having sex with strangers, hoping to make the world hurt as badly as he did.

Andrew was a shy, quiet young man who was secretly in love with his best friend, Jordan. He ultimately told Jordan how he felt and was rejected.

Finally, Christian was a writer who felt boxed in, trapped by the expectations of others. He believed his life was not his own, and that he would never be free. At the climax of *The Round Table*, Christian took his life in order to prove that he was still free to make his own choices.

When I began writing *The Round Table*, I firmly believed Christian was the character who represented me, even though I basically lifted Christian's entire story arc from *Dead Poets Society*. But I also saw pieces of myself in Jordan. I was angry and I was hurting *all the time*.

When Maddie and I would write to each other over e-mail, she used to sign off as Nara Star, and I signed off as Havok. Nara was a superhero identity Madelyne made up for herself for reasons that belong to her alone, but I chose Havok because he couldn't control his mutant ability—a powerful energy blast that exploded violently from his body—and he was terrified of hurting the people he loved. Which was how I felt. I buried my fear and shame deep inside. I played the part and pretended life was great, but I was scared to death that I was going to lose control and hurt someone.

In many ways Jordan was who I thought I would evolve into if I stopped caring, which was a real fear for me, seeing as caring about anything was growing more difficult with each passing day.

I focused mostly on Christian, Alissa, and Jordan in the early stages, and all I knew about Andrew was that he would tell Jordan he was in love with him, somehow contract AIDS, and quickly die. I knew even less about HIV and AIDS than I did about being gay, and I treated Andrew's character the way every movie and book I'd consumed had treated their gay characters. Like garbage. Like a thing. Like he was less important than the titular table around which the characters sat in every scene.

I followed the only writing advice I'd ever been given. I wrote what I knew.

That writing advice is bullshit, by the way.

My parents went away near the end of February for a couple of weeks, leaving me and my stepbrothers home alone, and we were thrilled to see them go. Not that we threw any parties or turned the house into an opium den or anything like that. My brothers had their own lives, and I wasn't in the mood to see anyone. Not even Maddie.

Date: March 2, 1996

From: Shaun

To: Maddie

Subject: Re: Shaun, please talk to me . . . .

I am not mad at anybody, I have just got a lot of things on my mind that need to be cleared up and unfortunately it has made it very hard for me to think about anyone else. I know that I am being kind of selfish but there are so many things going on right now that I don't know what to do. Last night I was so messed up thinking about this stuff that I got this pounding in my head that hurt so bad I almost went nuts.

I am very sorry that you all feel like I am ignoring you or are mad at you but there are some things that I have to deal with by myself and sometimes that means that I will not be acting like myself.

During the nine days that my parents were gone, I skipped a lot of school, stopped talking to my friends, drank a lot, and finished writing *The Round Table*. I'd scrapped most of the scenes with Andrew in them and began rewriting them, but something was different.

From *The Round Table*

Alissa and Andrew are sitting in their chairs when the lights come up.

ALISSA: What did you need to talk to me about Drew?

ANDREW: I don't really know if I can tell you this.

ALISSA: Tell me what Drew?

ANDREW: I mean, I trust you and all. You've never told anyone a secret that I gave to you.

ALISSA: What in God's name are you talking about? I get the feeling that you're talking right by me.

ANDREW: I just don't want to say anything unless I am absolutely sure.

ALISSA: (becoming frustrated.) Say anything about what?

ANDREW: (Leans over and kisses Alissa for about a count of 5)

ALISSA: What in the hell was that all about?

ANDREW: I just needed to see something.

ALISSA: Listen, Drew you know I love you like a brother and we even dated once, but if you don't tell me what the hell is going on, I'm gonna leave.

ANDREW: Don't leave! What I have to tell you, you can't tell anyone else. Not Christian, Not Jordan, not anyone. You have to promise me that.

ALISSA: O.K. I promise.

ANDREW: I kissed you just then to test myself.

ALISSA: Test yourself for what?

ANDREW: Tell me something: Did you feel anything when I kissed you?

ALISSA: Yeah, I felt your lips.

ANDREW: No, I mean; did you feel any emotions other than surprise.

ALISSA: Aside from the fact that it kind of felt like kissing my brother, it was actually kind of nice.

ANDREW: That's my point then. I didn't feel anything.

ALISSA: Nothing at all?

ANDREW: Not revulsion and not pleasure.

ALISSA: But it was a good kiss.

ANDREW: But for me I was just going through the motions. It didn't mean anything.

ALISSA: So what? We're more like brother and sister than anything else.

ANDREW: But still-

ALISSA: Still what? I don't understand where you're going with this.

ANDREW: Don't you see? My whole life I've just been going through the motions. I have never once really felt anything when I've been with a girl. It didn't matter if we were just making out or having sex. I have never gotten any pleasure from those acts.

ALISSA: Maybe you just haven't found the right girl.

ANDREW: And I never will.

ALISSA: Andrew . . . no.

ANDREW: I think I might be gay.

ALISSA: Oh, Drew.

ANDREW: Is that really such a bad thing?

ALISSA: I don't know what to say.

ANDREW: Tell me that you understand. Tell me that you are not repulsed by the mere sight of me. Better yet, tell me that I am some freak of nature. Just something. Anything.

ALISSA: You know that I will support you in anything that you do-

ANDREW: But you're not comfortable with it.

ALISSA: No Drew it's not that-

ANDREW: Then what is it?

ALISSA: I don't want you to be mad at me.

ANDREW: What is it?

ALISSA: I just don't think it's right.

ANDREW: What? Gay people in general or is it just me?

ALISSA: It's just you. I just don't see how you can be..

ANDREW: Say it, a fag, a queer, a homo, Say it!

ALISSA: Gay. You're just not the type.

ANDREW: What, is there this gay mold out there somewhere that I don't fit into? Well don't worry about it I've never really fit in before, I think that I can manage this one.

ALISSA: What will you do when other people find out?

ANDREW: No one else is going to know, unless you tell them.

ALISSA: You're not going to tell anyone?

ANDREW: Listen, I told you that I wasn't sure yet. I'm going to wait until college, when I am somewhere that I don't know anyone to see if it's true. Until then, I am going to keep lying to myself and dating whomever I want.

ALISSA: Drew, you shouldn't hide like this.

ANDREW: You don't have to tell me that. Don't you think I know? I am the one who is different here. Not you. You can flirt and go out with anyone you want. But me . . . I can't even date someone unless they are the same as me. I can't flirt with a guy I think is attractive because I am afraid that he'll beat the crap out of me. So don't tell me that I shouldn't hide. I know I shouldn't. I know that the more I keep inside of me the more I die each day. But at least I avoid being killed outright.

ALISSA: I didn't mean anything by it.

ANDREW: I'm sure you didn't Listen I've gotta get going. Thanks for listening. (Stands and leaves.)

ALISSA: Any time Drew. Any time.

The scene epitomized everything I feared. I feared being rejected by my friends. I feared that even if I came out, I wouldn't find acceptance with other gay people because I didn't feel like I fit the stereotype of how I believed gay people acted. I still lacked the vocabulary to understand being gay, but I was clearly struggling to find it. I was sounding out the words and trying to string those words into sentences, and I was failing miserably. Everything I believed about gay people was built on the stereotypes of fags. The type of person I'd been socialized for years to believe was the most horrible kind of person I could ever become.

Andrew from *The Round Table* was how I saw myself, and Andrew from my monologue of *I Hate Hamlet*, the way I'd played him, was who I feared I'd turn into, only, I wasn't self-aware enough to recognize the truth that kept throwing jazz hands in my face.

I didn't get it. Not until I wrote this scene:

From *The Round Table*

The room is dark except for a spot on Jordan's chair. Andrew walks in. He seems distraught. A spot follows him to the edges of where the lights to the table begin. The spot fades out; the table lights fade in. The spot on Jordan's chair MUST remain brighter than the other lights.)

ANDREW: I guess I'm the only one here. (He looks at Jordan's chair.) Maybe I can pretend your here. God, there are so many things I need to tell you. You never listened to me before, but dammit, you're going to listen to me now. (Falls to his knees and puts his head in his hands.)

God, I feel like such a moron. (Looks up at Jordan's chair.) You're so selfish, you are so damned selfish. You play in your world of make believe where you think everyone hates you, and here I am surrounded by people who truly do hate me, and for what. Because I am attracted to guys instead of girls. But you don't even try to see the hurt I'm feeling; you don't even care. I have spent so much time hating myself for what I am and loving you for all that you are. (He begins to imagine what Jordan would say if he were here.)

Don't stare at me as if I was some kind of freak. You haven't the right. I just wanted to tell you how I feel. I've been hiding for so long that it's hard for me to do this now. (Listens to imaginary response) You don't have to tell me that. I know you don't feel the same way about me. Don't you realize? I know that you won't . . . no, you can't, feel for me the same way I feel for you.

Everytime I see you with a girl on your arm, I die inside and imagine that it was me you were holding. (He begins to cry and pace around the room.)

What I want doesn't matter though. (Pause) What happened to us? When we were kids, there was nothing that could have stopped us. (Still hearing Jordan's voice in his mind) I know that we're not kids anymore, you don't have to tell me that. But what the hell, happened to us.

How did I become afraid of everything and how did you become, whatever it is you have become?

No. Don't try to answer. I remember the first time I saw you. I was only in the second grade and I wasn't burdened with all these feelings that I have now. But there were these older kids picking on a younger boy. I saw the way you walked over to them. I thought you were gonna join them; hell you could've been their leader. Not you though. No, you took the side of the smaller weaker boy. You fought fiercer than I have ever seen anyone fight. You earned a black eye in the whole ordeal, but from that time on no one ever picked on someone they thought you protected.

From that instant I knew I wanted you as my best friend. But when I look at you now, I don't see that little boy anymore. Where did you put him? (Pause) God, I need him now, I just can't stop the bullies anymore. Where did he go?

God! I feel like such a moron. (Stands and walks away. Spot on chair fades. Andrew gets to side of stage R. Turns back to chair.) I wish that I could tell you this is person but . . . Please just bring back the boy I used to know. (Exits)

Jordan has been in Stage L. Wing listening secretly. Walks on stage. Spot on him.

When I finished writing that scene, I printed it out, sat on the edge of my bed, read it aloud, and cried. I cried because I'd finally realized Andrew was me. I cried because I hated myself. I cried because, even though I wasn't in love with my best friend, I *was* terrified of rejection and of spending the rest of my life alone. I cried because I felt like my life was over.

Instead of being able to go out and buy a book about a closeted gay kid who's scared of becoming a stereotype while coming to terms with being gay that could have helped me understand what I was going through, I'd needed to write my own. And it wasn't good. It was flawed and awful and filled with the misconceptions I'd absorbed about the gay community, but it was all I had.

Stealing the *Playgirl* and spending hours looking at naked men should have been a giveaway that I might be gay, but self-deception is part of being human. Selfish people don't believe they're selfish, they just think everyone else is whiny. Mean people don't think they're mean, they just think everyone else is too sensitive. And far too often, queer teens will twist themselves into knots to avoid admitting that they're queer. Sometimes out of fear, sometimes because they've been raised with beliefs they can't reconcile, sometimes because it's all just shadows on a wall to them, sometimes because they're naive and simply lack the vocabulary to describe and understand what they're feeling.

But in writing *The Round Table*, in writing Andrew, I'd finally found the vocabulary I needed to say the words: I'm gay.

I still hated myself, but at least I could finally be honest about why.

COOKIE DATE

March 1996

Date: March 4, 1996

From: Shaun

To: Maddie

Subject: Maddie

I don't think you understand how fucked up I am right now. I am not walking around with a gun to my head, I am not one of those suicidal people on the movies that is crying to be save. I am not suicidal. I just don't care . . . AT THIS POINT. Hopefully I can get out of this but right now I am not even safe.

I am happy that you had a great weekend (and I want to hear all about it.) but that's not going to happen in my case. See, it's change that has messed me up. And it's not stuff that can ever change back. I'm stuck now trying to deal with it. It's like a guy trying to deal with a prosthetic (fake or what ever) leg. I want it to be like it was before, only I know that it can't be. I know that it is not going to be easy but I have to deal with this slowly. I just can't wake up one morning and go "Hey my problems are gone!" It's not the type that ever goes away.

I still know what I want and all of this has made me want it even more, right now though it is hard for me to do anything but care about me and it is hard for me to get past all the anger. I want to reassure you that I am not going anywhere. I just may not be all here all the time.

I do want to talk but I have homework to do now so I will call you later

Date: March 17, 1996
From: Maddie
To: Shaun
Subject: . . .

No matter what, you are still the same old Shaun that, when playing Gorgon(wasn't it Gorgon? :o) and letting me yell at him became one of my truest friends . . . nothing is going to change that. I promise you Shaun, in a few years things will get easier. We are just at an age when people can be cruel, and feel threatened by people that are different. That's just prejudice . . . which tends to be dropped in college. I know that you are worried that this is going to change your life, and it probably will, but people, your true friends, will always stand behind you.

March 25, 1996, 9:35 p.m.
Well, it has been almost a month since I have had the inclination to write anything in here, though I certainly have had enough to write about. I wrote in my first entry that I was doing this to look back on my senior year and see how I had changed . . . .. if only I had known that the changes would be so drastic.

In my las entry I was getting ready to be free of my parents for a week and just let loose. It was the worst week of my life. I did a lot of thinking and I came to the conclusion that I am gay. I still have my doubts, but I can't hide my feelings and that is what they tell me. I think that I am having a hard time accepting it, because I have been playing at being straight for so long. I was really forced to examine my feelings when I was writing a play (I finished!!!!!) it just dealt with everything in my life, and as I was writing these scenes, I realized that they were all me. So anyway, the only person I've told is Madelyne and she has been so cool. We, hang out alot and guy-watch and stuff. I am just afraid that I will change. I don't want to change. I want to stay who I am with just one added bonus.

Admitting to myself that I was gay was a huge step. It was a relief to finally understand why I hadn't been able to fall in love with girls the way my friends had, but it also felt like admitting to being a serial killer. It was something I didn't want, couldn't get rid of, and that I was convinced was going to turn me into someone I didn't want to be and hurt the people I cared about most. I felt like I was carrying a nuclear bomb in my chest that might go off any second and vaporize everyone near me. But still, I'd done it. I'd admitted it to myself.

Admitting it to others was a little more difficult, so I started with the one person I trusted more than anyone in the world. Madelyne.

The mall was quiet as we walked in. Madelyne hadn't said much on the drive over, and I'd been too scared to say much either. I'd printed out a copy of *The Round Table* and given it to her in the hopes that she'd pick up on the subtext and not make me say it, but so far she'd been coy, offering to accompany me on a cookie date if I wanted to talk.

She was going to make me say it.

"Cookies?"

"Sure," I said with less enthusiasm than she was looking for. I just wasn't certain if I could stomach cookies without puking. I'd already bitten my nails down so low, they'd bled.

"Come on. It's not a cookie date without cookies."

Maddie nudged my shoulder and motioned for me to follow her to Mrs. Fields. Maddie had always been aware without my needing to tell her that I didn't really like people touching me.

Growing up in a Southern household where people *loved* hugs and where "being polite" meant letting others hug me without making a fuss meant that I rarely mentioned how much I disliked being touched, but Madelyne had always seemed to know.

The cloyingly sweet smell of chocolate and cookie dough hung around Mrs. Fields like a morning fog. I got a bag of little semi-sweet chocolate chip cookies, and Maddie got a mixture. We fought over who was going to pay—she won—and we found a quiet spot outside to sit and eat.

"How's your mom?" I asked. Madelyne's mom had virtually adopted me into the family, and I loved her nearly as much as my own mother (and still do!).

"You know," Maddie said. "She works too hard."

"Yeah." I hated small talk then, and I still hate it now. When I go to a party, I either find those one or two people who are willing to get into a really intense conversation for a couple of hours about why the Oxford comma is the best comma or why Captain Janeway was superior to Captain Kirk, or I wind up sitting awkwardly by myself in a corner because I'd rather gag on a cocktail shrimp than spend five minutes discussing the weather or traffic.

That was another reason Maddie and I got along. We were as comfortable *not* talking as we were talking.

But when I'm nervous or scared, I babble mindlessly, filling the silence with my anxiety like a swarm of summer gnats.

"Did I tell you Mr. Carter asked me to speak at baccalaureate?"

Maddie laughed. “You?”

“Right? That’s what I said.”

“Who else?”

“Bella, though I’m sure she’s going to read a poem or something.”

“Probably.”

I wasn’t offended by Maddie laughing. She knew I could both write and give a good speech, but as a quintessential underachiever, I was an odd choice. There were other students who could also write and speak well enough to give the speech. I didn’t think I’d stood out enough for anyone to notice me. I also wasn’t particularly inspiring to or inspired by my classmates. I didn’t hate them, exactly, but I assumed they hated me, or that they would if they knew I was gay, so I preemptively wrote the majority of them off as mindless assholes who would lead small, unimportant lives.

“What’re you going to speak about?”

I shook my head. “No clue. I’ll probably write the speech the night before.” I dug into my bag of cookies and popped one into my mouth. They were still gooey and warm. “Have you heard from FSU?”

Maddie threw me side-eye and then glanced at the bag of cookies in her lap. Her long red hair hung loose over her shoulders, and she was dressed in jeans and a T-shirt. “I got in.”

“Congratulations!” I was waiting for her to smile or show some sign that she was excited, but her shoulders remain bowed and her expression guarded. “You don’t seem happy.”

"I don't think I'm going. I got a scholarship to PBCC. It's closer and it won't cost much."

"So you'll stick around here?"

"Maybe," she said. "I don't know. What about you? Any word from NYU yet?"

I loved acting, but along with my realization that I was gay came the realization that my true motive for applying to NYU had been to escape. I didn't feel like I'd die if I couldn't be an actor, but I did feel like I'd die if I didn't get out of Florida.

"Not yet."

"You'll get in."

"Maybe."

Maddie looked surprised by my answer. "You will. Don't worry. And if those admissions people are too stupid to accept you, you'll always have me."

"Thanks." We lapsed into silence, just eating cookies and listening to the water splash in the fountain behind us. "I don't know what I'll do if I don't get in."

"You'll be okay no matter what."

"But I can't . . . it's different here."

"It doesn't have to be."

"*I'm* different."

"No you're not," she said. "You've just added a new fun component to who you are."

"There's nothing fun about it."

"Why not?"

Too many cookies had started to sour my stomach, and I set

them aside and turned my attention to Madelyne. "Because I'm afraid of being . . . fun. People get beat up for being fun. They get murdered for being fun. They get laughed at and ridiculed. And 'fun' isn't the word most people use to describe them."

Maddie took my hand. "Fuck those people." She stopped and laughed. "Or don't fuck them. They don't matter."

"What if everyone hates me?"

"I don't hate you," she said. "My mom doesn't hate you."

"Your mom knows?"

Maddie nodded. "For a while now."

"Was it that obvious? Was *I* that obvious?"

Look, there are a ton of issues within the gay community—including toxic masculinity, misogyny, racism—but I wasn't socially aware of those issues back then. All I knew was being a fag, being Tito or Hollywood, was to be avoided at all costs. But if Madelyne's mom had sniffed out that I was gay, then it must've been because of my speech patterns or mannerisms or the way I dressed. And if Madelyne's mom had guessed, then it must've been obvious to everyone.

My mind started spiraling, and I thought I was going to throw up. Had anyone else figured it out? People from school? My parents?

"All that was obvious," Madelyne said, "was that you were hurting."

"Oh." I didn't quite know what she meant, but it kept me from having a complete mental breakdown. "But you know? That I'm fun, I mean?" I had some of the vocabulary now, but I was still afraid to say the word out loud where some random stranger might overhear me and decide it applied to me and attack me for it. So I latched onto Madelyne's word. I didn't have to be gay, I could be fun.

"The funnest."

There. I'd said it—sort of. Madelyne knew and there was no turning back. But this felt different. Sitting on the edge of my bed at home, reading *The Round Table* and realizing I was Andrew and that I was gay, had felt like dying. It'd felt like the painful death of the person I'd been before.

Sitting with Maddie, eating cookies and admitting to my best friend that I was gay felt like being reborn. It was scary and terrifying and I wanted to throw up, but it was also amazing. From now on, I could be myself around Madelyne. The only problem was that my perfect picture of what my future looked like was crumbling, and I had nothing to replace it with.

YOU-KNOW-WHAT

March 1996

HEATHER AND I HAD BEEN SLOWLY PATCHING UP OUR friendship since we'd kissed and I'd made the dumbass decision to ask her to be my girlfriend. Giving her a copy of *The Round Table* served two purposes. The first was that it erased the lingering awkwardness between us, since she knew that I was gay and therefore hadn't *really* hurt my feelings when she'd rejected me. The second was that it ensured that my other friends—and probably half the state of Florida—would know I was gay without the need for me to tell them.

I prepared for the worst. I expected to lose my seat at lunch and spend the rest of the semester eating in the library, I expected unknown assailants in masks to assault me in the creepy hallway between the north and south campuses, I expected to be spit on and called names and laughed at, even by the people who were normally laughed at by everyone else.

None of those things happened. My friends kept it in the family and didn't spread the rumor beyond the people who supported me. Debbie asked me to confirm it, which I did, and then we never spoke of it again. A few times, I thought I caught Bella checking me out from across a room, like she was trying to find the gay parts of me that she'd missed before, but she never brought it up.

No one refused to let me sit at my normal lunch table, no one shied away when I was next to them. It was like almost nothing had changed.

A couple of weeks after my cookie date with Maddie, I was sitting at lunch like I normally did and stood to toss out my garbage. Heather got up and followed me. Cornered me by the bushes on the senior patio and whispered, "I just want you to know that James told me he and the guys are cool with . . . *you-know-what*."

Of all of the guys in our group, James was the most reserved. He was shy and didn't talk much unless the conversation turned to art or comic books.

"He did?"

"Yes," she said. "I wasn't supposed to say anything, though." If the fate of the world depended on Heather's ability to keep a secret, the world would end in fire. But in this case, I was glad she'd told me. It was weird to think that *anyone* was sitting around talking about my sexuality, but a relief that they hadn't decided I was a disgusting, disease-carrying trash receptacle they needed to distance themselves from immediately.

Within a month, most of my friends knew I was gay. The biggest exception was Alan. But because he was away at college, I didn't feel like I needed to tell him, which was a relief since I doubted he'd take it well. I wasn't worried that he'd flip out and try to kill me. Instead, I feared that, because he thought so highly of himself, he'd assume I was totally in love with him, which I was emphatically not, and wouldn't be able to handle hanging out anymore. Luckily, I didn't have to deal with him right away.

Coming out was not the blood-splattered horror show I'd feared it would be, and while it wasn't the last time I would have to come out, it was pretty painless for a first time.

CRUSHED, PART 1

March 1996

MY FIRST GAY CRUSH WAS CHRIS O'DONNELL. YEAH, HE was cute in *Batman Forever*, but he stole my heart in the kind of obscure film *Circle of Friends*. I've always been a sucker for the nice guys. My first crush on an actual human person that I theoretically had a chance of speaking to was a guy at my school named JJ.

He'd enrolled at my school at the start of senior year—my graduating class was large enough that I didn't know the names of everyone in it, but small enough that I recognized when someone new popped in—and ate lunch with a group of football players who sat at a table across from mine on the senior patio. JJ had blond curls and rosy cheeks and farm-boy arms and shoulders. We were from different planets, and our orbits only came within shouting distance for forty-two minutes a day. Before I came out to myself, I spent lunch imagining what it would be like to be him. To be popular and good-looking. After I came out, I wasted lunch daydreaming about asking him to prom. I constructed elaborate fantasies where he'd get up from his table, walk across the patio, take a knee, and ask me out. I had long conversations with him in my mind about books and philosophy and music. I wrote poems to him and about him. My heart sped up when it was time to go to lunch, and it sputtered when the bell rang and lunch ended.

I'd felt different for so long but hadn't understood why until I'd learned the vocabulary. When I was finally able to put a name to what I was feeling and understood I was gay, I felt such a sense of relief to know. But knowing, in many ways, made me feel worse. I knew I was gay, but nothing had changed. Nothing *could* change. Before, when I was pretending to be someone I wasn't, I hadn't been aware I was pretending. Now I knew, and it was agony. Every day, I sat on the patio during lunch and wished more than anything that I could catch JJ's eye, smile and wave, and not worry that he and his football friends would come over and break my arms and legs and leave me in a bloody heap on the ground.

I'd even gone so far as to write him a letter.

March 25, 1996

Dear JJ (Don't ask how I know your name . . . . at least I hope that's your name)

OK, this is really weird for me, so bear with me. I doubt that you know who I am and I doubt that you share my feelings, but I had to know for sure. I see you sitting at lunch with your friends and I must tell you that you are gorgeous. OK, at this point you are probably going, "what kind of sick freak?" but that's fine, I'm going to have to get used to that kind of reaction. If you're not reacting in that manner . . . .. cool!

I don't want to scare the shit out of you, believe me, if some gay guy did something like this to me a year ago, I would have pissed my pants. So, feel free to think horrible things about me if you wish, but even just saying I'm gay is kinda big for me so I hope you don't think its bad.

Anyway, the reason I am writing this is because I see you at lunch everyday and again I feel compelled to tell you that I think you're really good looking. But I see you at lunch and even though you have given no signs that you were gay, and actually, judging by the people you hang out with, it is pretty clear that you're not, I felt I had to ask, nonetheless.

It would be a miracle, to find that the first guy I am attracted to is in the same boat as I, but if you're not . . . . . . well, just forget I ever wrote this. If, by some strange twist of fate, you happen to be gay, or even at that halfway mark, I would be interested in getting to know you better.

(If you are straight, just throw away this letter now. If not, read on.)

Unless, you are really open about this, which if you were it would have been easy to find out, I would appreciate you keeping this to yourself. I really haven't told anyone, except for my close friends. Well, if you are interested, give me a call and we can talk. As of yet, I only know that you look beautiful, you could be a psycho killer or something (just kidding) so anyway, thanks for being cool about this. (Unless you've tried to kill me or something, then . . . . Oh Well)

I kept the letter in my pocket, working up the nerve to get up in the middle of lunch, walk to JJ's table, and give it to him. But I never did. My friends might have been cool, but I didn't know JJ, and there was a very real chance that if I gave him the letter, he'd try to kill me.

And that's not hyperbole. I imagined handing him the letter in front of his friends. He'd read it right then and there, even though I'd tell him not to. His jock friends would make fun of him for being asked out by a guy. They'd call him a fag. JJ's fragile male ego would shatter, and he'd see no option to restore his masculinity other than kicking my ass.

To some guys, there's no difference between being gay and having people think they're gay. And while I hoped that JJ wasn't one of those kinds of guys, I wasn't prepared to bet my life on it. So I held on to the letter, and I held on to my dreams.

CRUSHED, PART 2

April 1996

SENIOR YEAR WAS COMING TO AN END MORE QUICKLY than I was prepared for. Classes were winding down, I was nearing opening night for the last show I'd ever perform in during high school—*The Lion, the Witch, and the Wardrobe*, in which I played Aslan—and most of the people I knew were already planning their lives beyond graduation. I'd spent my first three years waiting for the day when I could walk out of that school forever, but now that the day was near, I found I wanted to rewind my life and go back to the beginning.

I had a habit of magical thinking, especially when I was trying to sleep. I'd never been one of those people who could fall right to sleep the moment they closed their eyes. I was and am incredibly jealous of those people. Instead, I'd lay awake for hours, running scenarios in my head, replaying conversations where I felt like I'd said something absolutely mortifying and humiliated myself, or finally coming up with the perfect comeback to an insult that'd been flung at me weeks or months earlier. Some nights I prayed to God or the devil—I wasn't picky about which one answered—to make me not gay. Some nights I lay with my eyes closed for so long I believed I could see through my eyelids, like I had an extremely specialized form of X-ray vision. Then there were the nights I'd simply beg the universe to turn back time. To send me back to the fourteen-year-old version of myself eager to start high school, but to leave my memories of the last three years intact so that I could reclaim that time from my own ignorance.

I wanted to unfuck my life. I wanted to undo lying to Alex about losing my virginity. I wanted to take back sharing my first kiss with Tonia. I wanted to fix the hurt I'd caused Leigh by stringing her along when I'd never been biologically capable of feeling for her the way she felt for me. I wanted to be able to own who I was from the first day of high school instead of spending three and a half years flailing about like a dying fish.

"Please, just let me go back to the first day of school," I whispered. "I'll do things right this time. I won't screw it up. Please. Just . . . please."

And then I'd fall asleep, wake up the next day, and go to school, but everything was the same. I was still seventeen, and I still had no clue what I was doing. I was never going to give JJ the letter, I was never going to be popular, I was never going to be happy. At least not until I graduated. And then, only if I got into NYU.

For months I'd been replaying my interview over in my head, analyzing the myriad ways I'd failed. I'd applied for early admission and had been turned down and punted to regular admission. Maybe they thought I was good but not quite exceptional enough to warrant special treatment. It had hurt, yeah, but my soul was riding on getting in, and I couldn't fail.

It was overcast on April 8. The clouds had been hanging around all day and had grown darker by the time last period ended. I'd slipped into the habit of driving home immediately after school, no matter what other obligations I had. If I was scheduled to work, I'd just be late. If I had rehearsals, I'd hurry home and then back to school. But I needed to check the mail.

Every day that I drove to the bank of mailboxes at the end of my neighborhood and the letter wasn't inside, I felt a mixture of anxiety and relief. Relief because there was still a chance, but anxiety because I just wanted to know already.

April 8 was different, though; I felt it in my stomach as I drove east toward the beach. My hands were shaking so badly as I ran into the house and grabbed the mail key. No one was home, so I didn't have to bother pretending to care how their days had gone. A light rain began as I drove slowly to the mailboxes. I told myself that everything would be fine. I needed this, I deserved it, and the universe wouldn't let me down.

I slotted the key, opened the door, and reached into the mailbox. It was a Monday, so there was more mail than normal, but I didn't care about the bills or the junk because there it was. A letter bearing the torch logo and the letters: NYU.

My stomach dropped. I felt like I was going to vomit and crap my pants simultaneously. I wasn't holding a letter in my hands, I was holding my future. When I looked into the future, when I envisioned where I would be in five or ten years, the only place I saw myself with the ability to be happy was New York. People might not accept me there, they might make fun of me, but at least I'd have a chance of finding a place where I belonged. I couldn't say the same about my home. I needed to get out of Florida. There was no future for me there.

So that envelope was either a ticket to freedom or a writ of execution.

I stood under the awning by the mailboxes, shivering in the cool air. The drizzle turned into fat drops of rain.

I slid my finger under the flap, tearing it open gently. I pulled out a single sheet of paper, unfolded it, and read it.

I dropped the envelope and the letter onto the grass, got in my car, and drove away.

> *April 8, 1996, 2:43 p.m.*
> *Didn't get into NYU. Life sucks. Went down to the beach and sat in the rain for about an hour. That was fun.*

CRUSHED, PART 3

April 1996

April 11, 1996, 9:28 p.m.
I keep having a dream that my head is pounding and it hurts really bad and it's still hurting when I wake up and I just know it's the pain of not getting into NYU.

I lost my future. I lost myself. Without NYU, I didn't know what I was going to do or where I was going to go. I was desperate for something, anything, to cling to. All I really had left was that sappy letter in my pocket to a boy who didn't know I existed. It wasn't much, but it was something.

The senior patio was outside the theater, and I'd retreated there to go over my lines. Aslan wasn't a big part, but it was kind of fitting that it was my last. Not only because Madelyne was playing the White Witch, but also because I'd loved *The Lion, the*

Witch, and the Wardrobe when I was young, and the drama club had been the place I'd escaped to when the reality of life became too much. People like Ms. C. and Mr. Higgins and Maria had been a family for me when I hadn't felt like I fit in anywhere else. I hoped, as a senior, that I'd been able to make other misfits feel welcome.

I stood on the tables as I read my lines, using the height to help me find the perspective I needed for the role. I was the king of the animals, one of them but not *of* them. Regal and caring, but aloof. As I leaped from one table to another, I found myself standing on JJ's lunch table, over the spot where he normally sat. There was something written on the wood, and I crouched down to read it.

My initials were *not* KS. JJ had carved a heart onto the table and ripped mine out of my chest.

I didn't expect he was going to ask me out or talk to me or acknowledge my existence, and I definitely didn't think he was gay, but until that moment I could dream. I could touch the letter in my pocket and picture giving it to him and imagine him smiling as he read it and standing up and kissing me right there on the patio in front of everyone. Seeing that heart, seeing those initials, robbed me of what might have been. My lungs contracted. I felt like I was drowning.

I'd lost the life I'd hoped to have when I was younger. I was a freak, I was defective, I was worthless. Then I'd lost NYU and all hope of escaping to a place where I might find a world and people who would accept me. And now I'd lost JJ too.

I wasn't drowning; I had already drowned. This was my brain slowly shutting down. I might as well end it now.

"Shaun?"

The voice calling my name yanked me back from the ledge.

"Hey, Nina." Nina was a junior. She was kind of overeager and needy, but she also had a wicked sense of humor and was one of the most thoughtful people I knew.

"You okay?"

I needed someone to talk to so badly in that moment, but I didn't want to burden Nina or anyone with my problems, so I slid on my brave face and smiled. "Sure. Yeah. Everything's good."

"Do you have a minute?"

"I was just going over my lines." I held up my script and then motioned for her to sit.

"I'm sorry about NYU."

My insides clenched, but I kept that smile on. "It's no big deal. I'll just go to PBCC with Maddie."

"So you'll still be around for my senior year?"

"Looks like it." I glanced down at the heart under my hands. "So did you need to talk?"

Nina bit her lip and nodded. "There's something I wanted to tell you."

"Go for it."

"I like you."

Jesus Christ. The way she'd spit it out? Who does that? I'd spent hours and hours writing my letter to JJ—a letter that I knew in my heart I was never going to be brave enough to give to him—while Nina just came along and blurted her feelings out like it was the easiest thing in the world to do.

I was feeling crushed by a boy I'd never spoken to, would never speak to, and who didn't know I existed, while Nina had put her heart on the line without flinching. And the thing was, I'd known how she'd felt about me before she said it. Maddie had already confided in me that Nina'd had a crush on me for a while. This confession wasn't some spontaneous swell of emotion; it was one of the bravest things I'd ever witnessed.

But I didn't feel the same.

"I'm gay."

I'd expected shock, maybe tears. Instead, she said, "I kind of figured." She smiled. "How are you dealing with it?"

"With what?"

"Being gay?"

"Okay, I guess." I wasn't, actually, but Nina's casual courage had unnerved me and I didn't know what else to say.

Nina nodded along. "Well, if you ever need to talk."

I should have taken her up on the offer. I should have told her that I thought she was a superhero for having the courage to tell me how she felt even though she knew she might face rejection. I should have told her that I envied her. I envied that, even though I hadn't answered the way she'd hoped, at least she knew. At least she had the nerve to tell me. And I should have told her that I kind of hated her because she'd had that chance. A chance I would never have. I would never get to look into JJ's eyes and tell him I thought he was handsome and had a great smile and that I didn't know anything else about him but liked him anyway because crushes are stupid and irrational. I wouldn't even get to sit on a table as he gently told me he wasn't interested. That he couldn't be interested because he wasn't gay. I should have told Nina that I hated hurting her, but at least she got to know, while I never would. She got to move on from her crush, while mine lingered. While mine festered and rotted inside of me, tainting everything it touched.

But I didn't take her up on the offer.

"Thanks," I said. "But I'm all right."

LOVE, SHAUN

May 1996

EVERYONE GOT TO BE HAPPY EXCEPT ME. OR RATHER, everyone was allowed a shot at happiness except me. I didn't hate them for it, but, yeah, I kind of hated them for it. Partly because they had opportunities that I didn't, but mostly because they were so ignorant of it. They didn't realize how easy their lives were. They took for granted every moment spent holding hands while they walked down the hallway and every kiss in a public place. The only fear a guy felt when he asked out a girl was fear that she might reject him. He didn't worry that she might gather a few of her friends, surprise him afterward in a dark parking lot on his way home from work, tie him up, torture and beat him, and then leave him to die. He never had to worry that, even if she said yes, they'd have to pretend to only be friends when they were in public, because if they didn't someone might spit on them or call them names or attack them.

I walked through my last weeks of high school feeling like nobody, not one single person, understood how I felt. Not even Madelyne, though God knows she tried. I felt like most of them wouldn't *want* to understand. I also felt like I knew something nobody else did. Like I'd peeled back a corner of the universe and had seen the inner workings that human beings weren't meant to see. Like life was a lucid dream and I'd woken up within it, though I lacked the power to control it. Watching the rest of my classmates continue sleepwalking through their lives was infuriating. They had the audacity to act like they controlled the world when they had no clue what the world really looked like.

Fine, I hated them. *And* I envied them.

Being rejected from NYU had made me question my acting talent. Specifically, whether I had any. I'd played Renfield and Robin Hood. I'd played the role of a bumbling fool in a summer musical at a nearby school the previous summer. Madelyne and I had even staged a one-act play at the Kravis Center for the Performing Arts a couple of months earlier, and in each role I'd been fine. My acting was *fine*. I said the lines, I played the parts, I did the job. I could accept that it was possible I wasn't a good actor, but there were two moments that haunted me. Two moments that gave me pause and made me think I *could* be great. The first was my audition with Ms. C. That one minute as the funny freak Renfield. The second was my *I Hate Hamlet* monologue.

Those had both been moments where I'd shone. Moments where I'd drawn on a well of talent that existed somewhere inside of me. But the more I thought about it, the more I realized that those instances had been good because I hadn't been trying to perform. During my Renfield audition I'd acted on instinct, and during *I Hate Hamlet*, I had tapped into my anxiety of the person I feared becoming without knowing or understanding what I was doing.

My best acting came when I stopped trying to act. When I didn't even *know* I was acting.

Which was why life after coming out had become so much more painful. I hadn't really changed, I hadn't stopped acting, but now I knew I was doing it. And I was only doing it because I was terrified of how the other students and my teachers would treat me if I stopped.

So to recap, I was gay but too afraid to come out; my only escape route from Florida had been cut off, effectively stranding me in hell; I had a crush on a boy who I assumed would break my face and then murder me if he found out; and I blamed everyone for creating an environment where I felt terrified to be myself *and* for getting everything they wanted.

By the time baccalaureate rolled around, I was ready to burn my high school to the ground.

I'd only been mostly serious when I'd told Madelyne that I'd probably half-ass the baccalaureate speech and write it the night before. I was supposed to show a draft to my senior adviser, but he didn't chase me down when I never turned one in for his approval.

I spent weeks stewing in resentment before I sat down to write my speech, which I decided would begin with a poem I'd written.

Let me begin by saying that I was no poet. I wrote poetry, but none of it was good. Bella, who was speaking at baccalaureate before me, wrote decent poetry. Mine was purple and morose and appropriately teen-angsty. It was less Tori Amos and more William McGonagall, and it hasn't much improved since then.

But I was determined. I was determined to tell the truth without telling the truth. I was determined to point out the hypocrisy with which I, with which we *all*, had been living our lives. I was determined to tell them that there were consequences to their actions and that I was one such consequence. That when we stroll through lives of privilege without consideration of others, we risk hurting them irreparably, and that we must take responsibility for that hurt even if we aren't aware we've caused it.

That's what I was aiming for, anyway, as I stayed up all night writing and drinking iced tea and listening to Smashing Pumpkins and Tori Amos.

The day of the baccalaureate speeches, I was nervous as hell. The senior assembly was held in the gym, and I, along with the other speakers, was seated on a stage under bright, hot lights. The gym floor was filled with an ocean of folding chairs in which sat the other students, our parents, and teachers. Bella, who was a good and obvious choice, did indeed read some of her poetry, though I don't remember what it was about, who else spoke, or what they said. I was too busy thinking about my speech, sharpening the words I was about to murder my classmates with.

I sometimes wonder what kind of speech people expected me to give. When I wasn't sleeping in class, I usually spoke up only to crack a joke or argue some obscure point that no one else cared about. Without mincing words, I was an asshole. Smart? Yes. Clever? Not as clever as I believed I was. Funny? Sometimes. I held strong opinions and I loved fighting for them. For me, right and wrong were irrelevant. It was all about the debate. So, with that in mind, I have no idea why anyone thought giving me a platform to speak to my peers and their parents was going to end well.

Finally, it was my turn at the podium. The lights were hot and sweat rolled down my back. This was no different from playing Aslan, no more difficult than all those extemp rounds where I'd stood in front of strangers and bullshitted my way through a speech. More than any other speaker that day, I owned the stage. I was home.

I unfolded my papers and began to read.

I don't have video of the speech because about ten seconds in, my mom reached over to where my younger stepbrother was holding the video camera and pressed the stop button so that there was no evidence of the time I embarrassed her in front of my entire class. Madelyne's mom spent the entire speech whispering, "Don't do it!" under her breath because she assumed I was going to shout to the world that I was gay. I didn't, though I kind of wished I had. The speech didn't faze any of my friends, who were used to me being weird, and I honestly don't know if anyone understood what I was trying to say. I don't know if they heard my anger or my pain. I don't know if they heard me call them out for being awful people or heard the disgust I heaped upon myself. I don't know if they heard my challenge to face the truth of who they were and who they could be or to live with the consequences of an unfulfilled life.

I think, in the end, what they heard wasn't exactly the sentiment I was going for, but was one I could live with, and could best be summarized by the following:

To the graduating class of 1996,

Love,

Shaun

THE BIG GAY PAGE

May to August 1996

I GRADUATED HIGH SCHOOL WITHOUT BURNING THE place down, which I felt was a major accomplishment no one properly congratulated me for. Now that it was over, I felt a bit lost. Alan was coming home for the summer, and I left the Gap to work for a local computer company where I coded their first website, learned to build PCs from scratch, and tutored some elderly clients on how to use Windows 95.

I spent the majority of the summer hanging out with Madelyne and Alan. Nothing felt like it had the summer before, though. I'd changed. When I was with Maddie, I could be completely open. I could talk about guys I thought were cute and tell her how lonely and frustrated and angry I was all the time. I even told her how I'd been venting my anger by punching things. Walls, this metal filing cabinet in my bedroom, cement. It'd been difficult *not* to tell her, seeing as I'd shown up at her house with bruised and bloody knuckles often enough that she'd noticed. I was also cutting myself. I'd only done it a couple of times, but those were the only times I felt relief, and that scared me.

But I couldn't talk to Alan about *any* of that stuff. When he was around, I scurried back into the closet and slammed the door shut behind me. I spent the whole summer listening to him talk about the different girls he had crushes on and how they were all manipulative bitches because they toyed with him but wouldn't go out with him. And even though I knew what he was saying was awful and wrong, I was too scared to lose his friendship to call him out.

The worst was when Maddie and Alan started spending time alone together. They dated for a couple of weeks and eventually ended it, but I was still a total prick about it. Alan might have been an asshole, but he was one of my only friends. With him and Maddie dating, I assumed I was going to lose both of my best friends and spend the rest of the summer alone. I was also concerned because I knew Alan in a way Maddie didn't, and I didn't want to see him treat her the way he treated other girls.

The summer came to an end, and Alan went back to college. I thought a lot about telling Alan I was gay. I had the opportunities, and I felt like I was being a horrible friend by not being completely honest with him. But I couldn't do it.

When Ryan had come out the year before, I had told Alan about it one day after we'd finished gaming and the other guys had left. I hadn't planned to tell him, and I didn't yet know I was gay, but it had kind of slipped out.

"My brother's gay."

Alan paused with a handful of dice like I'd cast a Hold Person spell on him. "Weird."

"Yeah. It came out of nowhere. Like, we were driving and he just dropped it on me."

After a moment, Alan shrugged. "As long he's not too fruity, and he keeps it away from me, I don't have an issue with it I guess."

Alan had never met my brother, so there was absolutely a zero percent chance that my brother was ever going to hit on him, but that's the first place Alan went. He talked about being gay like it was a disease. Like "it" was something that he could catch if "it" got too near him.

So, when it was my turn to come out, I didn't believe Alan would be supportive of me, and I preferred to live the lie rather than lose a friend.

With the knowledge I'd learned from my summer job, I'd redesigned my website. My first website was a celebration of all the things I loved: *The Tick*, D&D, fantasy books, and writing, and it was decorated with awful graphics I'd designed in CorelDRAW. My new site was also awful and also celebrated my passions, but it included a page colored in rainbows that contained links to some queer sites I'd found and declared boldly that I was gay.

I wasn't worried about anyone discovering it because Google didn't exist at the time. Finding websites was difficult. Either it had to be submitted manually to one of the few places that were indexing websites at the time, or you had to know the address.

The only people I knew personally who were aware of its existence were Madelyne, Alan, and my brother Ryan. I wasn't worried about Maddie for obvious reasons. Alan hadn't visited my site in ages, so it didn't occur to me that I needed to hide it from him. And the only reason Ryan knew about the site was because I had sent him the link.

Date: May 3, 1996

From: Shaun

To: Ryan

Subject: Webpage

Ryan-

Sorry it took me so long. I had to figure out your address. So anyway, here it is, most parts of the page are not up, but it is still fun.

Gotta go to my play now

Shaun

And then I waited for him to reply. It was kind of a big deal, but also kind of not, if that makes sense. Ryan was my big brother, so I wanted him to know, but we were also basically strangers to each other, so there was safety in that.

Date: May 3, 1996

From: Ryan

To: Shaun

Subject: It's your big brother

For once in my life I am not going to criticize or second guess, or question you. I am more than a little jealouse tho. I wish that I had been as confident in who I am when I was 18. It took me 5 very long years to get to where I am today. I realized that I can't change who I am and if people don't like it they can hit the road packing. Thats why I came out. I got tired of being who everyone else wanted me to be.

Look you are a very smart kid and i know that you are going far in life. I have offered my freindship before and I offer it again-- if you need anything or you want anything if you need some one to talk to about anything. Call me.

I love you

Write back

Ryan

There were two problems. The first was that I didn't want a big brother right then. I wanted a friend. I've always been the kind of person who simply has to experience hardships on my own. It's not enough to tell me that the stove is hot. I'm going to touch the surface and burn my hand anyway. I might've been intelligent, but I was also incredibly stubborn. So the last thing I wanted was for the brother that I barely knew to come along and tell me how things were going to be. His intentions were pure, and he probably could have helped me understand myself if I'd been willing to listen, but I thought I was smarter than everyone else and could handle it alone.

The second problem was that since I didn't know my brother,

I assumed he was a fag just like every other gay person out there. I, alone, defied the stereotypes. Everyone else was a drug-addicted, sex-crazed, disease-harboring fag. And that included my brother. So even if I'd been willing to listen to him, I didn't think he had anything to teach me that I wanted to learn.

God, I was such an arrogant, confused asshole.

Ryan tried for about a month to start a conversation with me, but I responded with indifference, and eventually he stopped writing.

While I'd used my website intentionally to come out to Ryan, I hadn't meant to use it to come out to Alan. Or maybe I had. Just not consciously. I'd had to know on some level there was a risk Alan would see my site, but I'd posted it anyway and hadn't tried to hide it from him, so maybe I'd done it in the hopes that Alan would see it and save me the potential pain of having to tell him the truth to his face.

And see it he did.

I pulled my car in front of Madelyne's house and put it into park. She was already out the door and skipping down the pathway toward me.

"He knows," I said the moment she got into the car. "Alan knows."

"Knows what? The location of the secret government site where aliens are kept? That we secretly make fun of his hair? That I think he's the worst kisser who ever kissed?"

"He knows that I'm gay."

The levity fled Madelyne's face. "How?"

"My website."

"Oh."

"Yeah."

"And?"

I took a deep breath. I'd been holding this in for nearly a week, waiting to tell Maddie. It was rare that we didn't see each other every single day, but work had conspired to keep us apart. "Well, first he e-mailed me because he'd gone to my site to download some JavaScript I'd been working on. He saw the big gay page and asked if it was a joke or something I'd built on a dare."

"A joke?" Madelyne's eyebrow raised, and her lip twitched. She was slow to anger, but that only made her fury burn hotter when she set it free. And right then she was practically glowing.

I nodded. "So I wrote him back and explained that it wasn't a dare, and that I'd wanted to tell him for a while. I tried to make a joke about it and said something like, 'And before you ask: no, I'm not attracted to you.'"

"Because of course he's going to think you are," Maddie said.

"Of course."

"But you're not, right?"

Since I'd gotten that first e-mail from Alan telling me he knew, I'd felt like someone had stuck a corkscrew in my chest and had been slowly twisting it. I was going to lose one of my best friends, and there was nothing I could do about it. But Madelyne's question made me laugh.

"He's not *that* bad," she said after letting me cackle for a minute.

"I'm definitely *not* into Alan," I said. "Never have been."

Maddie crossed her arms over her chest, and I wisely quit laughing before she turned her anger on me.

"Did he write back?"

The corkscrew twisted deeper. "Yeah. Get this. He told me how he was so 'distraught' that he went to see this girl he's got a thing for, and used the story to get sympathy from her."

"Sympathy?" Maddie asked. "What the fuck does *he* need sympathy for? You're gay; you're not dying."

My shoulders slumped. "It's probably the same thing to him. But he said that as long as I don't go fruity on him, we can still be friends."

Madelyne was too angry for words, though I imagine she had a few words she wanted to say to Alan. But I didn't want her to, because I still held out hope that my friendship with Alan could survive. I was disgusted that he'd used my being gay to emotionally manipulate a girl who'd already told him she wasn't interested in him, but I was happy that he hadn't outright rejected me. Alan finally knew the truth, and he hadn't ended our friendship.

Except he kind of had; I just didn't know it yet.

Where Alan used to e-mail me frequently, and I was the one who took forever to respond, now it was my e-mails that went unanswered. And when he did reply, the e-mails were terse and impersonal. I figured it was because classes had started for both of us, and life was just getting in the way. But a couple of months later, I saw his mom in Publix, and we got to talking. She mentioned that Alan had been home the weekend before, and asked why I hadn't come around. I was devastated. I made up a lie about how I'd had to work, then said my good-byes.

Alan had come home for the weekend and hadn't bothered to tell me, something he'd never done before. We'd always hung out when he was home. And that's when I knew our friendship was over. Regardless of what Alan had said, he hadn't been able to accept that I was gay.

And even though, out of all the people who knew the truth, Alan was the only one who'd rejected me, that rejection filled my brain like a swarm of wasps. Depression sang a song that never ended, taunting me, telling me that Alan was only the first in a long line of friends who would eventually see me for the monster I was and abandon me.

FUTURE SELF, PART 2

September 1996

I WAS TRYING TO SEE THE FUTURE.

I had started attending classes at Palm Beach Community College at the end of August. It was a long way from New York City, but I held out hope that I could build some kind of life.

Coming out hadn't unfucked my brain. I worried straight folks would reject me for being gay and gays would reject me for not being gay enough. I was terrified that, in order to be accepted, I'd need to change the way I dressed, the way I spoke, my mannerisms, the kind of music I listened to. I liked Screeching Weasel and Operation Ivy. I liked Smashing Pumpkins and Natalie Merchant and Tori Amos. I did not like Madonna or Cher or ABBA or any of the music I believed gay people listened to. I wore baggy jeans and Docs. I bleached out my hair and started piercing things. I loved concerts and not clubs. I was desperate to have sex, but I wanted it to be with someone I could share my life with and not just someone I was sharing a moment with.

I was trying to see a future for myself where I could be gay without being a fag.

My mom's friend Barry died from complications due to AIDS at the beginning of September. I'd known Barry in the way that I knew most of my mom's friends. Which is to say, not well. He existed on the periphery of my life as someone my mom talked about occasionally and whom I'd met once or twice. I knew he'd been married and had two teenage sons, I knew he was gay, and I knew he had HIV.

I understood the last two facts in an abstract way. Barry being gay and having HIV didn't mesh with the man I'd met. Barry was tall and broad-shouldered, a successful attorney who was well liked. He was nothing like Hollywood or Tito. And, in a way, he was the reason I'd been able to hold on to the hope for so long that I could be gay and still have a normal life.

I didn't want to go to the wake, but I went out of respect for him and for my mom.

"We don't have to stay long," my mom whispered to my dad as we walked inside. The room was filled with people I didn't know, which immediately made me anxious, but I wandered in and haunted the walls and corners, trying to remain unobtrusive. Trying to stay away from the body.

"I don't know why they insisted on an open casket," I overheard someone say.

Next to the casket was an enormous picture of Barry, smiling the way I remembered him. Tall, handsome, built, broad-shouldered. “He played college football,” my mom used to say with a bit of awe in her voice.

That picture was how I remembered Barry. That picture was how I wanted to be remembered one day. That picture was a life preserver that I clung to when I couldn’t see my future.

Without meaning to, I got pressed into the line leading to the casket, and I didn’t want to dip out and seem impolite, so I let the current carry me forward. I’d lost sight of my mom and dad, and I was surrounded by mourners weeping. The room was filled with people who’d cared about Barry, loved ones who’d surely known he was gay and hadn’t abandoned him. Even as I was overwhelmed by the crowd, I was filled with hope by them. Hope that my life might also be filled with so many people who cared about me.

But then it was my turn to see the body and say good-bye.

I stepped up to the casket.

There was a man inside, but it wasn’t Barry.

There was a man inside who was gaunt and pale. A man who had wasted away. A man who was little more than skin on bones in a suit that was too big.

I glanced left at the photo, and then down at the body. It was the worst Before & After I’d ever seen.

The man in the photo was how I wanted to remember Barry, but the man in the coffin was how I *would* remember him for the rest of my life.

It didn't matter what he'd looked like when he was healthy, it didn't matter that so many people were there and cared about him. This was how his life had ended.

I'd finally succeeded in seeing the future, and it was in that coffin.

DEFENSE OF MARRIAGE

September 1996

ON SEPTEMBER 21, 1996, THE DEFENSE OF MARRIAGE ACT went into effect. Signed by Bill Clinton, DOMA defined marriage as *only* the union of one man and one woman and made it legal for states to choose *not* to recognize same-sex marriages from other states. This was mostly a response to the possibility that Hawaii might pass its own laws allowing same-sex marriages which other states would have been forced to recognize under the Full Faith and Credit Clause of the US Constitution.

I already hated myself for being gay, but the passage of DOMA simply reinforced the notion that everyone else would hate me too.

I've never considered myself particularly brave, but I occasionally suffer from wild, unexplainable streaks of fearlessness. I couldn't walk up to the guy in my economics class that I had a crush on and give him my number, but I could jump out of a plane; or give a speech to my entire class and their parents that essentially gave them the middle finger; or prepare an essay, and then read it aloud, dissecting the legitimacy of DOMA.

While I didn't find my first semester at PBCC particularly challenging, I loved my political science class. It was a natural extension of my love of debate, and my professor, Dr. March, was patient with me and often indulged my pain-in-the-ass questions. It was one of the few times in my life that I really engaged with a class, and Dr. March often gave me extra material on political theory and philosophy to read for fun.

Around the time DOMA was signed, Dr. March asked us write argumentative essays on a topic of our choosing, and I chose to explore whether a law must be moral in order to be a law. Dr. March's enthusiasm was infectious, and instead of waiting until the night before it was due to start, I worked on the paper for a couple of weeks, tweaking it right up until the day it was due. I even volunteered to read mine aloud in front of the class first, and to answer questions when I was done.

Abstract: The purpose of this paper was to define the terms "morality" and "law" whereby a set of values could be created for the purpose of determining whether or not a law has to be moral to be a law. It was determined, using a very narrow set of guidelines, that a law does not have to be moral to be a law.

I was damned proud of that paper. Using the skills I'd learned in debate, I defined the parameters of my argument—what a law was, when a law was considered legitimate, what justice was, how justice was applied, etc.—created a test against which any law could be examined, and then proceeded to run the Defense of Marriage Act through my test. I concluded that while DOMA might have been a valid law, it was most certainly not a moral law.

I held my paper in front of me like a shield while I read it, but when I was done, I set it on the table behind me and stood there feeling naked and alone. The classroom was silent. No one was looking at me. They looked at their desks and out the window and past me to where Dr. March sat in judgment, but never at me.

The silence was agonizing. But I stood there and waited. Finally, a question came.

"Are you gay?"

No one had raised their hand. The question had been shouted from somewhere in the room, though I couldn't pinpoint who'd done the asking.

"Excuse me?"

"Are you gay?" This time I saw the agitator. He was a stock character, a generic guy whose name I didn't know then and still don't know now. White skin, brown hair, forgettable face. I'm gonna call him Chad. He looked like a Chad.

This was the one question I hadn't prepared for. Yes, fine, I'd kind of hoped people would guess the truth due to the content of my presentation, but there was a difference between someone making an assumption based on subtext and them outright asking in front of the entire class. I mean, who the hell does that?

Chad. That's who does it.

I cleared my throat. "That's not relevant—"

"Yeah it is," Chad said. "So are you gay or not?"

"Again, it's not relevant because if you agree all people are equal, then—"

"Just answer the question."

Dr. March tagged in. "It's none of your business, Chad. Are there any further questions?"

I could have let Dr. March shut Chad down, returned to my seat, and moved on with my life like nothing had happened. But something in me refused to let a smarmy prick like Chad win the day.

"I am."

"There's no need—" Dr. March began, but Chad cut her off.

"See?" he said to the class. "It makes his whole argument invalid."

The righteous anger that had burned through me evaporated. I was boneless, spineless. I couldn't speak. Chad had disregarded my entire argument by simply disregarding me. I wasn't a person to him, I was a choice. A choice to be something the rest of the world didn't approve of, and therefore that rendered every opinion I had both suspect *and* unworthy of consideration. And this time I let him. I slunk back to my desk and counted down the seconds until class ended.

PANSY DIVISION

September 1996

MADDIE AND I HAD SETTLED INTO A ROUTINE. I HAD AN early morning class Monday, Wednesday, and Friday, after which we met at the mall for knishes and coffee. Then it was back to school for most of the day. But when we were done, if I didn't have to work, we'd go shopping at Toys "R" Us, Past Present Future Comics, or Music Xchange to feed our addictions to action figures, comic books, and music.

Back before Spotify or iTunes, I bought CDs. From stores. And they were expensive. I would've gone broke if it hadn't been for that run-down, smelly used music store located behind Circle K. Maddie and I spent hours pawing through the racks at Music Xchange, searching for some obscure album or new band to try.

I first noticed Ian working behind the register at Music Xchange one day while Maddie and I were browsing.

"Did she really accuse you of cheating?" Maddie asked.

"Yup." My Intro to Composition professor had asked us to write our first papers, and she'd handed me mine back with an F, claiming I'd cheated. "She said it was too well written."

"You're making this up."

"I've got the paper in the car."

"What're you going to do?"

I shrugged as I ran my fingers along the CD cases in one of the punk bins. My taste in punk music was pretty specific. I preferred punk with a sense of humor, or at least punk bands that didn't take themselves too seriously. They were surprisingly difficult to find. "I offered to show her some of the papers Mrs. Blankenship had me write last year as proof that I know how to string words together into sentences that aren't gibberish, but she said I'd have to rewrite my paper, and I'm not doing that."

Maddie gave me a frown that I knew too well. The one that said I was being a stubborn asshole. "C'mon, pookie. How long will it take you? An hour? Just write a new paper."

"But then she'll have won."

"So what?"

I didn't want to talk about it anymore. I understood the logic of what Madelyne was saying, but it was the principle of the matter. "We'll see. I made an appointment with the head of the English department to discuss it."

"Or you could write the paper and be done with it."

"I'd rather be done with this conversation."

I moved away from Maddie, and that's when Ian caught my

eye. He had platinum blond hair gelled into spikes, a stud pierced through his eyebrow, blue eyes, and he was wearing a torn white tee. He had that whole suburban, nonthreatening punk vibe going on. The kind that said, "I'm gonna protest fascism and the corporate control of the government, but I'll be home in time for dinner." I obviously fell immediately in love.

Over the next couple of weeks, I used every excuse possible to convince Maddie to go to Music Xchange instead of Toys "R" Us or PPF. She knew I was crushing hard on the guy, so she indulged me, even though it was getting to the point where we were as familiar with the store's inventory as its employees were. Sometimes, if Ian wasn't there, we'd walk in and then walk right back out. But when he *was* there, we'd stay for a good hour chatting about music. Ian's tastes ran toward the angry, screechy end of the punk spectrum, but he was sweet and funny, and I bought every CD he recommended. He could've convinced me to buy anything.

One day, I went in alone, determined to find an album by a queer punk band called Pansy Division that Ryan had told me about. They could have been a polka band—they were queer, and that was what mattered. It was the one time I actually hoped Ian *wouldn't* be there. Which seems counterintuitive, right? Yeah, buying a CD by a band called Pansy Division would have been a great way to clue Ian in that I was gay, but the whole idea made me uncomfortable. Like buying condoms and lube from my grandma. Either way, I was hoping to avoid it.

But the universe clearly hated me, so, of course, Ian was working.

"Hey." Ian gave me the chin nod as I skulked in.

"Hey." I could barely meet his eyes. I beelined right for the punk bins and flipped through them until I found Pansy Division stuffed in front of Propagandhi. Instead of buying it right away, I left the CD where I'd found it and browsed like I normally did, frequently returning to the *P*s like I was afraid the CD was going to vanish before I had the chance to buy it, even though I was the only customer in the store. Ian wasn't as chatty as normal, which I was grateful for.

I could still leave. I could leave and come back on a day when Ian wasn't working. Buy the album then. But that was stupid. I was already there, and it's not like I was buying a rainbow-colored cock ring. I could do this. I grabbed the CD, walked to the register, turned it facedown, and slid it across the counter to Ian.

Ian picked it up and flipped it over.

My heart. Oh God, my heart felt like it was going to explode. The boy I had a terminal crush on was holding a CD by a band called Pansy Division. And did I mention that the album's title was *Pile Up* or that the cover art was a photo of a gay orgy? Yup. Ian was holding a CD with a bunch of sweaty, naked dudes climbing all over one another like they were playing the worst (or best, depending on how you feel about gay orgies) game of Twister ever on the cover.

Forget what I said earlier. I would have rather bought an economy box of condoms and a barrel of lube from my grandma than that one CD from Ian.

"This is a good one," Ian said.

"What?"

He held up the CD, but he may as well have been shining a rainbow spotlight on me and shouting, "We got a homo here! Look at this homo! Everyone look at this fag!" I was mortified even though we were the only people in the store.

"I like this one," he said.

Was he flirting? Was that gay code for "Hey, I'm gay too, and I think you're cute. We should totally hang out sometime. We'll get coffee or Chinese and I'll tell you my whole life story, and you'll tell me yours, and then we'll make out and get married and spend the rest of our lives together listening to queercore bands and fighting the man?"

What was gay code for "Yes please. I've been waiting for you my entire life?"

"Cool" probably wasn't it, but "cool" is all I could spit out, because words were hard. Coming up with words and speaking words and doing both of those things without drooling or throwing up was impossible. If my Intro to Comp teacher had seen me at that moment, there would have been no doubt in her mind that I lacked the ability to write the paper she'd accused me of plagiarizing.

Instead of speaking, instead of pouring my heart out to Ian, I stared awkwardly while he rang up the CD. I dreamed our entire lives while he took my cash and counted back the change. For the first time since coming out, I glimpsed a future for myself that didn't end with me dying of loneliness or disease.

And then I ran from the store, because I was a freak.

The CD, by the way, was awful, but I didn't care because I was in love.

A couple of nights later, Maddie and I were at my house watching bad movies and eating cookies—chocolate chip for me, Oreos for her. We were obsessed with awful movies. We'd seen *Anaconda* at least three times in the theater.

"What happened with your essay?" Maddie asked when the credits rolled. I stretched out on my floor and turned to face her. She was perched across my bed, looking slightly sick from cookie overload.

"I wrote a new one."

"Told you."

"While Mrs. Harvey and the head of the English department watched."

"What?"

I shrugged. "I wanted to prove definitively that I didn't plagiarize anything. And, as a bonus, Mrs. Harvey said I can skip a bunch of classes since I clearly don't need the writing help."

"Seems like a waste of money."

"I can sleep in class or I can sleep at home. Home is comfier." I stifled a yawn. Maddie was getting antsy like she did when she was about ready to leave, and I'd spent most of the last couple of days trying to decide how to talk to her about Ian. I didn't want to lose my nerve, so I blurted it out. "Will you call Ian for me and see if he's into guys?"

Maddie stopped and stared. "That would be a no."

"Please?"

"Why on Earth would I do that?"

I explained about the Pansy Division CD.

"And you think him saying he liked it means he might be gay?"

"Don't you?"

"Maybe," she said. "But I'm still not calling."

"I'd call for you."

Madelyne laughed. "No you wouldn't, and I wouldn't ask." She smiled. "He is cute, though, so you better call him."

Maddie was right. It was a lot to ask of a friend. Besides, I didn't want Ian to think I didn't have the balls to pick up the phone and call him myself. That'd be a terrible way to start our life together.

I tossed and turned all night, running scenarios in my head, trying to think up the perfect opening line, imagining how he'd respond, visualizing the ways this was going to go wrong. And then the next day, when I got home from my classes, I picked up the phone and dialed. It rang and rang. And rang.

"Music Xchange. This is Ian."

"Yeah, hey. You probably don't remember me, but I was in there a couple of days ago. I bought the Pansy Division CD."

"I remember." There was a cautious curiosity to his voice.

"So I know this is weird and all, but I come in with my friend a lot—"

"The redhead," Ian said.

"Right. Madelyne."

"Is that her name?" he asked. "She seems cool. Does she have a boyfriend?"

Really? I mean, *really*?!

"Uh, she *is* cool, and she doesn't have a boyfriend. I can have her call you sometime if you want."

"Do you think she would?"

"Definitely."

There was a moment of awkward silence. Then Ian said, "So what'd you need?"

"Oh," I said. "Yeah, nothing. Talk to you later." And I hung up.

I was crushed. Absolutely devastated. The first time I'd worked up the courage to act, to say something, and I hadn't even gotten the words out before he'd shot me down.

I screamed into my pillow, and I punched my metal filing cabinet until the front was smeared with blood and the drawers were so warped they wouldn't open.

> *September 25, 1996, 10:41 p.m.*
> *Things are really bad for me right now. I have been keeping these journals as a record of how much I have changed. The changes have been disturbing. I pretty much want to write this entry in case I actually do decide to kill myself. I want my family to understand exactly what it was that was going on in my head. I don't know if I'll go through with it, but at this point I'm considering it in the same calculating way that I considered getting my ears pierced. Not as a fantasy, but as something I truly wanted to do and something I could do.*

A phrase keeps going through my head: "How can I believe in anything, if I can not believe in myself?" I don't believe in anything right now, because I can't seem to believe in myself. I actually got to the point of what I would write in my notes to my family and friends and I came really close to writing them. The fact that I am writing this shows how close I am.

Thursday night I got so bad that I just sat in a corner in my room and couldn't stop shaking. I just sat like that for about half an hour and then got up and went to bed. I'm losing it so bad and I don't know what to do. I keep having all these really bad dreams only I don't remember most of them only the impression of them. And I haven't been able to sleep a ful night's sleep in weeks. The only thing is that I really have been trying to ignore it because I want to have fun and be happy. I have been trying so hard but there's like this voice in the back of my mind telling me that it's all wrong. I just feel so lost. I don't feel like I have any direction. I know what I'm doing, but it doesn't seem like anything I do matters. If I had any courage I'd just end it, but where would that get me? I've gone over all that before but it's like this real uneasy balance. You've got this life that has very little worth holding on to and then complete oblivion. How could anyone choose non-existance when there's always a chance, however small, that something good might happen. I guess it's good that I still hold on to some bit of hope, but there have been brief seconds when it wouldn't have take much to convince me otherwise. I'm not completely insane, or maybe I am. I mean, I have more than a lot of people but I can't live for my computer or the fact that my parents don't beat me. Hell I would settle for abusive parents if I could just get some sort of order to my life. The harder that I try to do things the more I get knocked down. It's just getting to the point where I hate what I am. i am trying to be me but I just hate that person because he never gets anywhere. I really want to believe in myself but it's so hard to believe in something when everyone keeps laughing at you and telling you you're wrong.

I'm sitting here in a dead end town, going to a shitty college, my life is a waste. I have completely fucked everything that means anything to me. Right now I really want to die and there is very little that is keeping me from running downstairs and getting my dad's gun.

BEAUTIFUL THING

November 1996

SEPTEMBER 1996 TRIED TO KILL ME. I DIDN'T HAVE TO simply imagine what my future might hold any longer. The future was right in front of me, brandishing an ax. From Barry's death to the passage of a law that enshrined discrimination against queer individuals into the fabric of our country. No matter where I looked or what I did, I was being told that I didn't belong, that I shouldn't exist, that I didn't have a future.

I wasn't even asking for much. I could handle never being married, I could live with not being able to serve in the military, I could learn how to fight people who thought they could disregard me because of my sexuality, but I couldn't live without love. I wanted to fall in love. I wanted to *be* in love. I wanted to find someone I could share my life with and who would love me for who I was.

I was spoon-fed countless examples of what romantic love should look like. It was Sam returning from the dead as a ghost because of his love for Molly, and protecting her from danger with the help of Whoopi Goldberg; Lloyd standing outside of Diane's window holding a boom box over his head blasting "In Your Eyes"; it was Jack rescuing Rose from a loveless marriage and then saving her from freezing to death (though I call total BS on them both not being able to fit on that door). I was surrounded by examples of what romantic love looked like.

But none of those examples ever looked like me.

There were no happy queers in stories. There was one section in Barnes & Noble for Gay & Lesbian books. One row of one shelf out of that entire store. And it mostly consisted of erotica. But I still searched each and every book to find a story I could see myself in. I'd tiptoe to the aisle, look down to make sure there was no one around, and then casually stroll toward the section. If anyone walked past, I'd keep going, pretending I was looking at something else. Barnes & Noble may as well have set up a disco ball and a glitter cannon that went off each time someone tried to look at the Gay & Lesbian books.

Eventually I got my hands on a copy of *Magic's Pawn* by Mercedes Lackey, the first book I'd ever read with a queer person in it, but in addition to some sketchy sex with a talking horse, the story lacked joy. The main character still suffered for being gay. Even in fantasies, the gay kid couldn't be happy.

I was trying so hard to hang on, to build a future in my mind to look forward to. Straight people had countless examples of romantic movies, straight men got two—TWO!—movies showing them that it was okay for them to fall in love with mannequins and that they would find acceptance (three, actually, if you count *Lars and the Real Girl*, a movie in which Ryan Gosling falls in love with a sex doll), but I couldn't find a single example of a movie where the gay characters got their happily ever after.

The closest I'd seen was *The Birdcage*, which came out in March 1996. *The Birdcage*, while funny, was funny at the expense of gay people and culture. Yeah, I get that the movie is supposed to be a comedy, but all of the comedy requires the audience to think that men dressing in drag is *hilarious*. That Nathan Lane's feminine mannerisms are *so funny*. Not only did it reinforce every negative stereotype people held about gay men, it used them for laughs. Nathan Lane managed to imbue Albert with a humanity that I doubt any non-gay actor would have been capable of, and kept us laughing *with* him instead of solely *at* him, but *The Birdcage* still felt to me like it wasn't about the acceptance and celebration of queer culture so much as the exploitation of it.

My sense of what living as a gay man was like was obviously skewed, but it was typical for the time, especially for someone like me who'd lived a sheltered life. My views had been influenced by the ways in which media, including the news, portrayed the gay community. There was the sense that HIV and AIDS were the result of the promiscuous lifestyle led by those in the gay community, and that gay clubs were dens of iniquity where men had sex in dark corners and snorted lines of coke off of one another's washboard abs. I never questioned the assumptions I'd made about the gay community, partly because I was young and naive, partly because depression whispered to me that it was the life I deserved.

Either way, I didn't think I'd ever see a movie where two men were allowed to fall in love and have their happily ever after. Not in my lifetime.

And then I experienced *Beautiful Thing.*

Beautiful Thing was originally a stage play written by Jonathan Harvey, who also adapted it for the screen. It was directed by Hettie MacDonald (who directed the *Doctor Who* episode "Blink," one of my personal favorites of the new series) and filmed in the UK. Sony Pictures Classics picked up the US distribution rights, and it hit theaters in October 1996.

"I don't know what it's about," I said. "Just that it's gay."

I'd picked up Madelyne, and we were driving to our local movie theater, which wasn't known for showing indie or foreign films—when Maddie and I wanted to see those, we usually had to drive to a little theater over an hour away—so I was shocked it was playing.

"And it's British," I added.

"You don't have to sell me on it."

"It may not be any good."

"Will it be better than *The Rock*?"

I shrugged. "I don't see how it could be much worse."

"Then I'm in!"

Not that I'd doubted her. Maddie would have driven with me to Atlanta or beyond to see the movie if I'd asked her to.

My hands shook and my voice wavered when I walked up to the ticket booth and said, "Two for *Beautiful Thing*." I expected the young woman behind the glass to raise an eyebrow or snicker or sneer, but she took my cash, printed out the tickets, and slid them to me.

I wasn't just nervous because I was buying tickets to see a gay movie, I was nervous because someone might recognize me. I'd grown up in this town. The school where I'd attended kindergarten, first, and second grades was three miles west, and my high school was only two miles west. The Publix where I'd worked was literally across the street. People I knew worked in the theater. I could run into someone from my neighborhood who might tell my parents that they'd seen me go into a *gay* movie. I wasn't afraid my parents were going to disown me, but I still wasn't ready to come out to them.

When I found out I was going to fail geometry my sophomore year, I didn't tell my parents about it until I'd gone to see my guidance counselor, talked over my options with her, signed up for summer school, and created a plan to minimize the impact of the F on my education. That's who I am. I don't like to bring my problems to other people until I've figured out a solution.

When it came to me being gay, I didn't have *anything* figured out. I didn't know what being gay meant to me, and until I did, I didn't want to burden my parents with it.

So buying the tickets to a gay movie right there on my home turf felt incredibly risky. I kept looking over my shoulder as Maddie and I stood in line to buy Twizzlers for her and M&Ms

for me. I glanced around us as we walked toward the theater to make sure no one saw which one we went into.

It was the middle of the day on a weekday, so I'd expected the theater to be empty, and it was except for a couple of guys sitting in the second row and an elderly couple sitting in the middle. I assumed the elderly people had done what Maddie and I often did and had shown up and bought tickets to whatever was playing at the time even if they had no idea what the movie was about. The guys up front, I assumed, were like me.

Maddie and I sat near the back and joked around while we waited for the commercials to end and the movie to begin. I couldn't shake the feeling that I was doing something shameful. That police were going to bust into the theater, see me sitting there watching a film about two gay boys, drag me out in handcuffs, and splash my mug shot all over the news for the world to see and ridicule. That before the movie began, theater management was going to announce over the loudspeaker that the show had been listed in error and they would instead be showing *Space Jam*, a basketball movie starring Michael Jordan and Bugs Bunny.

"You okay?" Madelyne asked.

"Just hate these commercials."

Maddie frowned but didn't reply.

And then the lights dimmed and the movie played.

Beautiful Thing begins with Jamie, a teenage boy who lives with his mom—a bartender—and her hippie boyfriend in a working-class British neighborhood. He's a shy boy without many friends who spends his time reading gossip magazines and spying on the neighbors, who include Leah, a young woman who dreams of stardom, and Ste, an athletic boy who's abused at home by his father and brother.

As the movie unfolds, it's clear that Jamie knows he's gay, though he's not out yet, and that he's crushing *hard* on Ste, who doesn't seem to notice. Every time Jamie watched Ste with that look in his eyes, I melted. I understood. I felt crushed right along with him. This was everything I ever wanted. The boys weren't in the movie to be laughed at. They weren't there to be ridiculed or used as an object lesson. No one was addicted to drugs. No one had HIV.

I clutched the armrest during the scene when Ste stays over at Jamie's because his father has beaten him and kicked him out of the house—not because Ste was gay but simply because his father was an alcoholic asshole. They agree to sleep "top to tail," sharing the twin bed, and wind up talking. Jamie sees Ste wince from the bruises and offers to massage peppermint lotion into Ste's back. The scene is sweet and tentative. It's not about sex; it's about two young men who aren't sure how they feel or what their feelings mean, struggling to make sense out of chaos.

The elderly couple got up and stormed out during this scene, but I barely noticed them leave. I was too captivated by Jamie and Ste's story, and I was not going to let *anyone* ruin it. This movie, this moment, belonged to me.

The next morning, Ste, ashamed of what happened, sneaks

out, leaving Jamie even more confused. But it doesn't last long. Jamie confesses his feelings to Ste and convinces him to take a bus to a town where they don't know anyone. They wind up at a drag bar where there are other gay couples. The scene culminates with Jamie and Ste making out under the moonlight.

My heart soared!

Before the movie ends, Jamie and Ste have to face reality. They have to decide whether to keep their relationship secret or tell the world. They bring Leah into their circle of trust, and then Jamie confides in his mom, who accepts him. Ste doesn't want to tell anyone, because he's scared of what his father and brother will do to him if they find out.

Some movies might have ended there. With a scene that was downbeat but somewhat hopeful. *Beautiful Thing* was not just some movie. It was, after all, billed as an "Urban Fairytale," and fairy tales deserve their happy endings.

In the final scene, Jamie is standing in this little piazza in front of their apartments. Ste comes walking down the stairs toward him, dressed up and looking handsome. Mama Cass's "Dream a Little Dream of Me" drifts out of Leah's open windows. Jamie holds out his hand to Ste and asks him to dance. Ste thinks Jamie's joking at first—people might see them! His father might see them!—but Jamie isn't joking. Tentatively, Ste takes Jamie's hand, and they embrace. They dance.

When nosy neighbors begin to peek their heads out, Leah and Jamie's mom join the dancing, daring anyone to screw with their boys. And as the camera pans out, Ste rests his head on

Jamie's shoulder, leaving us with the image of two boys together and so totally in love. Happily ever after. The end.

Beautiful Thing was a revelation. I walked out of that theater smiling. I walked out of the theater *beaming*. I walked out of the theater shooting rainbows out of my ass and firing them from my eyes. Jamie and Ste were like me! They were just average teenage boys. Like me! I was able, for the first time since I'd written *The Round Table*, to imagine a future where I could have all the things I wanted. Where I could fall in love, where I could find someone to spend the rest of my life with and not be judged for it. Where I could be gay and not have to change who I was.

"When are we seeing it again?" Madelyne asked when we got out to the parking lot.

"Now?" I said. "Tomorrow? Every day until it leaves the theater?"

I bought the soundtrack, which consisted entirely of Mama Cass songs, and blasted it nonstop in an effort to hold on to the sheer, unadulterated joy I'd felt while watching the movie.

As I'm writing this, the movie *Love, Simon*, based on the book *Simon vs. the Homo Sapiens Agenda* by Becky Albertalli, is in its second week in the theaters. It is the first queer-centered romantic comedy in the US to receive the blockbuster treatment. There are billboards promoting it everywhere; stars like Kristen Bell and Neil Patrick Harris bought out entire movie theaters and gave the tickets away so that kids could see this movie. It's attracted the attention of fans beyond the gay community, and it's helped countless people come to terms with their own sexuality. The film's titular character, played by Nick Robinson, shared a story about how the movie helped his brother come out to him, and another of the film's stars, Keiynan Lonsdale, who also plays Kid Flash on the CW's *The Flash*, used the movie as a springboard to come out.

Whether *Love, Simon* makes money or not is irrelevant. It's created a cultural moment of acceptance for the queer community.

I wonder, if *Beautiful Thing* had had a cultural moment in 1996 the way that *Love, Simon* is having one now, would things have been different for me? Because the unfortunate thing about 1996 is that *Beautiful Thing* didn't inspire a moment. It didn't start a movement. No one bought all the seats in movie theaters. It didn't cause anyone famous to come out. It wasn't heaped with love and praise by Olympic athletes, and there were certainly no billboards for it in Times Square. Sometimes it felt like I was the only person in the world who even knew it existed. *Beautiful Thing* mattered to me, but as time passed, my memories of joy were crowded out by the memory of the elderly couple who'd been so disgusted by the idea of two young men in love that they'd left before the end. I began to see the movie not as an example of how my life could be, but rather as the fairy tale the movie billed itself as.

A fairy tale that would never come true for me.

QUEER, PART 1

December 1996 to January 1997

QUEER WAS THE WORD I USED TO DESCRIBE MYSELF. EVEN though I hadn't met a single gay person around my age other than my brother, I assumed, based on the stereotypes I'd absorbed, that I wouldn't get along with them. That we'd have nothing in common. I was an outsider amongst outsiders. I was queer.

I was also invisible. I was screaming on the inside, begging for someone to see me, but no one did.

That was, I believed, the problem. Surely I couldn't be the only queer boy living in South Florida or suffering through tedious classes at Palm Beach Community College. I imagined them hiding in the walls waiting for someone to come along and fire off a signal to let them know that they weren't alone. And I believed if I could figure out how to send up that flare, the queers like me would find me and embrace me and I'd discover my own beautiful thing.

"What am I doing wrong?" I asked Maddie while she sat with me on my break from Sunglass Hut. I'd finally had enough of the Gap and the impossible task of trying to keep the denim wall neatly folded, and I'd accepted a job at the Sunglass Hut a few stores down. My new manager, Carlos, was a youngish guy from Brazil who worked hard but didn't seem to take life seriously, and we'd hit it off immediately. Selling overpriced sunglasses wasn't much different from selling overpriced clothes, but it was a hell of a lot more fun.

Maddie gave me a constipated look, while noodles from the Chinese place hung out of her mouth. "What're we talking about?"

"There was a guy who came to the store," I said. "And I'm sure he was fun, but I got nothing from him when I flirted."

"I've seen how you flirt."

"Is it that bad?"

"It's cute."

"I didn't realize it was that bad."

Maddie held up her hands. "How did you know he was fun? Was he wearing a sign?"

"No—"

"Were you wearing a sign?"

I tilted my head and frowned at her. "Obviously not."

"Then maybe he just didn't know and was afraid you'd beat him up with your string bean arms."

"Maybe." I was starting to wish I hadn't brought it up. "You register for your classes next semester?"

I shoveled food into my mouth while I ate. With Christmas a couple of weeks away, the store was slammed, and I doubted I'd get another chance to eat until we closed.

"Mostly. I'm taking physics and photography."

My first semester grades had come in, and I'd gotten straight As for the first time in my life. I wasn't sure whether that meant that my classes were too easy or that I was finally being challenged. "I'm taking Mrs. Harvey again for comp two."

"Why?"

"Because she said I wouldn't have to come to class much and that she'd let me write a short story for an independent honors project."

"Well, okay then."

I shrugged. "I think I'm gonna transfer to FAU next semester."

"Really?"

"My other option is to go to the same school as Alan, and no thank you."

"Fair."

"What about you?"

"PBCC for another year."

The news made me smile. I was worried Maddie would take her brains to another school and leave me alone. "So we get to keep suffering together?"

"Suffer?" she said. "Every moment with me is a goddamn joy."

I laughed and then finished my lunch. Maddie took off and I returned to work. But I was still thinking about what she'd said. Not about school but about the signs. I'd seen a few cars with rainbow stickers on the backs like they were advertising, and I thought life would be easier if everyone wore their sexuality on their foreheads. Since that was never going to happen, I needed a different plan.

Look, I was a walking contradiction. I bought into the lies that movies and TV and books had force-fed me. I believed gay men were destined to die of AIDS, to die alone, to wind up the victims of hate crimes. I believed gay men were promiscuous, that they only cared about dancing, drinking, drugs, and dicks. I believed it was impossible for a gay man to live a "normal" life or find love. But I wasn't gay. I was queer. I'd seen my future, dancing to Mama Cass, and I was going to will it into existence if it killed me.

At the same time, I was still desperate to fit in. I rejected what I assumed gay culture would turn me into, while twisting myself into knots trying to figure out who I was supposed to be. I hated gay people until I learned I was gay. Then I hated being gay, and I hated myself. Then I turned my hatred toward gay culture and tried to hold myself apart from it.

I was a mess, and all I really wanted was a boyfriend.

Then, a week before the start of the new semester, I came up with a plan.

"Are you sure this is a good idea?" Maddie asked me. We were sitting at Denny's, eating our grilled cheese sandwiches and nibbling on fries.

"Good?" I said. "Probably not. But how am I ever supposed to find a boyfriend if no one knows I'm queer?"

Maddie gave me a little shrug. It wasn't indifference. Maddie had never been indifferent to anything in her whole life. The truth was that I sucked up so much of the emotional oxygen in the room that it left little for her. I'm not sure how our friendship didn't suffocate.

"Maybe work on being less shy," she said.

"Really?"

"It comes off as arrogance."

I would've laughed at that, if my brain had been able to process it before she'd continued speaking.

"I know you're not," she said. "But your shyness makes you seem aloof, and that reads as conceited sometimes."

Around strangers, my shyness and insecurity bordered on debilitating, but if they were interpreting that as arrogance, it was no wonder no one talked to me.

"Why can't people just see me for who I really am?"

"Because you don't let them."

"But how am I supposed to do that?"

Maddie pushed her plate away and tried to smile. This wasn't a new conversation, and I imagine she was both tired of hearing it and tired of saying it. "Walk up to them and introduce yourself."

I scoffed. "Yeah, because that worked super well with Ian." Not that I was bitter about the incident or anything.

"You can't let one rejection make you think it's always going to be so tough," she said. "There are other guys out there."

"I know. That's why I need to go through with my plan. So that they'll know I'm here. So that there won't be any doubts about who I am."

"Maybe. But is this really you, or is it who you want to be?"

I didn't have an answer, but I'd already made up my mind, so I changed the subject.

There were a lot of things I could have done that might have identified me as queer. I could have worn a rainbow flag pin, but people might have simply assumed I was supporting the cause. I could have dyed my hair flamingo pink, but people might've thought I'd lost a bet or simply liked the color. I could have covered my backpack with patches for Pansy Division, but it was unlikely that anyone would have recognized them. No, I needed to make a totally and utterly unambiguous statement. I needed to leave no doubt in the minds of everyone who saw me that I was absolutely, positively, 100 percent into guys.

It all went back to what Maddie had said while we'd been eating Chinese. If no one knew I was queer without me wearing a sign, then I'd wear a sign. It was an outfit, actually. And I planned to wear it to class on the first day of the new semester.

My style up to that point was a weird hybrid all my own involving a lot of ripped jeans and nice dress shirts worn over grungy tees. Whatever. It worked. The outfit I wore to class was weird, though, even for me. Jeans, my black-and-white Docs, black socks, a fresh white T-shirt, and black suspenders. But the pièce de résistance was the word QUEER that I'd stenciled across the front of the shirt in black block letters.

There was nothing I could do, short of wearing a string of dildos as a necklace, that would have made it more unequivocally clear that I was into guys.

I had to wear a shirt over my outfit to get out of the house without my mom or dad or stepbrothers seeing me. The whole twenty-minute drive to school, I felt my heart beating in my stomach. I wanted to puke. I kept hearing Madelyne's question in my head. Was this who I was? Was this who I wanted to be?

I pulled into the parking lot and sat in my car for a couple of minutes, blasting Dance Hall Crashers for courage. Finally, I shut off the engine, got out of my car, and walked across the parking lot to the English building. I kept my eyes forward, avoiding the stares, ignoring the giggles. It was too late to turn back; I'd committed to this ridiculous plan.

If you're reading this and thinking it's no big deal, you've got to remember that this was 1997. Not only did most people still consider "queer" a slur, but no one wore T-shirts announcing that the word applied to them. I assumed I was either going to find true love or someone was going to follow me to my car and beat me with a tire iron. And the truth was that I was so desperate that I didn't care which way it went.

I kept a journal recording people's reactions throughout the day.

> *January 7, 1996, 8 a.m.*
> *I'm walking around today with a shirt that says "queer" on it. The best reaction was from Mrs. Harvey. She was handing out the syllabus and while telling us about her vacation. As she walked by me she said, "This weekend my son got gay..um engaged."*

She said it right as she was walking by me and there was no mistaking that she was looking at me.

January 7, 1996, 10:20 a.m.
So I said I was doing this primarily so that there would be no doubt that I'm gay. I've turned heads and heard laughter and whispers, but I still feel confusion. I thought this would be some sort of magic queer suit and that, like Superman, I would be transformed, but it's not working. I may have screwed myself by wearing this shirt. Maybe I'm breaking some sort of taboo by bypassing the gaydar and wearing a sign.

In one way, I felt empowered. This was my response to Chad. This was my response to the old couple who'd been too disgusted to sit through *Beautiful Thing.* This was my response to everyone who thought there was something wrong with being queer. To everyone who wanted to silence me or tell me that I didn't matter because of my sexuality. At the same time, I felt like I'd willingly walked into a prison cell, shut the door behind me, and broken the key off in the lock.

No one cornered me in a dark hallway and attacked me, but no one tried to befriend me either. The outfit that I'd hoped would draw other queer people to me must have repulsed them instead. They didn't appear from the shadows in a burst of glitter, they sank more deeply into them, leaving me feeling as isolated and alone as I ever had.

I was sitting in the hallway waiting for my statistics class to start. I wasn't avoiding people or spending my time between classes hiding in corners. I made sure to plant myself in the middle of the most crowded buildings at every opportunity. A girl named Aimee that I'd met my first semester sat down beside me.

"Interesting shirt," she said.

"It's because I'm gay."

Aimee laughed. "I know. I knew."

"You did?"

"Yeah."

The day had gone much like I'd planned, but not at all like I'd hoped. In my dreams, I wore the shirt and the outfit, and it caught the eye of some cute, shy gay nerd like me. Seeing my shirt gave him the courage to approach me and introduce himself and ask if I wanted to go see a band play or catch a movie. I said yes and we went out and fell in love, and I got the happily ever after gay people like me never got in books and movies. I got to be sappy and messy like every straight person I knew.

"I just wanted to be seen, you know?"

Aimee frowned. She glanced at the people down the hall covertly watching me. "They don't see you. They see a word. That's all they see now. That's all they're going to see. Not you. Just a word."

"What was I supposed to do?" I asked. "How else was I supposed to let people know?"

Aimee shrugged. "I don't know, but sometimes it's better to whisper than to scream."

Funny. I thought I'd just been screaming on the inside.

WHAT I NEEDED TO SAY

February to March 1997

MY LIFE FELT MEANINGLESS. IT FELT EMPTY. DESPITE WHAT I'd hoped, my queer shirt hadn't acted like a magnet to other queer students at PBCC. I was, if anything, more isolated than I'd been before. I was cutting more frequently, and I was angry all the time. It was an awful cycle that I couldn't break free of. I cut myself because I had all this pain inside of me that I didn't know how to let out, but then I was so ashamed of what I was doing that it amplified my feelings and made me hate myself even more. Cutting wasn't helping; it was making things even worse. I wanted to stop, so I threw myself into work at Sunglass Hut and into the honors project I was working on with Mrs. Harvey, hoping the distractions would help.

I still hadn't given up on my dreams of acting, but where they had once seemed within my reach, they now felt impossibly far away. Instead, I focused on writing. Even though I'd been doing it since third grade, I'd never taken it seriously, but Mrs. Harvey was letting me write a short story for the honors project. Throughout January and February, we worked on character sketches and outlines together. Despite the rocky start to our relationship, I'd come to admire her.

"What is it you're trying to say with this story, Shaun?"

I shrugged. "Do I have to know that right now?"

Mrs. Harvey weighed the question for a moment. "Not necessarily. But you should consider your options so that you're not writing aimlessly."

Working with outlines was anathema to everything I believed about writing. Writing, I thought, came from inspiration, and inspiration appeared whenever it damn well felt like arriving. The best I could do was set the table and be ready when it decided to show. "I get it. I just don't know what I want to say."

"Then what do you *need* to say?" Mrs. Harvey leaned on her elbows and rested her head in her hands. She was an older woman with hair the color of an orangesicle.

"You okay?"

"Just tired."

"You didn't seem this tired last semester."

Mrs. Harvey looked up. "You've got good intuition. That's an important quality for a writer to have."

I shook my head. "I'm not a writer."

"Could've fooled me."

"Well, you're not fooling anyone," I said. "You're definitely not okay."

A wan smile spread across Mrs. Harvey's face. "My cancer's back. Breast cancer."

"Oh shit. I'm sorry. I didn't mean—"

"It's fine. I wasn't trying to hide it."

I felt like an ass. I should have let it go instead of pushing, but that's not how I was wired. "You're going to be all right, though? Chemo? Radiation?"

"All of the above," she said. "Don't you worry about me. This isn't my first dance." She tapped the pages in front of me. "Now back to your story."

I was supposed to turn in the story before spring break, but with only a couple of days until it was due, I hadn't written anything other than the outlines and sketches and a few random scenes. No matter how hard I tried, I couldn't make myself sit down and write the story I'd envisioned. I thought it was my old high school laziness reminding me that it was still hanging around and hadn't gone anywhere. There was nothing wrong with me and nothing wrong with the story, I was simply a lazy prick who couldn't get his head out of his ass long enough to do the work.

But my problem ran deeper than my laziness. There was also something fundamentally not working about the narrative I was trying to wrangle. The story was about two boys, Jamie and Nathan, who meet, fall in love, and decide to come out together at school. Only, things don't go as planned, and one of the boys is shot and killed, leaving the other alone. This was the story I'd been programmed to write. It should have been easy. But the words wouldn't come. I thought more about what I was trying to say with the story. I believed I was attempting to tell the truth as I saw it. That I would never find happiness; that if I did, it would end in tragedy; and that it was, therefore, pointless to try.

"Damn!" I slammed my fists on my keyboard, leaned back in my chair, and ran my hands through my greasy hair. It was late. Everyone else had gone to bed. I needed sleep too, but the story was due in the morning and I had nothing to show Mrs. Harvey that she hadn't already seen.

"It's no big deal," I told myself. "It's only an honors project." The worst thing that would happen is that I wouldn't get the honors designation. It wouldn't affect my grade at all.

I sighed and went downstairs to get a drink. My mom was sitting on the couch watching TV.

"I thought you went to bed?"

Mom looked over her shoulder. "I've got too much to do before we leave."

"Tahoe?"

She nodded. My parents were going skiing at Lake Tahoe, leaving me and my brothers home alone again. Like mine, my mom's insomnia was worst when she was stressed. She'd probably spent an hour in bed mentally packing, unpacking, and repacking her suitcases even though they weren't leaving for a week.

"Shouldn't you be in bed?"

"I've got a paper to finish."

"You'll get it done," she said. "You always do."

"I wish I shared your confidence. See you in the morning." I took my tumbler of water upstairs and sat on my floor in front of my CD collection. Music might inspire me. I considered Tori Amos, but landed on Veruca Salt instead.

I'd first heard Veruca Salt while working at the Gap. The mall didn't open until noon on Sundays, and Ginny had us come in at nine to clean the store, and for those three hours we drank coffee and blasted music. A lot of my music education had come from those mornings. The Sunday crew introduced me to Veruca Salt, the Breeders, Liz Phair, Bikini Kill, Concrete Blonde, and so many other amazing bands.

I popped in the CD and hit play. The reverb leading into the punishing drums of the first song filled my room, and I stared at my screen and waited for the magic. It didn't come. I didn't type a single word. Then, twenty minutes in, Nina Gordon sang, "Take me away . . . ," and I stopped to listen, enthralled.

The song was called "Benjamin," and for four minutes and five seconds, I remained transfixed by it. Maybe it was the plaintive tone of the music, maybe it was the way Nina Gordon's voice sounded when she sang "Benjamin," as if she was both making a statement and asking a question. I don't know, but that song latched onto something within me and refused to let go. When the last note faded, I reached over, returned to the beginning of the track, and put it on repeat. Inspiration had finally arrived.

"I was just waiting for the sunrise," Benjamin said in the opening line. And while my own sunrise crept slowly toward me, I told the story of why Benjamin was waiting. I told the story of

Ben and Noah. Of how they'd found each other as kids and had protected each other. How they'd drifted apart as they'd gotten older, but had stumbled upon each other again when they most needed to. I told the story of how they fell in love, fell out of love, and fell in love again, this time hopefully forever. Benjamin was waiting for the sunrise because, he said, "Every day gives us the chance to start again. Every sunrise is an opportunity to wipe away the things we fucked up."

Benjamin and Noah didn't dance on the beach while Mama Cass crooned in the background, but I wrote them a happy ending as Veruca Salt sang on repeat.

I trudged into Mrs. Harvey's class running on nothing but caffeine. I'd finished the story, read it, fixed the errors, and printed it out just in time to shower and leave for school. Mrs. Harvey looked up as I approached her desk. Her face reflected the exhaustion I felt in my bones.

"Your project?"

"Sort of," I said. "I know we've been working on Jamie and Nathan's story, but this isn't that."

Mrs. Harvey pursed her lips. "So then what is it?"

For the second time, a story had helped me understand myself. My knuckles were scabbed and bruised, my arms were lined with cuts, I was lonely and terrified of the future, but deep down I still had hope. I still thought I deserved to love and be loved. I still believed in my happily ever after.

"It's called 'The Magic of the Sun,' and it's what I needed to say."

PART 3

IDENTITY CRISIS

QUEER, PART 2

March 1997

I WAS EXHAUSTED WHEN I GOT HOME FROM WORK A FEW days before my parents were planning to leave for Tahoe, and the last person I wanted to deal with was my mom. Our relationship hadn't deteriorated the way it had when I was fifteen, but the pressure of keeping my secret from her felt like I was trying to contain an exploding grenade in my closed fist. Every time I saw her, I wanted to shout at her that I was gay and that I wanted her to know but didn't want to have to talk about it. But I knew *she'd* want to talk about it because coming out is, far too often, more about the person we're coming out to than it is about us. Not only do we have to expose this part of ourselves we've kept hidden, but we have to shepherd the person we're telling through and be careful not to hurt their feelings, and I just wasn't emotionally strong enough to do that.

When I got out of the car, I made a quiet wish that she'd be taking a nap or in the bathroom so that I could slip to my bedroom unseen. I walked into the house through the garage, rushed toward my room, and stopped cold. Spread out across the stairs was my queer shirt, the word staring at me like an accusation rather than my bold declaration.

"What is that?"

My mom was standing in the kitchen behind me, leaning against the counter. Her voice was sharp and short.

The truth was on the tip of my tongue, but a plume of anger rose in my throat and consumed the words before I could speak them. "What the hell? Were you going through my stuff again?"

"Only to get your laundry." My mom stiffened, her defenses snapping up.

She was lying, and I knew it because I'd stuffed the shirt in my top drawer way in the back. If she'd been hunting for dirty clothes, she would have had no reason to go through my drawers. My case was airtight, but I couldn't use the evidence against her because that'd be admitting I'd hid the shirt, that it was something to be hidden. We were both lying, and we both knew the other was lying, but neither of us could admit it without admitting truths we weren't ready to speak.

I grabbed the shirt and stuffed it under my arm. "It's nothing. A joke. Just stay the hell out of my stuff." I marched to my room and slammed the door.

I was so angry at her. What if my dad had been home? What if my stepbrothers had seen the shirt? I already knew what my dad thought of gay people because the only gay people that he was aware he knew were the creeps he arrested for having sex in public parks. And my stepbrothers still used the N-word and called people faggots without shame. They hadn't made a big deal out of Ryan coming out, but that was because he wasn't around. I had to live with them, and I couldn't bear being harassed in my own house.

Pressure and pain built behind my eyes. There was a shape to the pressure, a texture that felt alien, the way a word can look if you write it over and over again. It was like my entire body was beginning to feel unnatural to me, and I needed to get rid of it. It was almost like an extremely specific form of synesthesia. Like I was rolling a single grain of sand between my fingers, but the grain grew monstrously large, and I had to drop it but couldn't because it was stuck to my skin.

The pain didn't make sense, but I had to stop it. I had to release it somehow.

I turned on the shower and stood in front of the vanity mirror without my shirt. My face was splotchy red, but I wasn't crying. I wasn't going to cry. I'd tossed the queer shirt on the counter. The word stared back at me. I'd made the shirt and worn it for nothing. My plan had failed. I had failed. I was a failure, and now my mom knew it too, only I hadn't had the courage to tell her when she'd asked.

I hated myself so much.

I got my Swiss Army knife out of my underwear drawer, stood in front of the mirror while the steam filled the bathroom, and carved "queer" into my chest, one painful letter at a time. And when I was done, my chest and stomach and hands were smeared with blood.

I began cutting myself more frequently after that. Mostly on my upper arms, sometimes on my thighs and wrists. It made me feel in control. I couldn't wrap my mind around the shape of the emotional pain I was in, but I could understand the pain from a cut on my arm. Of course, using cutting to deal with depression is like snorting coke to cure cancer. The cocaine will probably make you feel great for a while, but now you're addicted to coke *and* you still have cancer.

Being smart didn't mean I always made smart choices. In fact, it often meant the opposite.

COMING OUT

March 1997

> *March 9, 1997, 8:50 p.m.*
>
> *Not much happening. Just a quick note to say that my parents now know that I'm gay. That's all.*

My mom and I didn't talk about the queer shirt after that, and a few days later, they left to go to Lake Tahoe to ski with their friends. I didn't have any big plans. My only real friend was Maddie, and there was nothing we'd do without my parents around that we didn't with them around.

At the time, I had a private phone line in my bedroom (cell phones weren't common back then) and an answering machine. Maddie was honestly about the only person who called me, so I often recorded silly messages to make her laugh. Sometimes I'd leave quotes from *The Tick*, other times I'd ramble about nothing until the tape ran out. At the time my parents were gone, my message said: *"You've reached Shaun's voice mail. He's been abducted by aliens that look like Chris O'Donnell, who are hopefully probing him, and might return your call when he returns. Toodles!"*

I never said I had *good* taste in men.

I got home late one night from a Denny's trip with Maddie, and I was surprised to see my answering machine blinking. Maybe Maddie had called while I was at work, or maybe it'd been Ryan, though I hadn't heard from him in months. Either way, I didn't think much of it as I pressed play.

"Uh . . . this is Mom."

Shit.

"Just checking to make sure everything's all right. I guess, uh, we'll talk when I get home."

Shit, shit, shit.

I immediately called Madelyne and told her what happened.

"The first thing you should do is change your message."

"Way ahead of you."

She went quiet on the other end of the phone. "Maybe this is a good thing. You've been wanting to tell her."

"I know, but—"

"She's not going to be upset; she's not going to kick you out. You know she loves you."

Those things were never in doubt. I knew there was nothing I could do that would make my mom stop loving me, but that's not what I was worried about. She was the one who'd taken me to watch *Mannequin*, she was the one who'd giggled with me at

Tito's antics, and she'd also seen Barry lying in his coffin looking nothing like the picture mounted beside him. She'd been the person who'd told me I could do anything because she believed I was someone I wasn't. She had the same information I did, and as soon as I told her I was gay, she'd know that I *couldn't* do anything. That I *couldn't* be anyone. That I was going to wind up like Hollywood or Tito or Barry.

"It's going to change the way she sees me."

"You're still the same person."

"Am I?"

Maddie didn't answer. Not because she thought I had changed, but maybe because she wasn't sure if the person I'd been had ever been real. It wasn't a coincidence that everything I loved involved becoming someone else. Theater, D&D, debate, writing. I found my truth in a character I'd written, and I think the games I played and activities I joined weren't ways for me to escape who I was by becoming someone else, I think they were ways to escape who I thought people wanted me to be by trying on who I thought I could be. I think I was more myself when I was pretending to be someone else.

But I didn't know, and if I didn't know, then I couldn't expect Madelyne or anyone else to know either.

My parents got home while I was in class, and I could barely pay attention to anything my professors were saying because I was so stressed out about what was going to happen when I'd exhausted all my excuses for avoiding my parents. My mom *was* going to ask me about the answering machine message, and I wasn't going to be able to lie to her.

I chewed my nails so low that my fingers were bleeding, and then I chewed at the skin around them. My stomach hurt, my head hurt. I felt like I was going to puke. I stopped at the beach after class, stood at the edge of the ocean, and let the sound of the waves drive the other thoughts out of my head.

I grew up on the beach, but I hated it. All that sand clinging to every crevice, and the smell of sweat and suntan lotion lingering in the air. It was disgusting. But there was still something about the ocean itself that I was drawn to. I'd never ride a rocket into outer space, so standing at the edge of the ocean was probably the closest I'd get to touching something boundless and greater than myself. For me, the ocean had a way of putting the rest of my life into context for a couple of seconds.

But I couldn't stay there forever, and eventually I went home.

My mom was sitting on the couch waiting for me. She looked travel weary and her smile was guarded, but she hadn't met me at the door with knives out.

"I guess we should talk," I said.

Mom scooted aside and made room for me on the couch.

"Is Dad here? The others?"

"They're gone."

"Right. So the message—"

"Are you gay?"

I hadn't expected her to ask. In a way, I was relieved that she'd saved me the trouble of having to spill it. On the other hand, I was annoyed at being rushed. I'd run this whole scenario where I reassured her that this wasn't her fault and then apologized for lying to her, but she'd just gone and tossed it right out there, blowing up my carefully thought-out plan. It was a scenario I hadn't prepared for, and the answer slipped out before I could come up with a way to break it to her gently.

"Yes."

My mom started to cry.

She hadn't cried when Ryan came out, and it was awful watching her cry about me. But, like I said before, sometimes coming out isn't about us. It's not fair that we have to carry the emotional burden of sharing our secret *and* making sure the person we're coming out to is okay, but we make concessions for the people we care about.

Besides, I may have run the scenarios for this conversation, but my mom had been running scenarios about my entire life since the day she learned she was pregnant with me. She'd imagined my life in a million different ways. She'd seen me go to college, become a lawyer, get married, have kids, and retire somewhere warm. She'd seen me drop out of college, wander aimlessly, but eventually find the focus my life had lacked, get married, have kids, and live a quiet existence. Maybe she even imagined that I, like the uncle with whom she'd said I shared many traits, would withdraw from society, spend my life alone in quiet contemplation, and read my days away. But me being gay was not a future scenario she had ever imagined.

"I really wanted grandchildren," she said through her tears.

Mom didn't say it to hurt me, but it still hurt. I'm not sure there's a thing in the world I could ever really do to disappoint her, but I felt like I'd disappointed her then. Like I'd stolen something from her that she'd never get back, and it gutted me.

"I'm so sorry."

She wiped the tears away and hugged me. "Don't be sorry," she said. "Just be safe. Just be happy."

My secret was out. I no longer had to hide. That *should* have been a massive relief. And, in many ways, it was. But I'd never been afraid of being completely rejected by my family. I hadn't lived under the specter of being thrown out of my house or sent to conversion therapy or anything awful like that. And my mom hadn't brought me up to be particularly religious, so I wasn't struggling with how to reconcile God and being gay. My fears were more about figuring out who I was becoming and who my family expected me to be.

In the beginning, my dad treated me like every time I walked out the door, I ran the risk of accidentally falling into a swimming pool filled with heroin and dicks.

"Be careful out there," he said as I walked down the stairs one night shortly after I'd come out. My mom had told him so that I wouldn't have to, and he hadn't really acknowledged it openly.

We joke in my family, especially my stepdad and stepbrothers. They're uncomfortable with actual emotions, so they use jokes instead. It's common knowledge that you're not part of my family until you've survived a Thanksgiving meal without crying. You had to be able to dish it out as well as take it. But my dad wasn't quite ready to joke about me being gay yet.

"I'm just going skating with Maddie."

Dad looked at me skeptically. "Still, be careful. I know how things are with your kind."

Logically, I understand that he wasn't trying to be offensive, but that one statement forced me to see myself the way he did. As a drug-addicted pervert. And the worst part was that I wasn't certain he was wrong.

OASIS

April 1997

I COULDN'T STOP SEARCHING FOR MY PEOPLE. TRYING TO build a family that not only accepted me for who I was, but who also understood me. Theater and debate and my D&D group had come close, but not quite. We were all misfits and outcasts, just not in the same ways. My friends might have understood how it felt to live in the margins, how it felt to have others look down upon or disregard them, but they weren't capable of understanding how it broke me when someone assumed Madelyne was my girlfriend or how tyrannized I felt by a random heterosexual couple casually holding hands in public. They couldn't fathom how I agonized over how I dressed and how I wore my hair, trying to find a personal style that fit me but that didn't look gay. They'd never get how I constantly analyzed my own voice to make sure it was deep and masculine enough. Even hanging out with

Madelyne and her boyfriend was painful because it felt like she was shoving in my face how easily the world accepted who and how she chose to love in a way that it would never accept me.

I didn't complain about those things, especially not to Maddie, because making her unhappy wouldn't have made me feel better; it would have just made us both unhappy. The best I could do was suffer in silence and continue to hope.

Nothing I'd done so far had helped me find people like me, not even advertising my sexuality on my shirt, and I was out of ideas, but the Internet offered the opportunity to expand my search beyond the confines of Palm Beach County. I'd already discovered a website called ELIGHT where I posted my poetry, but it felt like a one-way conversation, and I wanted someone to talk to. Then in April, I stumbled onto Oasis.

Founded in 1995, Oasis ran interviews with prominent queer performers like Anthony Rapp, Lea DeLaria, and Wilson Cruz; wrote about queer teens in their Profiles in Courage section; and offered queer youth a safe space to write about anything they wanted in a monthly column. I read every "issue" of the online magazine that first night, and I especially adored the columns, which were written by queer youth ranging from thirteen to their early twenties. I fell in love with all of them.

They wrote about their fear of being kicked out if their parents found out they were gay, they wrote about how unfair it was that they couldn't go to prom with the person they really wanted to go with, they wrote about the people who bullied them and how they were having trouble in school because they were scared. They wrote about how they couldn't tell whether the guy at Taco Bell had winked at them or if he'd just had something in his eye, and how they didn't ask, not because they were afraid of looking foolish, but because they were afraid. Full stop.

These were my people.

For a while, I was content to observe, but eventually I wanted to speak back. To start a conversation. My first column with Oasis appeared in the May 1997 issue. Calling it a column was being overly generous. It was a column in the same way that tomatoes are a fruit. You can call them a fruit, but you wouldn't put them in a fruit salad. My columns were explosions of words and feelings that had been building inside of me since my first vocabulary lessons. These were the early days of the Internet, so I had no fear about what I was putting out into the world. Just the idea that people like me were going to read what I was writing filled me with hope, and I floated around for weeks like a hot-air balloon.

May 1997

Platinum Blonde Queer

Muhahahaha!!!

So I'm happy right now. But I'm writing this, whatever you want to call it, and I'm staring at a couple of faint red lines on my wrist. Only one friend of mine knows that they're there (and now anyone who reads this article), but I see them. It was less than a week ago that I came within an inch of killing myself.

So why was I so low? In a word, I felt worthless. That's not exactly the word my father used, but it's how I felt. Actually, he told me that he was ashamed to be seen with me. I had only just "come out" to my parents a couple of weeks earlier. How did they take it? That's another story. But at that particular moment, my dad (my stepdad actually, but I don't make that distinction anymore) decided to just blurt out that he didn't want me to get into the drugs that were involved with my "lifestyle" and that, though he felt selfish saying so, he would be embarrassed to be seen in public with me.

That's when I started throwing my own private little pity party. Actually, I did take the opportunity, after beating the hell out of a metal filing cabinet and spraining my ring and pink fingers, to go see "The English Patient" for the second time. I went by myself, but sometimes movies are more fun that way. I cried at the end, and in the middle, and hell even in the beginning too. But when I got home, the hurt from my father's words wasn't gone, and I just wasn't in the mood to go to bed and sleep it off.

What's the point? Well, I talked to my mom the next day and she seemed to think the whole thing was a great big joke.

"Of course your dad wasn't talking about you being gay." That's what she said. What then? What could he have been talking about? "He was talking about your hair."

> Two days earlier I had gone from a light brown haired boy of 18 to a platinum blonde freak.
>
> So I'm happy now. I'm riding the manic-depressive roller coaster that every teenager rides. Sure, it's a little bit worse because, being gay, we have to deal with bigotry and "coming out" but that's life.
>
> My dad cared more about my hair than about the fact that I'm gay. So I came to a conclusion from all of this: I'm just not ready to kill myself over my hair.

I'm honestly surprised no one reported me to the police. Maybe they thought I was joking, but I wasn't joking. I had gone so far as to write a story that was a poorly disguised suicide note that began laying the groundwork for why I believed I didn't matter and deserved to die.

Even though I was discussing killing myself, I think writing for Oasis, having a place to vent, was one of the main reasons I didn't do it at that time, but it was definitely on my mind.

24-HOUR NOTICE

May 1997

"SOMETIMES I THINK ABOUT KILLING MYSELF."

It was dark out. Hot. Mosquitos swarmed around us and I slapped at them. I was wearing a green plaid shirt and jeans, and silver hoops hung from my ears. Madelyne was also in jeans, and a T-shirt and a cardigan. She'd recently cut her hair, and it was so curly I had to constantly remind myself not to make a single Strawberry Shortcake joke. We were wandering the boardwalks that zigged and zagged through the retention ponds and fake Florida greenery behind her housing community.

Madelyne stopped. "Like, for real?"

I shrugged. "I don't know. I mean, it's not like I've made a plan or anything."

"Is that part of it?" She motioned at my right hand. My knuckles were swollen and bruised. A flap of dried skin still hung off the knuckle over my pinky and was scabbed underneath.

"Maybe. I punched my filing cabinet." Again. It was no longer fit for holding documents and should have gone in the trash.

Madelyne led us to a wooden bench, and we sat. "Why?"

I chuckled. "If I knew that . . ."

"Then why do you want to kill yourself?"

I tried to come up with a way to describe the shape and texture of the pain inside of me. How sometimes the smallest injury felt like my body was being dragged across asphalt, skinning me down to muscle and bone. How when I closed my eyes I could feel the pain in my skull like a hot pebble in my shoe. How, no matter what I did, I couldn't seem to reach that pebble, not even when it grew so large that I felt like I was going to collapse under the weight of it. But, while my new vocabulary had given me words for some things, it hadn't given me the words for this.

"I'm just . . . I don't know. Everything feels pointless."

"Sometimes."

"Then why bother?"

"Because why not?"

I didn't expect Madelyne to have the answers. I wasn't looking for answers. Instead, I think I was hoping for reasons.

"I get it," she said. "There are days I feel the same way."

"You do?" This surprised me. I'd become accustomed to Maddie's black moods. The dark cloud that descended upon her from time to time. I recognized it, understood it. Hell, I felt a kinship with it. But I never considered she might've felt the same way I did about living and dying. I didn't think anyone did.

Maddie nodded. “Life really fucking sucks sometimes. No use denying it.” She smiled at me in this way that got me every time, because it was the one smile in my life that said, “I see you; I get you; I hear you.”

“But, listen. Promise me that if you’re ever serious about doing it that you’ll call me and give me twenty-four hours to talk to you about it. And I’ll promise the same thing.”

“So, like, a twenty-four-hour notice?”

“Exactly.”

It made sense in a way. And I liked knowing that if something happened to Maddie where she felt like life wasn’t worth living, she’d give me twenty-four hours to prove to her otherwise. So I grinned.

“Yeah. Deal.”

“Good.” She clutched her Muppet lunchbox that she used for a purse and said, “IHOP? My treat.”

In that moment, when I made the promise, I believed I’d keep it. I believed that I was in control. It wasn’t depression taking the wheel and making me feel like I wanted to die, that feeling was just a logical inevitability of my life to that point. I believed my suicidal thoughts were rational and that I could choose to ignore them, that the next time they surfaced I’d have the frame of mind to pick up the phone, call Maddie, and tell her I needed help.

FAGGOT FLAG

May 1997

I LIKED MY JOB AT SUNGLASS HUT, AND I LIKED MY BOSS, Carlos, but I wasn't out at the store. I didn't feel entirely comfortable being out there. The other employees were guys, and they often talked about women in ways that made me worry they wouldn't accept me if they knew I was gay. I didn't join in their conversations, but I didn't call them on the hurtful comments they made either. Instead, I melted into the background.

At school, even though my queer shirt had failed, I decided I still wanted to let people know I was gay, so I'd bought a little pride flag that I kept pinned to my backpack. Not one person had mentioned it since I'd put it on, and I'd mostly forgotten it was there. Near the end of the semester, I pulled into the parking lot at the mall, nearly late for my shift at Sunglass Hut. I had my final exam in statistics, and I'd have time to study if it was slow, so I grabbed my backpack and ran in.

Carlos was with a customer when I got to the store, and there were others waiting, so I tossed my backpack in the corner, clocked in, and got to work. Carlos and I were a great sales team. He was suave and funny, quick with compliments. And then I came along with all the technical details—lens materials, light transmission percentages, frame durability, distortion amount—and overloaded their brains. By the time we finished with a customer, they walked out feeling like they were wearing state-of-the-art sunglasses that made them look amazing.

I hated sales, but I was oddly good at it.

While Carlos rang up our last customer, another came in asking me to tighten the screws in their sunglasses, which I quickly did and sent the customer on their way.

Carlos stood by the register with his hands on his hips. He looked at me, then at the ground. "What's with the faggot flag?"

My heart skipped. I glanced to where Carlos had been looking, to where I'd dumped my backpack on the ground when I'd gotten to the store. I hadn't noticed that my rainbow pin was poking out, begging to be seen.

I liked and admired Carlos, and I didn't want to lose my job, but I also wanted him to respect me, and I didn't think lying to him was a great way to achieve that. The worst thing that would happen was that he'd fire me. Maybe not outright, but after writing me up for a string of minor infractions so that he could say he hadn't fired me for being gay but because I was a substandard employee. Not that it would have mattered; there were no protections for queer workers in Florida. But I could find another job. I'd still be able to eat, still have a place to live.

I straightened up, gritted my teeth, and said, "I'm a faggot. Is that going to be a problem?"

Carlos's face flushed red. He opened his mouth but didn't speak. I waited for what felt like a whole minute, and then I grabbed my bag and took it into the back room. It wasn't so much a room as it was a hallway, but at least I didn't have to deal with Carlos staring at me.

I leaned against the wall and tried to catch my breath. I was terrified but also exhilarated. I'd stood up for myself, and it had felt good.

Carlos knocked sharply on the door, which I knew meant there were customers to help. We were busy for a weekday, and it kept us from being able to talk to each other about anything but sunglasses for an hour, but eventually the rush died down, and we were alone in the store again.

"I don't have a problem with faggots," Carlos said. I was cleaning the fingerprints off the tops of the glass cases. "I just . . . I never would have thought you were one."

I stopped and turned to him. "Can you please stop using that word?"

"'Faggot'?"

"Yeah," I said. "That one."

"Sorry. It's common where I'm from."

"I get that. But I really hate it."

"Done."

"Really? Just like that?"

Carlos shrugged. "Is 'gay' better?"

"Yeah. Much." This conversation was not going the way I had expected, and I was happy but a little surprised.

Carlos spent the next hour peppering me with questions like when I knew and why I didn't act like other gay people he'd met and whether I'd been with another guy. "But the most important question," he asked, "is how does my ass look in these pants? Good, right?"

I busted up laughing. "I'm not answering that."

"You can tell me." Carlos turned around and pushed out his butt.

"Thanks," I said when I could breathe again.

"For what?"

"For being cool."

Carlos rested his hand on my shoulder. "We're friends. I don't care where you stick your—"

"Got it!"

"But c'mon. Check out my ass."

KEY WEST

June 1997

"I FEEL LIKE I'M COMING OUT OF MY SKIN." IT WAS WELL after midnight, and IHOP was empty except for us, our server, and the kitchen staff. We'd switched over from Denny's, because while the food was only marginally better, it was far quieter and we could actually hear ourselves talk.

"Boredom?" Maddie asked as she lingered over her wilted little salad.

I struggled to find the words. "No. I mean, Carlos is keeping me busy at the store, and I like having the money."

"Then what?"

"I don't know," I said. "I just feel like I'm going to explode if I don't get out of here."

"Then let's take a trip. Where do we need phone books from next?"

Maddie and I loved taking day trips together. We'd gone to Universal Studios and Disney. We'd even taken a trip to steal Orlando phone books. Why? Because we were going to become actors, and we needed the phone books to find agents and playhouses and to schedule auditions, and we got them from Orlando because it was the closest "big city" to us. After a terrifying crawl through downtown Orlando, I parked in front of the phone company offices while Madelyne crept inside. She came running back out a couple of minutes later carrying an armful of phone books, dumped them into my backseat, and dove in yelling, "Go, go, go!"

We needed one phone book; we brought back a half dozen.

I shrugged and shoved my own salad aside, determined to save most of my stomach space for the grilled cheese and fries we both had coming. "Don't you ever want to get away for a while? Go someplace no one knows you so that you can be yourself?"

"Sometimes."

"I guess that's kind of what I want now."

Maddie glanced up as our server brought us our sandwiches and cleared away the salad plates. We made small talk with her, asked about her daughter, and then dug in. IHOP's grilled cheese was not good once it began to congeal.

"How about Key West?" Maddie asked while I was midbite.

"Key West?" I said, though it came out sounding like "Kugh Est?"

"Sure. We'll drive down for a couple of days, get a hotel. It'll be great. I'll finally have the opportunity to snap a couple of early morning blackmail pictures to use against you when we're old and I need a favor."

I rolled my eyes. "You know you never have to blackmail me for a favor."

"Yeah, but where's the fun in that?" She was quiet for a second. "Well? What do you think? Can you get the time off?"

I'd been to the Keys a couple of times before. The last time had left an indelible stain on my soul because I'd gone with my stepdad and stepbrothers to dive for lobsters. I remember two things about that trip: getting incredibly seasick, and the sound a lobster makes when you detach its tail from its body while it's still alive. That high-pitched scream had crawled into my brain and I'd never been able to shake it loose.

But, as a vegetarian, I doubted Madelyne had any interest in diving for lobsters, and Key West seemed like it might be the kind of place where I could be myself without the fear of being ridiculed. I could fly my queer flag high, and no one would say anything about it, if they noticed at all. My only concern was being disappointed. What if Key West wasn't the accepting wonderland I'd heard it was? What if I got there and felt just as oppressed as I did everywhere else? It's not necessarily that I couldn't handle those things—hell, I'd come to expect them—it's that I didn't want to face disappointment and lose hope.

Which is exactly what would happen if we went to Key West and it sucked.

But I needed to escape. I was coming apart at the seams. Being out to my parents was a blessing and a curse. It was a blessing because I didn't have to hide anymore. There was no one of importance in my life who didn't know I was gay. But it was a curse because the way they treated me had changed.

Jokes, for example. They stopped joking with me. Before I came out, my dad would call, "Don't forget to use a condom," when I'd leave the house at night. When one of my stepbrothers would go out, he'd remind them not to get anyone pregnant, even if they weren't going on a date. If we were all watching TV and an attractive woman popped up on the screen, he'd make a bawdy comment about her, and everyone would laugh. After I came out, those jokes stopped around me. If my dad and brothers were talking about girls and I walked into the room, they'd suddenly go quiet and pretend they hadn't been talking.

Maybe they were acting differently because they knew that men could be dangerous. Because they hadn't worried about me when they thought I was dating girls. But I don't think their treatment of me changed because they saw the world as it was, but rather because of the way they saw me.

Still, I was happy that they knew. I was happy writing for Oasis and ELIGHT. I was happy that my second semester of college was done, that I'd finished with straight As again, and that I'd be going to FAU in the fall. Those were the little highs that sustained me during the nights when I'd cut myself and cry. But I needed more.

"Fine," I said. "Let's do this."

I pointed at the rainbow flags flying from the shops on Duval Street. "Look!" I felt like I was in a parade being welcomed home after having been lost at sea for a decade.

"It's very cool," Maddie said.

We'd gotten up early and made the five-hour drive, blasting Alanis Morissette and Dance Hall Crashers to keep awake. Madelyne's mom had surprised us by paying for our hotel, which was a brief walk from Sunset Pier, leaving us unexpected extra money for shopping and food.

But the first thing I'd wanted to do after we'd checked into our room was simply walk around and see if Key West was going to live up to my expectations or disappoint me. So far I was definitely not disappointed.

When you're used to being hungry, a single bite of food can feel like a feast. I'd gotten used to subsisting on crumbs for so long—a magazine, a dozen queer youths posting once a month, one movie out of thousands—that I didn't know what to do with the riches that surrounded me. Key West wasn't just tolerant or accepting; it was really, really queer. Stores hung rainbow flags off their buildings and posted rainbow stickers in their windows. I felt, for the first time in my life, like I was real. Like I was valid. Like I could hope for more than for people to shrug and roll their eyes and pay lip service to acceptance. If an entire island like this existed, then there had to be more places out there for me.

"Wanna shop?"

I nodded, too happy and excited to speak.

"What do you think?" I stood in the middle of the sitting room in our suite, held my arms out, and twirled.

Madelyne was wearing a corset dress with knee-high black boots and black-and-white striped stockings. "I love it."

"You don't think it's too much?"

"For home? Maybe. But it's perfect for here." Maddie grabbed the camera off the counter and took a quick picture before I could ruin it by making a silly face.

I went back into the bedroom and stood in front of the floor-length mirror. "I don't look ridiculous?"

"You look like you belong."

I ran my hands along the stretchy, shiny black shirt. It was short-sleeved and so tight that I could see the lines of every muscle. Fine, mostly the lines were my ribs. Instead of black, the shoulders were bright silver and flashy. I'd paired the shirt with my jeans and my black-and-white Docs. I'd bought the shirt, along with three others, at a cute little boutique that sold shirts covered in sequins and glitter, shirts in every color and pattern imaginable, shirts that *definitely* would have embarrassed my dad if I'd worn them in public with him. The silver shoulders were as flashy as I'd been brave enough for, but just knowing that the other options existed and that I was allowed to wear them made me feel alive.

"You ready?"

Maddie and I weren't club people or bar people or party people. We were the kind of people who walked to the edge of the pier and watched the sun set over the water. The kind of people who paused to admire the murals and talked quietly.

"Do you think anyone's staring at us?"

"Probably," Maddie said. "But they're tourists, so we don't care what they think."

"It'd be nice if no one stared at us for any reason ever."

"Yes it would."

But I knew that as soon as I got home, I was going to take the clothes I'd bought and put them in the back of a drawer with my queer shirt, because people back home *would* stare, and I *did* care what they thought, no matter what lies I tried to feed myself.

DANTE, PART 1

June 1997

WRITING FOR OASIS HADN'T CREATED THE CONVERSATION I'd hoped it would. I thought I'd pour my heart onto the page and that people would crawl through the screen after reading to be my friend. I was so lonely and my only audience was the world. But the world wasn't listening. Or so I thought until I got an e-mail from Dante.

"He's so sweet," I said one day while Maddie and I were driving out to the comic book store. I usually did the driving, not because I was a better driver—Maddie was always the better driver—just because that was one of our habits.

Madelyne watched me skeptically. "But what do you know about him?"

"I know that he's in college to be a teacher. I know that he loves books and is from Puerto Rico and is twenty. I know that he doesn't think I'm worthless."

"*I* don't think you're worthless."

"You don't count."

"Since when?"

I shrugged instead of answering. Dante and I had been e-mailing back and forth for a couple of weeks, and sometimes I stayed up until dawn composing replies to his e-mails or sitting at my computer waiting for that little *ding!* to let me know he'd written me back. I hated being where I couldn't check my mail, but just the idea that there might be a Dante letter waiting for me when I got home made me grin like a fool.

"He could be some weirdo living in a cave in Alaska who gets off on trying to dupe people into believing he's someone he's not."

"How do they get Internet access in Alaskan caves when my connection hardly works half the time?"

"You know what I mean."

I couldn't help laughing. "I know, I know." The Internet was so new that most still embraced the utopian ideal that it would bring out the best in humanity and join people together in ways we couldn't yet imagine. Dante told me who he was, and I believed him.

"I just don't want you to get hurt."

"Don't worry," I said. "I won't."

Dante would never hurt me. I believed that with all my heart, and I held nothing back from him. I told him about my past, about how I despised myself and cut myself and often wished I were dead, about my family and town. I cracked open my chest and poured my soul into every e-mail. And Dante did the same. He wrote me thousands and thousands of words about his life. He told me how he'd been born in Puerto Rico but had grown up in Florida, and how he'd never felt connected to either of his homes. About how he wanted to teach younger kids so that he could protect them from bullies in a way that teachers hadn't protected him. How when I told him I felt queer but not gay, he understood *exactly* what I meant.

Our conversations were raw, often filled with the hurt we felt, but I never felt self-conscious sharing it with Dante because he understood the source of that pain. He understood it because he felt it too.

This was what I'd wanted. *This* was what I'd needed.

Despite how close we'd gotten, we'd been dancing around the idea of meeting in person.

"He lives in Daytona," I told Carlos while we cleaned the shelves inside the display cases. It was a tedious job, but it was late on a weeknight and we were bored. "It's only three hours away."

Since I accidentally came out to Carlos, our relationship had grown into a true friendship. Sometimes the way he said things or the questions he asked might have sounded offensive, but I knew him well enough to understand that his intentions were good, and he never got upset when I corrected him.

"You gonna bone?"

"What? No! Jesus, Carlos. You can't ask someone that."

"Why not? Me and Nat—"

"Nope," I said. "La la la la." He was only joking, but in the off chance he wasn't, I plugged my fingers into my ears to block him out.

Carlos was on the floor laughing, and I gave him the finger. Fine, I admit it, I had a teeny tiny crush on him. Not that I would have ever told him. It would have made his ego bigger than it was, and our store was already too small.

"So do you think I should go or not?"

"You like this guy, right?"

"Yeah."

"Then go!"

"But what if he's a serial killer?"

Carlos shrugged. "Then I'll need to hire a new assistant manager."

I threw the object nearest to my hand at him, which happened to be a tiny bottle of lens cleaner. "Come on, Carlos!"

"You're young and stupid," he said. "Go be young and stupid."

It's not like I'd needed permission, but getting it from Carlos made me feel like it was the right thing to do. He might have been vulgar and silly and insensitive, but he was also thoughtful and smart, and I knew if he believed it was the wrong thing to do, he would have said so.

"Then it looks like I'm going to meet Dante."

"Not this weekend, though," Carlos said. "I need you to work."

"Asshole."

Dante and I arranged our schedules, and I volunteered to drive to Daytona to meet him.

I blasted Natalie Merchant and Veruca Salt and PJ Harvey as I drove up the coast. I killed time running scenarios. What if I didn't like Dante? What if he didn't like me? What if we ran out of things to talk about? Talking to a live person was different from writing an e-mail. I wouldn't have hours to craft the perfect response. I couldn't linger over a sentence, tweaking it until it sounded just right. I might drool on the table or snort while laughing and choke on a french fry. Dante might actually be a creep. No one knew exactly where I was. I'd told Maddie and Carlos about Dante, but not where I was going, and I hadn't said anything to my parents. They probably assumed I was at work.

As I neared the Applebee's where we'd agreed to meet, a voice in my brain started yelling, *"What are you doing?! Turn around! Run! Don't do this, you're going screw it up!"*

I pulled over at a rest stop to breathe. I got out of the car and leaned against the hood and tried to catch my breath.

All I had to do was go home. Go home and write Dante and tell him something came up. Tell him I'd changed my mind and that we shouldn't meet. I wanted all the things I'd missed in high school—a first date, a first kiss, a first awkward screw—but what Dante and I had through e-mail was perfect because it existed in a quantum state. Every possibility was still on the table. The moment we met, the possibilities would collapse and lock into place, and that scared me so badly that my stomach churned and I felt like I was going to puke.

And then I thought of Nina. Of her bravery. She'd known when she'd told me how she felt that I probably didn't feel the same way about her, but she'd done it anyway because it was better to try and fail than live in a perpetual state of what-if.

So I got back in my car and started driving again.

I sat in the parking lot for ten minutes after I arrived, working up the courage to go inside. I checked my hair, I made sure I hadn't spilled anything on my shirt, I ate a handful of breath mints. And then I walked into Applebee's to meet the boy I hoped would change my life.

Though Dante didn't look exactly like the picture he'd sent me, I recognized him immediately. His style was aggressively normal—he was a little shorter than me, a bit squishy around the middle, he had brown hair, a goatee, brown eyes, and he was wearing a plaid button-down with cargo shorts.

"Shaun?"

I smiled shyly, not sure what to say. "Hey, Dante."

"Should we get a table?"

I liked that he asked rather than assumed. Almost as if he was giving me an out in case I'd taken one look at him and changed my mind.

"Definitely."

Our server led us to a table near the window and took our drink order. To keep my hands busy, I emptied about a dozen packets of sugar into my iced tea and stirred the sludge around, knowing it would never, ever dissolve.

I'm not sure which of us was more nervous. We'd been talking for weeks and had shared incredibly personal secrets, yet there we were, unable to look each other in the eyes for more than a moment, fingers dancing on the table, shifting anxiously in the booth. It was cute and a little pathetic. But mostly cute.

"So, uh, how was the drive?"

"Long."

"Sorry," Dante said. "Next time I'll come to you. If there is a next time. I'm not assuming there will be, but if there is *and* you want me to, I'll drive."

It was the most adorable word vomit I'd ever experienced. Red crept into Dante's cheeks, and he kept looking at the table. I wanted to reach over and hug him so badly.

"Have you seen *Con Air* yet?" I asked. Dante shook his head. "Oh my God. It was awful! We have to go see it. And, yes. I'm assuming we will go see a movie at some point in the near future."

Dante looked me in the eyes and smiled, and what a beautiful smile it was.

We kept talking in fits and starts, but somewhere between ordering our food and the server delivering it, our conversation shifted from awkward to effortless. We finished our lunches and moved on to dessert. Then to coffee. Our server's shift ended, and our new server introduced herself. Dante and I talked until our throats were raw and laughed until we cried. The world evaporated. We were the only two people left alive, alone at an Applebee's in Daytona Beach, Florida.

And then it was time for me to go home.

I didn't want to, but my parents would be wondering where I was, and I had work the next day. Dante and I lingered in the parking lot for another hour trying to figure out how to say good-bye to each other. The thing was, I didn't want to say good-bye. I didn't want to leave him, not when I'd just found him. But I had to. Dante hugged me and it felt like the first time someone had ever touched me. Like I'd been marooned on a deserted island for the first nineteen years of my life, and Dante had seen my signal fire and found me and I didn't have to be alone anymore.

I drove home wearing a smile as big as the moon. I checked my e-mail when I got home, and Dante had written me a long letter telling me how much fun he'd had and how he hadn't wanted me to leave, and how he'd wanted to kiss me in the parking lot. I wrote back telling him that I wished he had.

XY

July 1997

I LEARNED ABOUT *XY* THROUGH OASIS. *XY* WAS A PRINT magazine created and edited by Peter Ian Cummings that featured photo shoots of attractive and often scantily clad young men making out with each other or posing suggestively. It was basically soft-core porn with a few articles and opinion pieces thrown in. I loved it.

But while it was basically jerk-off material, it was also the first time I saw queer life normalized. The boys making out on the pages weren't ashamed; they were openly displaying who they were. Yeah, it was posed, and no, most people don't ride their skateboards through their neighborhood in their underwear, but it made me feel seen the way I'd felt seen and normal in Key West. Like I wasn't something dirty that had to remain hidden. Obviously, I bought a subscription.

Though I was out to my parents, I still wasn't comfortable being *out*. I didn't want to do anything to remind them that I was different. So I rented a mailbox nearby for my monthly *XY* subscription to go to, as well as anything else I didn't want them to see, like the pride pins and shirts I bought.

My success with my honors writing project for Mrs. Harvey had given me the confidence to keep writing, and when I saw that *XY* was accepting submissions, I threw together a few opinion pieces on topics ranging from "pride" to "the future," and mailed them in. Yes. The mail. Printed paper, folded and stuffed into an envelope. And then I waited.

XY printed my essay about coming out in the July 1997 Pride issue. It was an incredibly bad essay about what I considered the dangers of young people coming out too early to be, but I was so proud of that piece that I actually went into a Barnes & Noble and bought a copy. From a real live person. No stealing this time. Yes, the cashier threw me some funny looks, but I'd actually been able to purchase something I'd written in a bookstore, so I was bulletproof for the rest of that day. Nothing could hurt me.

Seeing my name and something I'd written in the pages of a magazine dedicated to being gay, a magazine that was sold at Barnes & Noble, made me feel powerful. It made me feel like maybe being queer wasn't so bad.

At the same time, *XY* exemplified everything about the gay community I feared I would have to become. Sure, it was both body and sex positive, but it made me feel ugly that I didn't look like any of the barely clothed boys on its pages. The party-hard, fuck-and-run lifestyle it sold wasn't the lifestyle I wanted. In my essay for *XY*, I talked about how kids seemed to be coming out at a younger age, and how I worried coming out too young meant they were missing the opportunity to experiment. It was a massively flawed essay that ended with the line, "Whatever it means for our future though, if I start getting hit on by eighth-graders while I'm at a club, I'm gonna be pissed."

The irony of that ending salvo was that I had never, not even once, been to a gay club. But I wrote as if I had. I wrote as if going to clubs was something I did all the time, because that was, I believed, the expectation. Especially from the readers of a magazine like *XY*. If they'd only known I spent hours in my bedroom reading books and coding websites and playing video games and hanging out with <gasp> *a girl*, they never would have let me into their club.

The image that had been crammed into my brain of gay men as sex-addicted, drug-using party whores who were destined to die alone of AIDS or at the hands of people who hated us hadn't been changed by *XY*, they'd just glossed it up and made it look like I was going to have *so much fun* doing it. I'll always be grateful to *XY* for being the first to publish me and for giving me something to jerk off to, but they really distorted my concept of what being gay meant.

DANTE, PART 2

July 1997

DANTE AND I KEPT TALKING. BY E-MAIL. OVER THE PHONE. When I was at school or work, I couldn't think about anything other than getting home to see if Dante had written me. I talked Madelyne's ear off about him. I wondered if I was in love.

Maybe it sounds silly to wonder if I was in love with someone I'd only met once, but I had no basis for comparison, and no one had ever made me feel as squishy on the inside as Dante. I was intoxicated by emotions I wasn't equipped to handle, but instead of shying away or overthinking it, I leaned into the feelings. Maybe it was love, maybe it wasn't, but I didn't care.

Not only that, but growing up in the closet meant that I was experiencing many of these emotions for the first time. Where my friends had had their first loves at fourteen and fifteen, I was nineteen. I might have always been ahead of the curve when it came to my vocabulary, but I was woefully behind when it came to dating and love.

A couple of weeks after our first meeting, Dante drove south to my hometown. We met at Applebee's again—it was sort of a joke now—and I showed him around where I'd grown up. There was none of the awkwardness of our first meeting. Being with Dante was easy and fun and comfortable.

After dark, we parked near the beach and walked up and down the shore. He slipped his hand into mine, and I didn't flinch. Our fingers settled together like they belonged. It was the feeling of putting on a favorite pair of shoes. I wasn't worried who saw us or what they might be thinking.

When we got tired of walking, we set out a blanket in the sand and watched the stars and the moon. I leaned against Dante's chest, and he wrapped his arms around me. I didn't know it was possible to feel so happy and so *safe*. I was living my own beautiful thing. I was only missing Mama Cass singing from heaven, her voice surrounding us like a captive breeze, but I imagined I could hear her anyway.

Dante and I sat on the beach for hours, just talking. Just existing. This was it. This was the happiness I feared I couldn't have. It was the beautiful now that others had been taking for granted for centuries. It was knowing I wasn't alone, that I wouldn't have to be alone, that there was someone out there who was nerdy like me and shy like me and queer like me. It was knowing I could be who I was even if I didn't know who I wanted to be. It was knowing that happily ever afters actually existed for people like me, despite how hard the world had tried to convince me they didn't. Fuck the world. They didn't want me to know I *could* be happy so that they could hoard happiness for themselves. But I was onto them now, and I wouldn't be fooled again.

There was a moment when we were sitting there, and I was watching the moon, and I swear it danced across the sky. It swooped up and then back down into the water and then disappeared. I might have been overexhausted, or it might have just been a reflection on the water. Hell, it could have even been a UFO, but when I told Dante, he didn't laugh. He listened in all seriousness, because he always took me seriously.

"I can't believe this is real," I said. "I can't believe *you're* real."

"Why?"

"Because I never thought I'd meet someone like you. I never thought I was good enough to deserve meeting someone like you."

Dante shifted so that we were facing each other and looked me in the eyes. "You're more than good enough. You know that, right?"

I shook my head because, no, I didn't know it. I didn't believe it. When Dante said it, I *wanted* to believe. But I wanted a lot of things I could never have.

"I wish you could see yourself the way I do."

"Me too," I muttered.

"Shaun?" Dante cupped my face in his palm.

"I really like you," I said.

“Can I . . .” Dante hesitated. “Can I kiss you?”

I couldn’t get the word out. I just nodded, and then he kissed me, and I knew. This was what kissing should feel like. It’d been different with Tonia and Leigh and Heather, and not because Dante had facial hair. It was the feeling of finally finding a puzzle piece that fit into place. Of bursting through the surface of the water and taking the breath that had been burning in my lungs. Of remembering the word that’d been on the tip of my tongue for decades. This was the feeling I’d been missing all those years.

Dante was a terrible kisser, but I didn’t care. I wrapped my arms around his neck and pulled him closer and kissed him back.

In that moment, I saw the future. One where I could fall in love and get married and buy a house and rescue a shelter dog and grow old with someone who wanted to grow old with me. We’d work during the week, cook dinner together at night; I’d read on the weekends while he did the yard work because I hate yard work and would, of course, only marry a guy who’d never make me cut the grass or pull weeds. Maybe that person was Dante, maybe not. It didn’t matter who was in that future; it only mattered that I believed that future was attainable.

Eventually we walked to my house and snuck up to my bedroom where we lay on my bedroom floor talking. Sex was the furthest thing from my mind. Yes, we kept kissing, but that was as far as it went. Near dawn, Dante had to drive home. I walked him back to his car, he kissed me good-bye, and then I slept for a couple of hours before going to Sunglass Hut.

My mom was waiting for me when I got home after work.

"You were out late last night," she said.

Just because I was still living at home didn't mean I felt it necessary to explain where I'd been. I was nineteen; old enough to do what I wanted. "Yeah."

"I know you brought your *friend* here."

"Dante," I said. "We were hanging out."

My mom's lips pinched and her eyes got a bit beady. "Well, that's not okay. What if your brother had heard what you were doing?"

"Talking?" I asked. "I'm sure he's heard people talk before."

"You know what I mean."

I dug in for a fight. "Sex? Do you really think I'd bring a guy into the house and have sex in my bedroom?"

My mom was flustered. After a moment she said, "No more," and ended the conversation.

I stormed upstairs. At first, I was pissed because she'd assumed I was having sex when I wasn't. I thought my mom knew me better than that. I'd been honest with my parents about my drinking in high school—I hadn't done it often, but I told them every time I was going to a party where there would be drinking—and I'd done it responsibly, I hadn't done any drugs, and I'd never been in serious trouble. Sure, I was a rebellious, contrarian asshole in some ways, but I'd never given my mom reason to believe I'd do something like bring a guy home and have sex with him in my bedroom. Yet that's exactly where her mind went.

Before I'd come out, when I was dating girls, my mom had

never assumed I was having sex with them when I brought them to my room. She'd believed I was the kind of person who respected both her and the girls I was with enough that I wouldn't have sex in my bedroom, especially while there were other people home. She'd trusted that I understood her rules and would follow them. But, suddenly, now that I was gay, she no longer trusted me.

The high I'd felt the night before vanished. Even my own mother believed being gay meant I was destined to become someone else. Someone who brought men to the house and fucked them while my younger brother slept in the next room. She probably expected that next I'd be doing coke off a go-go boy's ass and having orgies while she slept on the other side of the house.

I tried to put my mom out of my mind. I tried to recapture how I felt when I was on the beach kissing Dante. To feel happy again. But the voice in my head told me I didn't deserve to be happy. I didn't deserve Dante. He was too kind and too good for a wreck like me. He deserved to be with someone sweet and stable. Someone who didn't despise themselves.

Dante had wanted me to see myself the way he did, but all I saw was my reflection, and I knew that's not what Dante saw. Because if Dante saw me the way I saw myself, he'd run. He'd dump me so fast and I'd never see him again. But one day he would see it. He'd get annoyed with my pessimism and my moods. He'd peel back the illusion he'd draped around me and see me for who I really was. He'd give up on me the way I'd given up on myself. At least, that's what the voice kept telling me. That's what depression whispered at three in the morning when I should have been sleeping because I had an early class. That's the poison that drip, drip, dripped into my bloodstream every minute of every day.

I could still see my future, but it no longer looked the way it had when Dante had kissed me. The darkness had infected it. I would never be happy, never be loved. If I continued seeing Dante, it would only end badly. He'd grow to despise me the way I despised myself. The way everyone despised me.

So I dialed my ISP, opened Eudora, logged into my e-mail account, and wrote Dante an e-mail. Unlike nearly every other e-mail I'd written to him, I kept this one short, simply explaining that I wasn't the person he thought I was, and that I needed to end our relationship before he realized it and his feelings for me turned to hate.

Then I pressed send and broke both our hearts.

THE BOY WITH THE DRAGON TATTOO

August 1997

TRANSFERRING FROM PALM BEACH COMMUNITY COLLEGE to Florida Atlantic University wasn't a huge leap, but it made me feel like I was doing *something*. The one thing I hated most about my new school was the commute. It was forty-five minutes from school to home if traffic wasn't awful. Longer if it was, which was normally always.

School ate up a large chunk of my time, and work devoured the rest. I slipped into a routine that numbed my mind and kept me from thinking too much about my life and how much I hated it. And then I met the boy with the dragon tattoo.

Though the Sunglass Hut I worked at was one of the busiest in the state, they still gave us solo shifts during the weekday mornings and evenings. There was a period of overlap in the afternoon, but we worked alone for three or four hours. It was an inconvenience, yeah, but I got a lot of homework done without Carlos or any of the other employees around to bug me.

I was working alone on a particularly slow night, doing the assigned reading for my literature class, when I heard the clomp of shoes on tile that told me I had a customer.

"Hi! Welcome to Sunglass Hut!" I forced cheer into my voice even though cheery was the last thing I felt.

"Hey." Standing at the edge of the store was a guy about my age. Slim with blue eyes, long lashes, curly brown hair, and a stylized dragon tattoo peeking out of his left sleeve. He was dressed casually, and he had a metal stud piercing his lip that I thought was sexy as hell. "I need sunglasses, I guess?"

I shrugged. "Sorry, all out. Can I interest you in a gently used and totally useless early British literature textbook?" I held up the thick book with a grin.

"Sunglasses would be more useful."

"True," I said. "Let's see what we've got."

I ran through the standard list of questions I asked every customer who came into the store with exactly zero idea what they were looking for, and narrowed the selection down to a few choices for the guy to try on. He slipped a pair of black plastic shades on, stood up straight with his hands on his hips, and turned toward me. "Do you like them?"

Oh, I did. I liked them very much.

"They're great" is what I managed to spit out.

"That's what's important," he said.

Was he flirting? Did he smile at me or was he smiling at

himself in the huge mirror that covered the back wall behind me? Of course he wasn't flirting with me. Why would anyone in their right mind flirt with me?

The first time I went to Paris, I stayed in a little hotel in Montmartre, near the Sacré-Cœur. Each morning, I walked from my hotel to a pastry shop for espresso, where I attempted to speak to the owner using what little French I'd taught myself from a book. The owner was polite, and served me with a smile, defying the stereotype of the surly French I'd been warned to expect. Finally, on the third or fourth day, she said, "I speak English. You don't speak French. You butcher the language." While she was saying this, she made violent chopping motions with her hand. "Thank you for trying; please stop."

Flirting is its own language. Some people are fluent, the words rolling off their tongues beautifully. Others are like me. They butcher the language. But that didn't stop me from trying. Or from trying to try. A million words whirled in my brain as I attempted to come up with something to say that was witty and clever and wouldn't make me sound like a fool.

And then, even though I hadn't had another customer for at least an hour before Tattoo Boy had shown up, an annoying tourist couple chose that moment to wander into my store.

"Hey," I said with an uninviting nod in their direction. I gave them the kind of look that told them that I was going to make shopping in my store an incredibly disappointing experience, but they were undeterred. I bounced back and forth between them and my tattooed boy, my smile fading each time I had to help them and reappearing when I talked to him, but the tourists began demanding more and more of my attention. Normally I enjoyed discussing the technical details of sunglasses. This was not one of those times.

"You're busy," Tattoo Boy said. "I'm just gonna get this." He held up a sunglass cleaning kit for sunglasses he didn't seem to own.

I wanted to shout, "Don't go!" I was tempted to throw the cleaning kit at the stupid tourists and spew profanity at them until they were so outraged that they left in disgust. I did neither of those things.

"Cool," I said. "Here you go." I rang him up, gave him a receipt, and watched him leave.

I sold the interrupting couple the ugliest, most expensive sunglasses I could convince them to buy as punishment for costing me . . . for costing me what? It's not like I was going to ask Tattoo Boy out. I didn't know if he was gay, and even if he was, he wouldn't have been interested in me. The most likely scenario was that he would have continued trying on sunglasses, I would have continued butchering the language, and he would have gotten bored and taken off. Probably.

I only had an hour until closing, which meant it was time to start cleaning up and preparing to leave. Technically, we were scheduled forty-five minutes to clean the store, count the register, fill out the end-of-day paperwork, and make the deposit, but Carlos and I had a running contest to see who could get out the fastest, and I held the record at nine minutes. I was on track for a smooth, quick close, when Harold showed up.

Harold was a mid-fiftyish, over-tanned, slicked-back-hair sugar daddy looking for a new toy. He stopped by frequently when I was alone in the evenings and spent hours bragging about his expensive cars and his mansion, and he'd drop not-so-subtle hints that he loved spending money on young men. He once asked me if I was interested in watching his house while he was away on vacation, and offered me an obscene amount of cash to do it, but I assumed he'd probably installed hidden cameras throughout the house so he could watch me, and politely but firmly declined. Still, he was a persistent man and kept returning to the store, always when I was alone.

In addition to being gross, Harold was yet another example of what I thought I had to look forward to. Cruising the mall for a boy thirty years my junior, bribing them with money and gifts so they'd spend time with me, and refusing to take no for an answer. Hell, my feigned ignorance about what he was after only seemed to encourage him. When I said, "No," he heard, "Try again later."

While Harold swaggered around the store, trying to impress me by talking about his new Corvette, I started running scenarios, wondering what might have happened if Tattoo Boy hadn't been driven away by the tourists. In one scenario, I asked him out. I learned that he loved art and music, and we traveled the world attending concerts and operas and symphonies and wandering aimlessly through museums for days. We fell in love and spent the rest of our lives together.

In another, we dated for a few weeks, but then I grew bored and broke up with him.

In another, he asked me out, and I said yes. We made plans to meet up in the parking lot after I was done with work. I sped through my closing duties, eager to see him, and broke my own record. He was waiting for me at my car, but he wasn't alone. He and his two friends jumped me and forced me to the ground where they kicked me until I was an unrecognizable mass of blood and meat and broken bone, and then he left me to die.

Tattoo Boy and I lived countless lives in an hour.

But the one scenario I hadn't imagined was that he'd come back.

Minutes before closing, after I'd finally gotten rid of Harold, Tattoo Boy ran up to the counter, smiled, handed me a napkin, and then dashed away again. It was ridiculously cute, but it happened so quickly that I barely believed it. The proof, though, was the napkin. The one in my hand with his phone number written on it in a gentle, looping script. And his name. Jonas.

I spent the rest of the night smiling, and called Jonas the second I got home.

Jonas worked at a bagel shop about thirty minutes south of where I lived. I met him at his store after my morning classes later that week, and he introduced me to the tasty wonder that is chocolate chip bagels slathered in honey butter. Jonas, as I learned, was eighteen. He'd dropped out of high school because he'd been bullied so badly and often that he couldn't bear returning. He smoked Newports. He wasn't Dante. We didn't have much in common. I easily read eighty books a year, he hadn't read eight books in his life. I loved Natalie Merchant and Dance

Hall Crashers and the Cure. He loved Daft Punk and other techno groups I didn't recognize. Over chocolate chip bagels, we chatted awkwardly. I presented myself the way I wanted Jonas to see me. As someone confident, smart, and worthy.

"So, uh," he said, stumbling a bit. "Any chance I could take you out? On a date?" He looked around like he was embarrassed about where we were. "Somewhere classier than here, obviously."

This was what I wanted, right? A boy, a cute boy, was asking me out. He knew what I looked like and had talked to me, and he hadn't run screaming. In fact, he actually wanted to spend *more* time with me. But did I want to spend more time with him? We'd hung out for a total of less than an hour, but I already felt like we were running out of things to say. Talking to Jonas was nothing like talking to Dante. The conversation lacked that easy, eager flow.

I was so lonely, though, and Jonas was right there and seemed to like me.

"Definitely," I said.

On our first date, Jonas took me to a gay bar but hadn't checked their schedule, so we happened to show up on the one night of the week they catered to lesbians. Which, if I'm being honest, I was glad for. I held a lot of misconceptions about the gay community for a long time. Misconceptions that made me feel uncomfortable around other gay people. It wasn't until I started hanging out with a group of lesbians I met a few years later that I really came to appreciate the companionship and diversity present within the community that I'd held myself apart from for so long. The night of my first date with Jonas,

I was glad because it meant we could talk without any distractions.

Dinner that night didn't convince me that Jonas and I were meant to be together. I convinced myself of that. I wanted to be with someone, anyone, so badly that I deceived myself into believing Jonas was more than he was. Sexual attraction, for me, begins with a mental and emotional connection. It's a stereotype that gay men are promiscuous and hypersexual, but it's a stereotype we've earned, though we don't deserve the judgment that comes along with it. I, however, never understood it. I believed that that's how I was supposed to be, but it wasn't how I'd ever felt. The idea of having sex with someone I didn't genuinely care about was weird, and I had to convince myself that Jonas and I had forged that kind of bond.

After dinner, we parked on a strip of grass at the airport, where people lined up to watch planes take off, and had sex in the backseat of my Mustang.

I was irrationally happy at first. It was one thing to believe I was gay, but another to get naked with a guy and know with absolute certainty. Though let me be clear: sex isn't a determining factor for sexuality. For me, however, it was the last item on my checklist of things I needed to do to prove to myself that I was actually, undeniably gay. I'd thought that by lying to the *Dracula* cast about losing my virginity back in ninth grade, I'd robbed myself of the privilege of talking to someone about my first time, but I found that I didn't want to tell anyone about what I'd done with Jonas.

I was ecstatic that I'd done it, but I wouldn't say I enjoyed it. A) It was in the cramped backseat of my car. The seats folded down into the hatchback, but Jonas and I were both around six feet tall, so it was still uncomfortable. B) I had no clue what I was doing! Did blow jobs require actual blowing? What the hell was a top and what was a bottom? Do all gay men bite like that? Was he serious about rimming?

Look, this country is shameful when it comes to sex education. It's even worse when it comes to educating teens about sex that doesn't involve a penis inside a vagina. Nothing had prepared me for sex with another man. Nothing.

But the primary reason I didn't enjoy it was because C) I wasn't into Jonas. He was hot, he could be funny, and he had good taste in bagels and bagel spreads, but that wasn't enough. I kept going out with him, though, because I was lonely. We went to movies and we went shopping and out to eat, but mostly we spent a lot of time having sex. We both lived with our parents, which made finding places to do it difficult. But that's all we did. Look for places to do it where we wouldn't get caught. In one moment of desperation, we even spent the night at a sketchy hotel in West Palm by I-95.

I hated every second of it.

It's what you deserve.

That's what the voice whispered whenever I wondered why I stayed with Jonas.

He's who you deserve.

This was what I'd imagined being gay would be like.

Meaningless sex with someone I didn't love or enjoy spending time with. I didn't even bother using condoms because I hated myself so much and figured getting sick was a fate I was unworthy of escaping.

I'd hated myself because I was gay and lonely. I hated myself even more because I was trying to fill that loneliness by sleeping with a guy who meant nothing to me and to whom I meant nothing.

Maybe you're sitting in your room or in the hall between classes, and you're screaming at me and at the book, "But you could have had better than Jonas! You had Dante! He was sweet! Why didn't you stay with him?"

Because depression works best when it creates an environment where it can't be detected. It wants you to wonder if you're depressed because you have depression or because of external circumstances in your life. Depression told me I didn't deserve someone like Dante, that I wasn't good enough, and that I belonged with someone like Jonas. That he was the kind of guy I could expect to spend my life with and the kind of guy I could expect to become. Depression made sure I chose the path that would make me the most miserable so that I would believe I was unhappy because of my life and not because of unbalanced brain chemicals.

I might have stayed with Jonas for longer than a couple of months, but we went to a party at the house of one of his friends, and I caught him doing coke. My standards were low, and I didn't have a problem with drugs like pot and acid and ecstasy, but hard drugs were my Rubicon, and Jonas had crossed it. Gathering what scraps of my dignity remained, I walked out the door and never talked to Jonas again.

I should have been able to consider breaking up with Jonas a victory. My way of declaring that I didn't have to be a stereotype, that I didn't have to compromise myself. But it still felt like a loss, and I still felt like a loser.

MY BLOODY VALENTINE

September 1997 to December 1997

SMOKING IS A DISGUSTING HABIT. I STARTED DOING IT TO catch the attention of a guy I'd never said a single word to but had a crush on nonetheless.

I was nineteen and should have known better. About smoking and about the boy. He was in my Practical Logic class at FAU, and he wore one of several different My Bloody Valentine T-shirts to our lectures on Mondays, Wednesdays, and Fridays. I didn't even know his name, but in my head I called him Winston. He had this sort of curly, grungy brown hair, a plain face, and black painted fingernails. He looked like he could be my type, which, after breaking up with Jonas, was any guy who would talk to me.

Losing my virginity in the backseat of my car had convinced me that just about everything I believed about being gay was true. I would need to compromise if I hoped to find any kind of happiness before someone beat me to death. I'd need to be more like Jonas—screw a bunch of guys or put every white powder I could find up my nose—before I died of AIDS. But while I could tell myself I needed to change, I couldn't do it overnight. I couldn't ignore nineteen years of insecurity. I needed a plan.

I arrived early to class every day and noticed that Winston did too. Usually he stood by the door and smoked while waiting for the class before us to be dismissed. I tried to devise a way to approach him that wouldn't make me look like a weirdo. I considered asking him about one of our assignments, but he slept through more classes than I did. The band My Bloody Valentine seemed like a good opening. Thinking Winston and I could bond over our shared love of odd music definitely had merit. Or so I believed until I purchased a My Bloody Valentine CD at Music Xchange. You could call what was on that CD music, but I wouldn't have. It was kind of new wave screechy. Not my thing. And not that I had much room to talk. My taste in music was, and still is, pretty questionable.

But I couldn't simply walk up to Winston and talk to him. Bad things happened when I improvised.

The answer came to me when I discovered an empty cigarette pack Jonas had left behind crumpled under the seat of my car one day while cleaning it out. I could ask Winston to bum a smoke. The plan was cool and casual, and if it didn't lead to us falling in love and spending the rest of my potentially short life with him, then at least I wouldn't look like a complete jackass. Right?

There was only one problem with my idea. Okay, there were multiple problems with it, but only one that I saw at the time. Winston and I had been in class together for well over a month, and he'd never witnessed me smoking. He'd see right through my subterfuge, know I was only pretending I smoked in order to talk to him, and would rightfully write me off as a freak. I needed to establish my bona fides. I needed Winston to see me smoking for a while before I asked him for a cigarette.

What ridiculous moron pretends to smoke just to get a guy to talk to him?

Me.

I did.

I was that moron.

Everything I knew about smoking, I learned from Jonas. He smoked menthols, so I bought and smoked menthols. The first few times I lit up, I felt like I was sucking minty hornets into my lungs from a fire hose, and I coughed until my eyes watered and burned. But I powered through. I smoked in the car on the way to and from school, I smoked between classes, I walked to the beach at night and smoked by the water so that my parents, who had both quit smoking years before, wouldn't find out.

And, slowly, I began smoking in front of Winston.

"Hey, can I bum a cigarette?"

I pulled off my headphones and said, "What?" to the guy blocking my view of Winston.

"Cigarette?"

"Yeah, sure." I flipped the pack open and let the guy take one, ignoring his attempts to speak to me so that he'd leave and I could continue pretending to smoke and to also be completely and utterly disinterested in Winston.

My plan was working. I no longer coughed when I lit up, the heaviness in my chest that I used to only feel when smoking had taken up full-time residence, and my mouth no longer tasted like a smoldering tumor because I no longer tasted much of anything. I was officially a smoker.

"You're not this guy," Madelyne said one Saturday as we strolled through Toys "R" Us. "Really. Who are you?"

"Me," I said. "Just with a higher risk of lung cancer."

Maddie shook her head. She'd cut her hair to her shoulders and let it go curly, and she was wearing combat boots, striped leggings, a long skirt, and a T-shirt. She looked like a punky, Wiccan, Muppet-loving goddess.

"No," she said. "You're the boy who sleeps during class and wears socks with sandals and thinks spiking the fake tea during *Little Women* with powdered Gatorade was both scandalous *and* hilarious."

"It wasn't?"

"No." We stopped walking to look at the action figures and dolls. Maddie was a collector. I collected so that I could spend time with her. "Why did you start smoking?"

She'd smelled it on me when I'd picked her up from her house. I promised not to smoke around her and hoped she'd drop it. She didn't, though, but I didn't want to explain about Winston. I'd told her about Jonas because my neck had looked like I'd lost a fight with a Cthulhian tentacle god after our first date. All she'd seen when she'd looked at Jonas was a tattooed high school dropout with no goals, no plans, and nothing to offer me. I'd tried to describe in detail his positive attributes, but she hadn't been interested. So I was afraid if I told her I was only smoking so that I could use it as an excuse to strike up a conversation with Winston, it would unfavorably color her initial opinion of him.

"Don't know," I said. "Because I felt like it?"

"Well, that's stupid."

She wasn't wrong. It would have been stupid if it had been my actual reason, but since it wasn't, I ignored her. I happened to believe my reason and plan were brilliant, and if Winston and I were still together with our dogs and kids and grandkids when we were old, the story of me taking up smoking for love would make everyone with feelings clutch their hearts and coo "Awwwww."

I did wonder at Madelyne's original question, though. Who was I? It was a relief to be the Shaun who smokes around Maddie, but Shaun who smokes was only a character I'd created for Winston. If I was that Shaun around Maddie now, who had I been before and where had he gone?

I didn't think Maddie was only talking about smoking. I was the Shaun who smokes, the Shaun who dates cokeheads with dragon tattoos and has sex with them in his car. I was the Shaun who lies to his mother about where he's spending his nights. The Shaun who traded Belly and Alanis Morissette for Dance Hall Crashers and Pansy Division. The Shaun who carved lines into his upper arms and wrists and thighs with razor blades and glass.

She said I wasn't that guy, but I'd done those things, and actions make the man, yes?

I lit up in the parking lot, and Maddie sat in the car while I finished.

Two days before final exams, I was waiting outside of Practical Logic. I was smoking. It was one of those rare freezing Florida days that made me hate that I couldn't smoke inside and hate that I'd become one of those people I used to laugh at for shivering in the cold or rain to feed their nicotine addiction.

I stubbed out my cigarette when I saw Winston approaching, and I shoved my mostly full pack of Newports into my backpack.

Today was the day. I was the Shaun who smokes. I was the Shaun who walks up to boys in My Bloody Valentine shirts and asks them for a cigarette. I was the Shaun who was grateful for sweatshirts to hide the hash marks on his skin. I was the Shaun who talked to cute boys and went out with them even though we had no future because I ruined everything I touched.

I was the Shaun who stood and walked toward Winston.

He looked up. Stubble painted his upper lip and chin, but his cheeks were smooth. His eyes were blue. And he was shorter than he'd seemed when I was the Shaun who watched from afar.

"Hey," I said. My voice felt deeper. Probably a side effect of torturing my vocal cords with superheated smoke and tar and whatever other chemicals I'd been sucking into my lungs.

"Hey?" His voice was wispy. Breathless like he'd just woken up.

"I saw you smoking over here. Maybe you've seen me smoking over there?" I rambled. I was a rambler. I'm still a rambler. He stared. Clearly not a rambler. "Anyway, I left my pack at home and I was wondering—"

Winston shook his head. "All out. Sorry."

I didn't know what to do or say. I'd spent the last two months preparing this cover, and every single time someone asked me for a cigarette, I'd opened my pack to them. The possibility had never occurred to me that Winston would refuse, and now I was stuck in this scenario I hadn't planned for and thought I might vomit or cry or skip the final exam because who cares anymore? I only knew that I had to do something, because seconds had passed and I was still standing there.

So I motioned at his shirt and said, "You like My Bloody Valentine?"

He did. He just didn't like me. Any version of me. All my careful planning, and all I'd gotten for my trouble was addicted to cigarettes.

POUNDING AND POUNDING AND POUNDING

January 1998

FAU WAS AS FAR AS I COULD GET FROM HOME, BUT IT wasn't far enough. Look, I didn't hate my parents, they weren't monsters, but every question felt like an interrogation. Every time they asked me where I was going or what I was doing or who I was seeing, I felt like they were strapping me down and waterboarding me to extract the answers, and I wanted them to stop. I wanted everything to stop.

It'd been difficult enough to hide being gay from them, but now I was hiding that I smoked, and after Dante I'd hid dating Jonas from them. If I went out, I changed in my car so that they wouldn't comment on what I was wearing.

They were drowning me without realizing it. And it wasn't their fault. At some point in their lives, they'd learned how to breathe underwater, and I hadn't.

I needed to escape, so I did the only thing I could. I presented a carefully crafted and reasonable argument about how the long commute to and from FAU was preventing me from being able to take the classes I needed and how the only solution was for me to move into a dorm on campus. It didn't take much convincing, seeing as I'd been stranded at school on more than one occasion by the migraines I'd started suffering from when I was young, and in January 1998, I moved into my new dorm room.

My roommate was a short young boy from the Bahamas named Jason. He was dating a tall Swedish girl he frequently snuck into the room after he thought I was asleep so they could have sex, which was both gross and annoying because it made it difficult for me to get up in the middle of the night to use the restroom. And speaking of the restroom. My building was arranged in a series of suites. Each suite consisted of a small common area with two desks and two rooms accommodating two students apiece. There was one bathroom between two suites, which meant eight boys sharing one toilet, which quickly got gross.

Still, I felt a sense of freedom living on campus that I hadn't felt at home. I could eat what I wanted, do my laundry when I felt like it, make my bed (or not) when I was in the mood. I took on six classes instead of the normal five, convinced I could easily handle it. I'd gotten a 4.0 during my first semester at FAU, so an additional class shouldn't have been a problem.

During my first week, I came out of my morning class to

discover a man calling himself Brother Jim preaching from the grassy area between the social sciences building and the breezeway. At least a hundred students had gathered, standing or sitting wherever they could find a spot, to hear this man speak. So, obviously, I figured I'd stop to see what the fuss was about.

Over the course of an hour Brother Jim called young women "sluts" and "whores," told Jewish people they were going to hell, explained that Catholics were the spawn of Satan, and spent a curiously inordinate amount of time lecturing us about sex and masturbation. But this was not sex education. According to Brother Jim, anyone who performed oral sex on a man was a "sperm-sucking sinner," and anyone who performed oral sex on a woman was a "vaginal-fluid-sucking sinner." He might not have understood how sex actually worked, but I couldn't deny that he painted quite a lurid mental image.

And when he was done shaming heterosexuals, he moved on to "fags, queers, and ho-mo-sexuals."

Brother Jim told us, his "congregation," that there were three essential building blocks to becoming a queer.

First, you must believe in evolution. Anyone who believes in the scientifically proven and observable process of evolution is on their way to becoming a ho-mo-sexual.

Second, you must discount the existence of God. Belief in evolution is incompatible with theism, therefore those who believe in evolution are atheists, and an atheist is two-thirds on their way to becoming a ho-mo-sexual.

Finally, the third building block is a belief in secular

humanism, which is a belief that mankind is capable of living moral and self-fulfilling lives without the interference of a higher power. According to Brother Jim, only an atheist could believe it was possible for a person to be happy and morally upright without God, and only someone who believed in evolution could be an atheist. And if you consider all three of these things to be true, then *congratulations*, you're gay.

Brother Jim was preoccupied with his subject. He told us that one of the characteristics of queers was that we were unmerciful, which was why when we had sex it involved so much "POUNDING AND POUNDING AND POUNDING!" He also explained that ho-mo-sexuals were stupid, since we hadn't figured out what a rectum was for, and that we were the "inventors of evil devices," such as the dildo.

For the record, dildo-like devices have been discovered in archeological digs dating back as far as thirty thousand years, and there is evidence that dildos were commonly used by the ancient Greeks. In fact, phallic dildo-like devices have been discovered in nearly every civilization throughout history, made from a creative variety of materials, some of which, I'm sure, were devised by ho-mo-sexuals. Most, however, were likely created by women forced into marriage by or to a man like Brother Jim.

Brother Jim also accused gay men of being murderers because, according to the Bible, God said that any man who hated his brother was a murderer, and all fags hate their brothers because when we have sex it involves so much "POUNDING AND POUNDING AND POUNDING!"

Brother Jim possessed an unhealthy obsession with the pounding.

I'd decided to skip class so I could sit outside and continue listening to Brother Jim and write down his "wise" words to ponder later. As I was listening, near the front, I found myself surrounded by a group of people, one of whom was wearing a rainbow flag pin on his backpack. They seemed to know one another, and I made certain that my own rainbow pin was prominently displayed.

After a couple of hours, I started to get bored, so I pulled a button off my bag that read YOU STRIKE ME AS SOMEONE WHO DOESN'T KNOW WHAT THE FUCK YOU'RE TALKING ABOUT, walked it up to Brother Jim while everyone watched, and handed it to him. It was a weirdly satisfying, petty, and pointless act, but when I returned to where I'd left my bag, the guy with the pride pin was waiting for me.

"That was funny," he said. "I'm Parker."

"I'm Shaun." Parker was tall and thin with a mop of brown hair and kind of weaselly eyes. Cute if I squinted the right way. I, on the other hand, was turning bright red as he stood there staring at me.

"You're gay?" he asked.

"What gave me away?"

Parker laughed and motioned to his friends. "We're in Lambda United, FAU's gay/straight alliance. You should come to a meeting sometime."

"Sounds cool. Maybe I will."

Parker tore a sheet of paper out of a notebook, wrote the time and room for the next meeting, and passed it to me. "Hope to see you there."

I took the paper and ran before I did or said something stupid. I mean, I'm sure he invited every queer person he met to the gay/straight alliance because queers stick together, but I still felt like his invitation had been a little more personal. That we'd been the only people on the quad, and that he'd invited *me* and not just another queer kid. It probably wasn't true, but I rode that feeling all the way to my next class.

By the time I returned to my dorm, the high had vanished, replaced by self-loathing. I'd spent the afternoon listening to Brother Jim and writing down the ridiculous things he said, but they'd burrowed into my head. Brother Jim, alone, was a caricature. He was a joke to be laughed at. But he wasn't alone, was he? He wasn't just one among many. I knew that not all Christians believed the same thing as Brother Jim, but I also knew that there were quite a few who did. People who devoted their lives to picketing the funerals of queer people with signs that read GOD HATES FAGS. Strangers who didn't know me but hated me anyway because I was a guy who liked making out with other guys.

And I wondered if maybe they were right to hate me. I didn't believe in God, but maybe those queer-hating folks were right to think that I was an aberration. Maybe I'd be better off dead.

That's the first sensible thing you've thought in ages. Might as well get on with it, right?

I sat outside my dorm, lit a cigarette, took a couple of drags, and pressed the red-hot end into the top of my hand until the pain drove away the pain. Until everything hurt and nothing hurt.

January 16, 1998
I identify as gay, but I don't identify with gays.

I made up my mind to go to a meeting of Lambda United. That's what was missing in my life. A sense of community. I was never going to belong anywhere if I didn't make an effort. And this was the perfect opportunity. I was being invited to a group full of queer people. It helped that Parker, who'd invited me, was kind of cute, but that's not the reason I was going.

Okay, maybe it was a little.

January 16 was a Friday. I sometimes went home for the weekends, but I liked staying on campus when I could. There weren't many people there, I could skate everywhere, and it was just nice being able to do what I wanted without my mom leaning over my shoulder constantly questioning my decisions. When I finished my afternoon classes, I showered and got dressed for the meeting. It took me forever to find the perfect outfit. I needed one that said, "I know I look good, but I swear I just threw this on and *definitely* didn't put any real effort into it."

Besides, I didn't know which Shaun I wanted to present. Was I super-gay Shaun in tight black Lycra? Punk-rock Shaun in a band tee and ripped jeans? Preppy Shaun in glasses and a button-down? Was I the Shaun who smoked or the Shaun who huddled in corners listening to 10,000 Maniacs? Which Shaun would impress the other queers the most? Which one would they accept?

None of them, asshole.

C'mon. That's not helping.

You're a loser, and everyone will see through you.

I sat on the end of my bed and buried my face in my hands. Maybe I shouldn't go. I'm not going to like anyone and they're not going to like me. It's just that simple, so what's the use in trying?

"Hey, Shaun. What's happening?" Jason walked in and tossed his backpack on his bed. His locs hung to his shoulders, and he was always smiling.

"Nothing. Just thinking about going to a meeting for some club." I hadn't told Jason I was gay, but I hadn't exactly hidden it either. I was sure he'd seen the rainbow pin stuck to my backpack, and I figured if he wanted to ask me about it, he would. He hadn't, which was weird seeing as he forced me to listen to *his* sex life every time I woke up in the middle of the night. I mean, I knew he was straight, but did he really need to shove it in my face?

"You thinking about not going?" Jason asked.

I shrugged. "Maybe."

"You should go," he said. "You need friends."

I guess my nights of sitting in and playing on the Internet or watching *Buffy the Vampire Slayer* had earned me a reputation as a loser.

"Anyway, I won't be here this weekend," he went on. "So the palace is yours."

Jason was a good guy, and he was right. I should go. I was scared, but so what? I'd done way scarier stuff than going to a meeting. I'd driven three hours to hang out with a guy who might have been a serial murderer, and I'd eventually kissed him. I'd had sex. At the airport. In my car. Where lots of people had probably seen it. Yes, just thinking about how many people likely watched me having gay sex for the first time *does* still keep me up at night. Just like not going to this meeting would have if I'd chickened out.

"Fine, I'll go," I said to Jason. "See you Sunday."

I smoked three cigarettes on the five-minute walk from my dorm to the building where the Lambda United meeting was being held. My stomach was in knots, but I forced myself to climb the stairs and go inside.

Parker wasn't there. The girls he'd been with weren't there. There was an older man, probably a professor, and a few people I didn't recognize. I stood in the doorway, watching, afraid to enter.

The older man spotted me shaking in the doorway. A friendly smile lit up his face, and he beelined toward me.

"Hi. You must be new." He introduced himself as Will, Lambda United's faculty advisor, and then he ushered me around the room. I'd never been in a space with so many queer people my age at the same time. I couldn't say anything except my name, and I couldn't remember the names that were rapidly fired at me.

While Will was showing me around, Parker and the girls I'd

seen him with earlier showed up, and the meeting began.

It was . . . disappointing. As the meeting progressed, the conversation devolved into a gripe session about queer life. How annoying clubs were and how everyone went anyway. I had nothing to contribute, which was definitely out of the ordinary for me, and I couldn't wait for the meeting to end. I felt so out of place. None of these people were like Madelyne. Hell, none of them were even like Dante. I was in a room full of Jonases, and I couldn't wait to escape.

The meeting finally ended, and the others broke into impenetrable cliques. I stood on the periphery for a minute and then tried to make my exit, but Will caught me at the door. "What did you think?"

"It was okay."

"It's not always like this," he said, sounding a little embarrassed. "We do a lot of good work here."

I tried to imagine what kind of work they might actually do, but couldn't. "I'm sure." I kept trying to drift toward the door.

"Next month, Ronni Sanlo is giving a talk. A couple of us are taking her out to lunch first. You should join us."

I had no idea who Ronni Sanlo was, but I really wanted to leave, so I told him I'd go.

"Good," Will said. "And I hope we'll see you next Friday too."

"Sure. Definitely."

I smoked another three cigarettes on my way back to the dorm and spent the rest of the weekend alone.

RONNI

February 1998

I THOUGHT I COULD HIDE FROM MY PROBLEMS IN A DORM room that constantly smelled like sex and sweaty feet, but I couldn't. The exhilaration of living on my own quickly faded, and the voice crowded in again, reminding me that I was ugly, that I was worthless, that I was never going to have the life I wanted.

Look, the voice said. *Look at where you expected to be when you were seventeen, and look at where you actually are.*

The voice was right. I thought I'd be living in New York City, attending NYU, acting. Instead, I was still stuck in South Florida, attending a local state college, and working at Sunglass Hut. The guys who wanted me only wanted me for sex, and the one who'd wanted more, I hadn't deserved.

It didn't help that moving to the dorms had made it even

more difficult to see Maddie. She was busy with her own life, and the physical distance between us created an emotional distance that hadn't been there before. No one was to blame; it was simply that we'd grown so accustomed to seeing each other every day that spending time together less frequently made things weird.

I kept trying to find friends. There were a couple of girls in my dorm that I talked to occasionally, but we didn't have a lot in common. Sometimes I hung out with a guy who'd been in my political science class at PBCC who'd transferred to FAU and was in one of my classes. But he was creepy, frequently asking invasive questions about what it was like to be gay, and dropping subtle hints that he might be open to the possibility of getting a blow job from a guy. I was so desperate for human contact that I might have offered if I hadn't been utterly oblivious. When he mentioned that he could be okay with the idea of a guy blowing him, I never imagined that he meant me.

It was probably for the best that I was so dense.

I hadn't gone back to another Lambda United meeting, but I passed Will on my way to class one day, and he reminded me about the lunch with Ronni Sanlo. Honestly, it sounded boring, and I didn't want to hang out with those catty queers again, but my alternative was to sit alone in the noisy cafeteria and read while pretending I wasn't lonely, so I agreed to go.

Over lunch, I sat at the end of the table and listened while Ronni told us a little of her story. How she'd come out as a lesbian, and that her husband had divorced her and been awarded custody of their children by the state of Florida. The courts believed that just because she was gay, she didn't deserve the right to see her children. But Ronni continued fighting, and had been speaking and advocating for others ever since.

I watched while Will and the other Lambda members ate their meals and listened to Ronni, wearing these inspired smiles of awe. They heard Ronni's story and saw someone who'd refused to quit in the face of adversity. Someone who'd shrugged off the horrible names she'd been called and ignored the death threats. Someone they could look up to and aspire to be.

They saw a future that was bright and hopeful.

I did not see those things. I saw exactly what I feared. Yes, I thought it was wonderful that Ronni had found the strength to fight. But what about the people who didn't? What about me? I didn't want every decision I made to be challenged by some homophobic asshole who assumed their religious beliefs were more important than my right to live freely. I'm happy that Ronni Sanlo fought for her kids, but I didn't want to live in a world where that fight was necessary.

Listening to Ronni wasn't inspirational to me, it was depressing as hell. I didn't see a future that was bright and hopeful. I saw a future where I'd have to crawl through broken glass naked with a smile on my face if I wanted to achieve anything. Where my worth to society was determined by who I loved, and where my basic rights could be stripped because of something I had no control over.

The life Ronni Sanlo described seemed like a fight I had no

hope of winning. An exhausting, never-ending struggle from which I could only escape through death.

By the end of lunch, I decided I was better off not attending any more of Lambda's meetings or events. If I could have chosen not to be gay, I would have, but since that wasn't an option, I decided it was best to stay away from other queer people. And then, as I was leaving, Parker sidled up to me, asked me for my phone number, and told me he'd call sometime.

PART 4

DEPRESSION MATH

SPRING BREAK

March 1998

IF I'D BEEN MORE OBSERVANT, I WOULD HAVE SLEPT through the month of March. I'd stolen the *Playgirl* (and been caught) in March, I'd written *The Round Table* in March 1996, I'd been outed to my parents by my answering machine in March. Even though some not-horrible things had come from those events, they'd been pretty traumatic for me. I was a nineteen-year-old queer boy with depression who'd spent years pretending to be whoever I thought I'd needed to be to make people like me and was so terrified of being alone that I often thought I'd be better off dead.

Despite that, and despite my history with March, I was excited about spring break. I'd been looking forward to going home and hanging out with Maddie. We saw each other when possible, but it was never enough. I was less enthusiastic about spending time with my parents, but that was the sacrifice the gods had demanded, and I was willing to pay it.

Then March came along and took a steaming hot dump all over my happiness.

The food court at the mall was crowded, but I'd been working for the last two hours on my philosophy term paper attempting to prove that fear, not faith, was the foundation of western religion before I was scheduled to work. I'd been inspired by Brother Jim, though not in the way he'd likely intended.

"Heya, Pookie!" Maddie slid into the seat across from me, bearing a tray of fries for each of us.

"How were your classes?"

Maddie shrugged. She'd leaned into her love of history but was flirting with archeology too. I figured she'd just wind up majoring in everything until her money ran out, which didn't sound like a horrible plan to me. I might have despised FAU and South Florida, but I loved school.

"So I was thinking next week we could do some movie binges. Maybe rent *Anaconda* for the hundredth time? Murder a bag of Oreos? I asked Carlos for some days off, and he actually gave them to me."

"About that . . ." Maddie pushed her fries away and stared at the center of the table. "My dad asked me to come to Illinois to visit him. He's not doing well, and I haven't seen him in a while, so—"

"You're going," I said. "Obviously. You have to; it's your dad."

Maddie glanced at me through her lashes. "You're not upset?"

Of course I was upset. Didn't everyone know that the

goddamn world was supposed to revolve around me? Clearly not. Clearly, Madelyne's father hadn't gotten the message. "I'm sad, sure, but I get it."

"If I could stay—"

"This is important, Pookie. I totally understand." Understanding was one thing. Being okay was another. Logically, rationally, I understood that I wasn't the only person in Madelyne's life. I understood that I wasn't even the most important. She had parents and a brother and other friends. She had herself. I would've been a selfish asshole if I'd demanded she stay, and I understood that. But that didn't stop me from wishing she wasn't going to leave. Understanding didn't stop me from feeling like the universe was conspiring to fuck with me.

Wednesday night, a week before spring break, I was sitting outside, smoking on a picnic bench near my dorm room. I should have tried quitting, but the truth was that if I ignored the way my mouth tasted like a septic tank in the morning and the way my lungs felt like they were filled with hot sandspurs, I enjoyed smoking. Not because I thought it made me look cool, but because it was mine. A moment in time that belonged to me. Look, smoking is stupid and awful, and starting—especially to impress a guy—ranks as one of the top five stupidest things I've ever done, but I didn't particularly care if it killed me. In fact, I kind of hoped it'd hurry.

While I was smoking, my phone rang—cordless landline, not cell. The bench where I smoked was just within the range of my phone's base station, and I carried it with me in case one of the three people I knew called. I was expecting it to be Maddie. She wasn't due to leave for a couple of days, and I figured she was home and bored and wanted to talk.

"Hey!" I said, not waiting to see who it was first.

"Uh, is this Shaun?"

The voice on the other end was definitely *not* Madelyne. "Yeah?"

"It's Parker."

From Lambda. Oh. Oh! I hadn't actually expected him to call. If I had, I'd have been an anxious wreck. Instead, his call caught me by surprise. "Hey! What's up?" I quickly lit another cigarette and got into character.

"Nothing. Hanging out. You?"

"Same." I was trying to play it casual. Interested but nonchalant.

"Do anything good last weekend?"

"Worked. Saw a movie with a friend. You?"

"Yeah, work. Went to a party. It was cool."

This was my longest conversation with Parker, and I wanted to dig out my teeth with a rusty nail. But he was a sort-of-cute, real live person on the phone who seemed interested in talking to me, so I kept chatting and smoking.

After three cigarettes, we ran out of things to say. This was the point where I expected Parker to fake diarrhea to get off the phone and then burn my number and never call me again. Instead, he said, "Wanna go for a ride?"

"Sure."

"Pick you up in ten minutes."

I raced inside, changed my shirt, finger-combed my hair, and threw on some deodorant. I looked messy, but Parker hadn't given me time to make myself pretty, so whatever. When I came back out, he was waiting in front of my building in his Civic, blasting rap. I don't have anything against rap, but I did have an issue with preppy white boys who blasted rap because they thought it made them edgy.

Parker turned down the music when I jogged toward the car. "Get in."

The moment I slid into the seat, but before I had the chance to buckle my seatbelt, Parker peeled out of the parking lot. Oh God. Was this how stupid I looked when I spent ten minutes cuing up the perfect song to blast out my open windows when I finally started the engine and took off? It was. It really was.

"Where're we going?" I probably should have asked before I'd gotten into the car, but I'd been so excited by the prospect of going out with someone that I hadn't bothered. Based on Parker's outfit—plaid pajama bottoms, flip-flops, and a tank top—I assumed we weren't going to a club or any place where we might see people, but I couldn't guess at our actual destination.

Parker had cranked the music back up, effectively killing our ability to carry on a conversation. Not that I was complaining. By this point, these were the things I knew about Parker:

He listened to rap.

He wore pajama bottoms in public.

He was a living, breathing gay human male.

Not the stuff great romances are made of, but I was willing to work with the limited resources available to me.

We drove to a nearby hotel on the ocean, and Parker pulled

up in front, parked the car, and got out. "Back in a sec."

"Okay." What else was I going to say?

While Parker was gone, I found his CD case on the floor and flipped through his music catalog. It was . . . disappointing and uninspired. A lot of movie soundtracks, more rap, Madonna, some club music. Aside from the rap, it was basically the CDs I would have expected to find in a 1990s Gay Boy Starter Pack, alongside cheap lube, a handful of condoms, and a copy of *To Wong Foo, Thanks For Everything! Julie Newmar*.

"What're you doing?"

I didn't see Parker approaching, and I was a little embarrassed that he'd caught me snooping. "Great taste in music."

He grabbed the binder from me and tossed it in his backseat. "I forgot my wallet."

"Where?"

"Here." Parker gave me a look like I was the dumbest person he'd ever met. "That's why I came." Then he held up his wallet.

"Oh," I said. "Cool."

"I work here."

Information that would have been helpful earlier. "I work at Sunglass Hut. I'm an assistant manager."

"Good for you." Parker didn't seem as impressed as Jonas had. "Thanks for coming with me."

"No problem." I mean, I know how difficult that ten-minute drive would have been for him to have had to make alone, and I was just happy I could be the warm body in the passenger seat on his wallet recovery adventure. "You want to hang out?"

"Can't," Parker said. "Early classes." He cranked up the music again and drove back to school.

The entire trip back to campus I kept wondering why the hell he'd called me and why he'd asked me to ride with him to get his wallet. It seemed clear he wasn't actually interested in me. I'd tried to talk about books, but he didn't read. We had no common ground when it came to music. I don't even remember what he was majoring in—probably something like business management—and he had zero interest in literature or writing or philosophy or politics or *anything* I liked. The only thing we had in common was that we both liked dick, and even then, I wasn't interested in casual sex.

I spent years looking down my nose at the gay community for its emphasis on casual sex, and for a long time I confused sex and love. It wasn't until I was older that I realized, once again, I'd simply lacked the vocabulary to describe how I felt. The truth was that I didn't feel sexual attraction without romantic attraction, and I assumed others felt the same way. For me, sex and love *are* the same thing, but that's not how everyone else is wired.

All of which is to say that I didn't understand why Parker was spending time with me when he seemed pretty indifferent to me.

Less than thirty minutes after he'd picked me up, Parker was sitting in front of my dorm again.

"Thanks for the company."

"Anytime."

"Got plans for spring break?"

I shook my head, already missing Maddie even though she hadn't left yet. "Mostly work. There's a used record store out west I want to check out."

Parker's eyes looked a little glazed over, and he nodded. "Sounds fun."

"What about you?"

Parker reached his hand across and rested it on my thigh, slowly inching up. "Hanging out."

The move had thrown me. I hadn't received any signals from him indicating he was interested, and I was pretty damn sure I hadn't sent any. But maybe I was wrong. Maybe I'd judged Parker too harshly. Maybe he was nervous and shy, and he compensated for it by being incredibly boring.

"Yeah?"

He kept moving his hand up until he was rubbing my crotch. Then he unbuckled his seatbelt, leaned over, and kissed me.

When it came to kissing, my experience was admittedly limited. Tonia had kissed like she was trying to extract my tonsils. Leigh had approached kissing methodically, like she might be quizzed on it later. Dante was the kind of kisser best described as eager. And wet. Like making out with a cocker spaniel. Jonas treated kissing like a contact sport, and I'd come away with the bruises to prove it. Parker, on the other hand, kissed me like he'd spent weeks on a desert island without food and he thought I had a potato chip crumb wedged somewhere between my molars. There was a lot of tongue involved. I'm not sure how someone so little could have a tongue that long. He must've kept it wound up on a spool in his mouth.

And while Parker was kissing me, his hands groped at me like he was checking for tumors.

I went along with it because I felt lucky that a boy was interested enough to want to kiss me. The voice in my head was going, *I don't know why he likes you either, but you best get some before he realizes what a disgusting troll you really are.*

We made out for ten minutes, and then Parker pulled away and said, "See you around."

It felt like a dismissal. Was he mad that I hadn't invited him into my dorm room? Jason was probably there with his girlfriend, which might have been awkward. And I definitely wasn't going to have sex with him in his car. We were in front of my dorm, not at the airport.

"Uh, sure." I grabbed the handle and opened the door. I was barely out of the car before Parker took off and was gone, leaving me wondering if I'd imagined the whole stupid adventure.

COOKIE MONSTER

March 1998

SPRING BREAK BEGAN, MADELYNE LEFT FOR ILLINOIS, I broke the news to my mom that I'd decided to stay in the dorms, and I told Carlos I didn't need time off. I planned to work so much that I didn't have time to think. But, of course, I always found time to think. Depression affects everyone differently. It frequently turned me into an insomniac, and I'd find myself awake at three in the morning, smoking cigarettes and searching the Internet for people to talk to. I'd stopped writing for Oasis back in December, not because I'd run out of things to say, but because I suspected no one was listening. I didn't think I'd ever find someone online who wanted to talk to me, but I kept trying anyway.

I told myself I wasn't hanging around school waiting for Parker to call, but that's exactly what I was doing. He'd kissed me, and I assumed that it had meant something, though I wasn't sure what. But if it had, why hadn't he called? What was he waiting for?

I ran the scenarios. He'd gotten home after kissing me the other night and had thrown my phone number away, because he'd been so disgusted that the thought of seeing me gave him diarrhea. He wanted to call, but he'd spilled cereal milk on the paper with my number on it and now he couldn't work out whether the last two digits were 73, 49, or 05. I was just one of the many guys he sometimes made out with, and my name wouldn't pop back up into rotation for a few more weeks.

The what-ifs were exhausting, and I wasn't getting anywhere, so I finally worked up the nerve to call him.

"Hello?"

"Hey, Parker. It's Shaun. From Lambda? We hung out the other night."

"I know who you are." I couldn't tell whether he sounded angry or high or annoyed or simply uninterested, and it was freaking me out.

Bravery isn't always a good thing. We stare down something scary, march forward, and pat ourselves on the back for not giving in to fear. But fear has its uses. It's meant to keep us from marching into dangerous situations we'd be smarter to run from. It's meant to prevent us from making self-destructive decisions like calling a guy who clearly wasn't interested in me and had probably only made out with me because he was bored or thought it would stop me from talking so much. I wished I had listened to my fear because now all I wanted was to travel back in time, smack my past self, and tell him to put down the phone, go inside, and do some laundry or something.

"So, I had fun the other night. Driving. And talking. The other stuff was nice too."

For the next ten seconds all I heard was some kind of muffled voices. Then Parker popped back on. "Right, I'm kind of busy. I'll talk to you later."

"Cool," I said. "Later." But by the time I finished the words, he'd already hung up.

Fuck.

I lost it. I sat outside and smoked and cried. I was wiping tears away when a girl who lived in my building saw me and headed my way. Carly was someone I ran into in the laundry room but not someone I'd ever taken the time to get to know.

"You okay?"

I hoped I'd dried my eyes and wiped my nose and that I just looked miserable and not like I'd been crying.

"I guess. Just some stuff."

"Girl stuff?" I shook my head. "Guy stuff?"

I nodded without thinking. I was still afraid of admitting I was gay to other people, but I'd just told Carly, and she hadn't freaked, so that was cool.

"Come out with us," she said. "Me and a couple of friends are going to Fort Lauderdale. It'll take your mind off the stuff."

"Thanks," I said. "But I'm not in the mood."

Carly shrugged. "Well, sitting here waiting for him to call isn't going to help you either." And she took off.

She was right. I knew she was right, so I strapped on my roller-blades and skated around campus. There was something wonderful about speeding along the slick cement halls that were usually filled with people running from one place to another. I felt like I owned the school. I'd actually gotten pretty good on my skates, taking turns way too fast, jumping benches and other obstacles in the dark, just begging to get hurt. Kind of like with smoking.

I guess you could say I was passively suicidal. I wasn't going to kill myself, but I wasn't going to stop dumb luck from taking me out either.

When I returned to my dorm, sweaty but still wide awake, I had a message on my answering machine. From Parker. I immediately returned his call, and he told me he was hanging out and making cookies and asked if I wanted to come over.

I told him I'd be there in fifteen minutes.

So here's the thing. Did I actually want to hang out with Parker or did I just want Parker to want to hang out with me? That's a question I still don't know the answer to. I think it's probably closer to B) than A). I was lonely. I wanted someone to believe I was worth spending time with. The voice in my head told me I was utterly worthless, so I derived any value I had as a human being from others. I wanted to belong, I wanted to be wanted, and Parker was the only gay person I knew who could provide that. Or so I thought.

I showered in record time, got dressed, and drove to Parker's. He also lived on campus, but he lived in the nicer and much more expensive student apartments.

Parker opened the door when I knocked. He was in shorts

and a tank top and was wearing a baseball cap that made his ears look flappy and huge. "Hey," he said, and then wandered into the living room like he'd already forgotten he'd invited me over.

The house smelled like cookies, which was an immediate turn-on.

"Nice place." It wasn't that nice. I mean, it was nicer than my room, but still reeked of dude-bro funk. Like feet and body spray and old pizza and at least one questionably crusty sock stuck between the couch cushions. It was basically a studio with a kitchenette, and a bunk bed over the couch. *The Craft* was playing on the TV, which I gave Parker points for, and he had a computer set up on his desk.

"Want a beer?"

I didn't, but I took one anyway and sipped it while we sat on the couch and watched the movie. Parker seemed comfortable around me, almost like I wasn't there. Within five minutes of arriving, I wanted to leave. I should have left. But I didn't, because, as pathetic as it was, it was better than being alone.

"So what's your deal?" Parker asked.

"What do you mean?"

"You single? You ever even dated anyone?"

I shrugged. "I broke up with a guy a few months ago for being a cokehead."

Parker, who'd polished off at least three beers since I'd arrived and who'd probably had a couple before then, nodded along. His eyes were heavy and his lids fluttered. "So you're not with anyone now?"

"Nope. How about you?"

"Not really."

"Not really" is not really an answer. That's like saying "it's complicated." No shit. Everything's complicated. I've always maintained a strict policy of not cheating on guys. I've never done it. Once, I was dating a guy named Tim who I only really stayed with to kill time, and I met another guy at a club through a friend of a friend. Carter and I hit it off, spent the night dancing and joking, but when Carter tried to kiss me, I made him wait, found a payphone, called Tim, and told him we shouldn't see each other anymore. He threatened to hunt me down and kill me and called me a terrible human being who deserved to die, and then when he was done, I hung up, went back inside, and spent the rest of the evening making out with Carter outside on the club's patio. All of which is to say that I wasn't comfortable with Parker's gray-area answer.

"Do you have a boyfriend?" I asked.

"Nah."

"Okay," I said. "Then is there someone who'd be hurt or pissed if you fooled around with me?"

Instead of answering, Parker kissed me. Or rather, he tried to kiss me. What he really did was lean toward me and fall into my lips and then grope at me. Clearly, Parker was drunker than I thought, and I wasn't actually that into him physically, so I tried to disentangle myself from his grabby hands.

"Maybe we shouldn't," I said.

"Whatever."

I took "whatever" to mean that he understood and was cool just hanging out. I turned the TV to one of the late-night shows and started planning my exit strategy. But Parker had been doing some planning of his own.

When I sat back down, Parker closed the distance between us. "I'm not really *with* anyone."

I didn't believe him, but I wanted to. I wanted to believe he'd invited me over because he was interested in getting to know me. Because I'd said something that he'd found intriguing and not because he thought I'd have sex with him.

Parker took my hand and rubbed it against the bulge in his pants. There was no mistaking what he wanted and why he'd invited me over.

"I'm gonna go." I stood, but Parker pulled me back down onto the couch and climbed on top of me. He kissed me and rubbed his crotch against my arm.

"C'mon," he said.

I didn't want to have sex with Parker. I just wanted to go home.

If you leave now, he'll never talk to you again, said the voice in my head. *If he likes you enough to want to fool around, you'd be an idiot to turn him down. It's not like the boys are beating down your door.*

And what if it led to something more? What if sex before conversation was just how things worked in the gay community? What if fucking was the ho-mo-sexual equivalent of shaking hands? If I didn't give Parker what he wanted, I might miss out on the chance to really get to know him.

So I shut my eyes and kissed him back. Parker tugged off his shirt and ground against me, sliding into my lap. We shifted until I was on my back on the couch, and he was on top of me. So far all we'd done was kiss, and it was fine. At the time, Parker wasn't the worst kisser I'd ever been with, so at least he had that going for him. After twenty years of experience, I can now officially rank Parker in the bottom five. He was awful.

I lost track of time. My body responded to Parker's in a way that felt like betrayal. I didn't want this, but I wanted to want it. It reminded of me watching *The Little Mermaid* with Tonia. The difference being that I could see myself being attracted to Parker if I got to know him better. But rather than fight it, I gave in.

Parker unbuttoned his shorts and tugged them down around his knees. He rubbed his dick against my thigh three, maybe four times, his body stiffened, and then he came on the leg of my jeans.

"Sorry," he said with an insincere shrug.

"Uh." I grabbed Parker's discarded tank top and mopped up the mess he'd squirted onto my pants. Then I went to the bathroom to wash my hands. When I returned, Parker was asleep.

I got out of there and sat in my car and cried, shaking so badly that I couldn't drive until I'd calmed down.

Parker had used me. He hadn't wanted to get to know me better. He hadn't even wanted to have sex with me. He'd lured me to his apartment with the promise of cookies so he could treat me like a jizz rag. The cookies had been a lie and Parker had been a liar.

EVERYTHING'S GOOD

March 1998

THE NEXT NIGHT I WAS ALONE AT SUNGLASS HUT, SITTING behind the long glass case mostly listening to 10,000 Maniacs' unplugged album for the seven billionth time, and trying not to cry.

What're you doing? You're an imbecile. And ugly. Have you looked at yourself? It doesn't matter what color you dye your hair, you're still a grotesque freak.

The same voice that had convinced me to dye my hair blond was now attacking me for it.

He was using you. He never liked you. And you didn't even get a cookie. How have you survived this long?

The pressure started building in my gut. A tightening that spread to my eyes. My stomach hurt and my eyes hurt and I felt the voice's poison spreading through my blood to my arms and legs like a trillion tiny spiders searching for an escape route, and if they couldn't find a way out, they were going to rip their way free.

I ducked into the back room, pulled down the toolbox, and dug around until I found the pack of box cutter blades. I peeked my head out to make sure there were no customers. There weren't, and I didn't expect there to be many on a Wednesday night. I pushed back the sleeve of my black Polo, exposing my right bicep. There were a dozen lines across my skin. Some were little more than scars. Some were scabs.

You ought to cut a lot farther down your arm if you ask me.

My skin was expanding. It was tight like a balloon and it hurt and I just wanted it to stop hurting for one second. I slashed across my arm with the razor and gasped. A two-inch-long vertical line of blood welled up. I cut again. And again. Three lines. The second was the deepest I'd ever cut. I wondered if I might need stitches. Blood wept. The spiders retreated.

"Hello?" a voice called from the store.

Damn. I grabbed a wad of paper towels and wiped up the blood before pulling my sleeve down and walking back onto the floor. I was expecting a customer, but it was only John, a part-timer who worked a couple of shifts a month so he could keep his employee discount.

"What's up, Shaun?" John was short but built like a bulldog. I was pretty sure he was from Brazil like Carlos. Maybe. He had long surfer-blond hair, and he played the guitar when we closed together.

"Slow night." I kept my right arm turned away from John.

The cuts throbbed and stung. The pain was worse than usual, which was good. The more I felt that pain, the less I felt the pain.

"Don't you usually have a class?"

I nodded. "Spring break."

John's face lit up. "Any good plans? Hot girls—" He stumbled. Cleared his throat. "I mean, hot dudes you're going for?"

I liked that he tried even though it clearly made him uncomfortable. "Nah. Maddie went to Illinois, so I'm mostly hanging out in the dorm."

"Dude. Go have some fun."

Was he looking at my arm? I couldn't check or it would definitely draw his attention. But it felt like he was looking. I hoped he didn't see the blood.

"I have fun," I said, trying not to sound defensive. "Skating with the guys and movies and stuff."

"What about dates?"

Tell him about Parker.

"I had a date last night," I said.

You call that a date?

John smiled with his eyes and his cheeks and his chin. He had a pretty great smile. I tried to smile too, but it never felt right on me. "So you're good, then? Everything's good?" The way he said it was confusing. I wasn't sure whether he was asking me, telling me, or trying to convince himself.

"Of course."

To John, there was nothing he could imagine that was better than being nineteen and single. The world was a buffet of places to explore, adventures to have, and people to have sex with. I could have explained what had actually happened on my date with Parker. Told him how embarrassed I was that I'd fallen for Parker's pathetic performance. How ashamed I was that, even knowing Parker was using me, I'd still called him and left him a message to see if he wanted to hang out again. That I was so pitiful that I needed Parker to call me back in order to stop feeling like I was worthless.

I could've told John all that. I could've let go of my smile and pulled back my sleeve and showed him the blood and told him what the voice in my head kept repeating. But all he would've heard was that I was squandering the best years of my life, and he would've offered me some half-baked hippie wisdom like, "You just need to lighten up, man," or "Drunk people make stupid choices." He wouldn't have understood, because he was incapable of seeing the world the way I did.

Or so I assumed. I never found out because I never gave him the chance.

Instead, I smiled. I told him everything was good. I kept my sleeve tugged down, and we tried on the dumbest looking sunglasses in the store and trash-talked each other until his wife came to collect him. He waved bye, she waved bye. I waved. Bye.

And then I waited. I ducked into the stockroom, I peeled back my sleeve, and I added another line to make it an even four for the night.

CONTENT WARNING, PART 2

I KNOW THIS STORY HASN'T BEEN UNICORNS SHITTING Fruity Pebbles, but what comes next is my attempted suicide. Sorry if that's a spoiler, but I want to make sure that you're okay to continue. It lightens up after that, but getting through it is going to be rough. If you'd rather skip ahead to page 329 where I'm in the hospital, I won't be offended or upset. Your well-being is more important than a story. It's more important than any other consideration.

SUICIDE

March 1998

I WAS GIVING PARKER A CHANCE TO REDEEM HIMSELF. Yeah, that's what I was doing. When I returned to my dorm after work, I was hoping I'd find a message from him begging me to call him, which I'd do, but only after making him sweat it out for a couple of hours. He'd explain that he'd been drunk and was sorry for the way he'd acted. Or he'd tell me that he liked me but had been afraid that I didn't like him back and thought trying to have sex with me was, in its own screwed-up way, how he was trying to show me how much he liked me.

I would have accepted any explanation that would have allowed me to reframe what had happened at his apartment the night before into something other than a meaningless five-minute pathetic couch hump that ended in disappointment.

But the light on my answering machine was a solid red. Parker hadn't called.

I threw my backpack onto my bed and poked my head into the bathroom to see if Jason was around, but it looked like I had the room to myself.

I considered going home. Throwing a bag together and spending the rest of spring break at my parents' house. It would have been the smart thing to do. Instead, I turned on the television and tried to watch TV. When that didn't distract me enough, I went rollerblading until my legs were wobbly. I smoked an entire pack of cigarettes, went out and bought another, and made a dent in that one too. I smoked so much that my lungs felt like I'd turned them inside out and scrubbed them with broken glass.

And each time I walked back into my room and checked my messages, Parker still hadn't called. I hated that I needed it. I hated that I'd had no problem writing Dante an e-mail and cutting him out of my life, but I couldn't stop thinking about Parker. I hated that how I felt about myself was determined by a phone call from a guy I hardly knew.

I sat at my computer to see if Maddie had e-mailed me, and spotted the bottle of Extra Strength Tylenol on the shelf over my monitor. I grabbed the bottle and carried it to my bed. Dumped the pills out and counted them. Sixty. 10,000 Maniacs played in the background. Natalie Merchant asked, "What's the matter here?"

Go on, the voice said. *This is the inevitable conclusion of your life. This has always been your future. Not NYU, not the theater, not writing. This.*

Everything fell into place and seemed so logical to me. I was used to picking apart and tearing down arguments, but the argument I'd been building for years that had led me to this moment felt unassailable.

The world would never accept me. Gay men were murdered, gay men were deemed unfit to serve openly in the military, gay men weren't allowed to get married to other men, gay men died of AIDS, gay men could play no role in life other than that of the celibate comic relief or the tragic victim. I'd tried to blend in. I'd tried to be myself while also playing the role society wanted me to play, but it hadn't worked. I'd been rejected from pursuing my dream at NYU, hadn't been able to escape Florida. Even my ideas were dismissed by my peers when they found out I was gay.

My parents were good people, but they couldn't help how they felt. My dad was embarrassed to be seen with me. He didn't know how to relate to me because I didn't play football or fish or care about mowing the lawn. Every time the phone rang, he probably expected to hear one of his cop buddies on the other end telling him I'd been arrested for soliciting sex in a public restroom. And I know my mom loved me more than anything, but she'd immediately assumed the worst the one time I'd brought a guy home.

My best friend was a beacon, but she had her own life to live. I'd been holding on to her so tightly that we'd fought whenever she'd gotten a boyfriend, not because I didn't want her to be happy, but because I was terrified of losing her. And even as I struggled to hold on, I knew I was only going to end up driving her away. If every day could have been like Key West, I might have been happy, but Key West was a fading memory in the rearview. Madelyne was eventually going to have to leave me behind. She wasn't responsible for my happiness, and it wasn't fair to expect her to be.

I'd spent so many years feeling like I didn't fit in. Feeling like an outcast. But I'd lacked the vocabulary to understand why. When I'd finally learned the right words, when I'd finally learned that I was a fag, that I was gay, that I was *queer*, I'd hoped and prayed that I'd find a place where I belonged. That I'd find a group of people who accepted me and understood me and wanted to get to know me. I'd hoped that I'd find a boy I could love who would love me back.

I found Dante, who was too good for me. I found Jonas, who only cared about drugs and sex and bagels. I found Parker, who'd only wanted a warm body he could jerk off onto. I could have been anyone that night, and I doubt he would have noticed.

The world was never going to allow me to be happy. My family was never going to accept me. My best friend was eventually going to leave me. I would never find acceptance in the gay community unless I fundamentally changed everything about myself. It's not like I hadn't done it before. I'd taken up smoking just for the chance to talk to a guy I knew nothing about. I could get drunk and dance to music I didn't like, take a couple bumps of coke and screw some guys whose names I didn't want to know.

But what would my future look like then? Would that make me happy?

No.

The best-case scenario was that I'd wind up like Harold. Rich but lonely. Trolling the mall for barely legal boys whom I'd have to lavish money on just to get them to spend time with me. The worst-case scenario wasn't death. It was becoming exactly what my mom and dad and the world assumed I'd become.

The things I wanted were simple. I wanted to study English, I wanted to find a nice, preppy boy with a hint of a punk side, I wanted to spend Sunday mornings in bed listening to Natalie Merchant. I wanted to grow old and get jobs and buy a house and sell the house and all our belongings so we could travel around the world. I wanted someone I could jump out of a plane with. I wanted someone I could share a book with. I wanted someone who could argue with me, and someone who knew when to let me win.

I wanted normal. I wanted a normal life. I wanted what every non-queer person takes for granted. I wanted the rights non-queer people are given without hesitation.

But you'll never have those things.

I would never have those things. When I looked into the future, I saw nothing but pain.

Either I changed everything about myself in order to fit in, or I continued on my miserable path. The math was simple. It always added up to the same solution.

I couldn't control how society treated me, I couldn't control how my parents felt, I couldn't control my friends' lives, I couldn't control how other gay men saw me, but I could control my own life. In fact, my life was the only thing I had full control over.

And the logical way for me to stay true to myself and not compromise who I was, was to end my life on my terms.

It made perfect sense. If I was never going to be happy in life, then what was the point of living?

March 11, 1998

I think I'm finally ready.

That's how my suicide note began. I wrote it in a green journal Maddie had given me for Christmas. I laid out my reasons for wanting to die. I wrote my mom, Maddie, my brother, Carlos, friends I hadn't seen in a while who might wonder. I left each of them advice that I thought might help them. Why? Because I believed I was so much smarter than they were. I believed I was seeing the world the way it truly was. Life was nothing but a game, and I'd found a loophole. A cheat code that would allow me to bypass the pitfalls and the pain the future had waiting for me.

I cried while I wrote my note. I sobbed like a child. I smoked cigarettes. I went to the vending machine by the cafeteria and bought a canned orange juice. I finished writing my note.

March 11, 1998

I guess I'm out of things to say. Again, I'm sorry, but this is the only way to save me. I've thought it over and over, and this is my final conclusion. This is how I can live my life; this is how I can be free.

My hand shook as I sat cross-legged on my bed and stared at the little mound of Tylenol. I'd done everything I needed to do. I grabbed a handful of the gel caps, stuffed them in my mouth, and chased them with orange juice. I scooped up the rest of the pills and swallowed them, too.

There. It was done. I'd done it. I was going to die. I had an erection, which felt really inappropriate and weird, but also, whatever. I was done trying to figure that thing out.

I put on the Cranberries' *Everybody Else Is Doing It, So Why Can't We?*—a perfect album from the first song to the last—pressed play, shut off the lights, lay down, and closed my eyes, expecting never to open them again.

I waited for Dolores O'Riordan's siren voice to lure me to sleep, but after fifteen minutes, I was wide awake and still alive.

My mind raced. I had no idea how the Tylenol was going to kill me. Would I die in agony? Would I drift off in painless sleep? Thinking about it made me anxious, so I got up and went outside for a cigarette. I lit one and smoked it. It was cold, and I wrapped my arms around my body and shivered.

Now that I'd done it, I was eager for it to be over. I'd made the decision, finally, and I didn't want to have to wait any longer than necessary. I figured I should stay in my room, but I couldn't sit still, so I lit another cigarette and took off walking. I should have been at peace with my decision, but my mind lingered on Parker. How the night might have been different if he'd called me back. If spring break might have been different if he'd wanted to cuddle and watch a movie rather than watch a movie and then jerk off on me. When I'd gone to see him, I hadn't been looking for someone to screw, I'd been looking for someone to love. For someone to love me.

I lost track of where I was walking and ended up at an outdoor amphitheater in the grass with tiered seating. I lay down on the stage and smoked, blowing the smoke into the air and imagining it was my life slowly leaving my body.

This. This is where I should die. It seemed fitting that I'd die on a stage, playing yet another role—this time that of the martyr.

I began to laugh. A belly laugh that filled the night and wouldn't stop. It was even less appropriate than my suicide boner. Everything was so absurd. Life, my life, the people in it. It was absolutely irrational. Nothing about life made a goddamn bit of sense, yet we kept pretending we understood what we were doing or what we were supposed to do when the truth was that we didn't have a clue at all!

Oh shit. Maybe *I* didn't have a clue. This was for real. This was me taking my life. Once I died, there was no coming back. No do-overs. No extra life at the end of the game. "Oh God. What have I done?"

My laughter turned to tears, and my tears to panic.

I rolled off the stage and tried to throw up. I stuck my fingers down my throat, but nothing happened. Jonas had joked about me not having a gag reflex, but it wasn't a joke now. I couldn't force myself to puke.

I got up and walked again. Tears streamed down my face. Snot dripped from my nose. I stumbled along the pathways between the trees, stopping every couple of feet to shove my fingers down my throat. Nothing happened.

I fell into the grass and crawled on the ground until I found a tree branch the width of my thumb, and I put it in my mouth until it hit the back of my throat and—

What the fuck am I doing?

I stopped.

This is ridiculous.

I threw the branch aside, stood up, and brushed my hands on my pants. I lit a cigarette and smoked until I regained my calm.

This was okay. I was okay. Everything was okay.

Okay.

When I finished my cigarette, I shoved my hands in my pockets and walked back to my dorm room. This time when I lay down and closed my eyes, I fell asleep immediately.

911

March 1998

I WOKE UP IN AGONY. I FELT LIKE A PAIR OF ANGRY RATS were trying to claw their way free of my stomach. I jumped out of bed before I was fully awake, ran to the bathroom, closed myself in a stall, knelt on the disgusting floor, and puked. My vomit was a slimy Mello Yello color and smelled like acid. I hadn't eaten much the previous day, so there wasn't any food in me to come up, but I couldn't stop vomiting.

I'm alive. The thought occurred to me after one of the waves of nausea ended and I was sitting on the cool floor that was definitely covered in dried piss. I'd taken sixty Tylenol and survived. I felt like I was being slowly turned inside out, but I could deal with that because I was alive.

I don't believe in God or fate or any type of predestination. But I do believe that every single thing we've done leads to everything we do, and that it's kind of pointless to regret the past when it's the cause of our present. Which, I get seems stupid if your present sucks, but the present will soon become the past. The thing you hate now, the thing that's making you feel like you can't go on today might become the reason you're speaking in front of a crowd or taking a class or applying for a job or writing a book.

At nineteen, sitting on that disgusting bathroom floor, I hadn't really crystallized my philosophy on life, but I began to think that while I might not be particularly thrilled with my current situation, I was mostly okay with still living.

And then I threw up again.

"Shaun?" Jason called. "You okay in there?"

It was two in the afternoon. Over twelve hours since I'd taken the Tylenol. I'd gone back to bed and slept for a while, but I was up again puking, and my stomach hurt worse than before. The rats had bred. There weren't two in my belly, there were twenty, and they were on fire.

"Fine!" I yelled. "Just a stomach bug."

I lost track of time sitting on the floor. I began to wonder if I still might die. If this was just how Tylenol worked. There would be no quick death in sleep for me. My death would be slow and long and agonizing. That initial spark of wanting to live I'd woken up with had faded, probably because of the pain. Not even the voice of depression could cut through so much pain.

Eventually the puking stopped. I tried to drink some water but couldn't keep it down. I tried to go back to bed, but the rats continued breeding and clawing and biting, and they were still on fire. They were balls of fighting, fucking, fiery fury, and I just wanted them to stop torturing me.

If I said that I finally picked up the phone and called 911 because I was desperate to live, I'd be lying, and I swore when I started writing this that I would only tell the truth. What I wanted when I called 911 was for the pain to end. I didn't care how.

"I took too many Tylenol," I said.

The woman on the other end of the phone had a sweet, kind voice, and she spoke to me like we were discussing my favorite pizza toppings rather than how I was dying. "Where're you at?"

"FAU."

"I'm sending paramedics to you now," she said. "Why'd you take so many Tylenol?"

"My stomach hurts. I think I'm dying."

"The paramedics are on their way. You just stay on the phone with me, okay?"

"Okay." I started crying, and I couldn't stop. So long as I'd been suffering alone, I'd been able to bear the pain, but now that I was talking to someone who cared, I couldn't handle it anymore. I wanted to pass the pain along, let another carry the burden for a while. It didn't matter that I didn't know this person or that they were on the other end of a phone or that they were being paid to be kind and might not actually care whether I lived or died. I just wanted her to take my pain.

"Can you tell me how long ago you took the Tylenol?"

"Hours."

"What time?"

"I don't know. Two?"

"This afternoon?"

"In the morning. Two in the morning."

Sirens wailed outside.

"The paramedics are almost there, sweetie."

"I hear them."

Everyone in the building was going to know. They were going to see the paramedics bust down my door and carry me out on a stretcher. They'd know I'd tried to kill myself. Parker might even find out. I tried to care, but my stomach hurt too bad for the shame of it to break through for more than a second.

I don't know how the paramedics got through the door—maybe my RA let them in, maybe they really did break it down—but suddenly they'd crowded into my room and surrounded me and were asking so many questions that I didn't want to answer.

"Why? When? How many? Why? Why? Why?"

"Everything's going to be okay now," the 911 operator told me.

But I didn't want to let her go. The medics were looking at me like I was trash. Like I was a broken boy who'd tried to kill himself and had managed to fail at that too. But the operator was nice, she was kind. She understood.

"Thank you," I said.

And then I was being strapped to the stretcher. Someone slid an IV into my arm. I was in the back of the ambulance being taken to Boca Raton Regional, which was so close I could have walked there if I'd been able to stand. The medics kept demanding answers, and I just wanted them to stop. I wanted the pain to stop. But all I could do was cry and tell them I didn't know and beg them to leave me alone.

And then I was in the emergency room. A brown-haired nurse wearing *Looney Tunes* scrubs was talking to me. Where the paramedics had been serious and distant, this nurse was like my 911 operator. She spoke like we were old friends catching up on lost time.

"Is there anyone you want me to call?"

I was nineteen. Legally an adult. No one had to know about this. I didn't have to tell a soul. The situation wasn't totally out of control. I wasn't really going to die. I could handle this on my own the way I'd handled everything else. But I didn't want to handle it on my own. I didn't want to be alone.

"My mom. Call my mom."

And then my mom was there.

I swear to God my mom must have magic powers or the ability to open portals between two locations, because only a few seconds passed between me begging for her and her appearing. I've never asked my mom what happened when she got that call. Did she leap into her car and break every speed limit, managing to make the forty-five-minute drive in fifteen? Did she get my dad to drive and use his lights and sirens even though it was against regulations? Did she drop the phone when the nurse called her or did she take her fears and anxieties and lock them in a box to deal with later?

I've never asked because I don't want to know. And maybe I

should ask because this is a memoir and I'm trying to get it all right, but I'm honestly not sure I can deal with that truth from my mom. I'm not sure I can hear what she would tell me. Digging through my old e-mails and journals and stories and poems has opened my eyes to a lot of things I didn't realize about myself; it's forced me to remember and admit to things that I'd blocked out or forgotten. It's been an education—one I've embraced despite the pain—but, in this case, I'm okay remaining ignorant.

My mom didn't ask why. She didn't ask how. She just hugged me and told me I was going to be okay.

I was dying for water. Some of the rats in my stomach were trying to crawl up my throat, and all I wanted was a single sip of water. I begged the nurse and my mom and anyone who would listen.

The nurse returned with a cup of thick black liquid instead, because, despite her jaunty scrubs, she hated me and was trying to prolong my agony. "It's charcoal. You need to drink this while we wait for your blood tests to come back."

"I just want water," I pleaded. I was pathetic. I would've lapped up water from the dorm toilet and then gone back for seconds.

The nurse shook her head. "Charcoal first. It's probably been too long for the Tylenol to still be in your stomach, but just in case, this will bond to it and get it out of you." She held the cup forward.

"Please just let me have some water."

"You can have some ice chips after you drink the charcoal."

"Why're you doing this? I just need water."

Calmly, like it was merely a suggestion, she said, "If you don't drink the charcoal, I'll have to insert a tube down your throat and pour it directly into your stomach."

"Ice chips after?"

She nodded.

I took the cup and tasted it. Oddly, it was kind of sweet. But it was the consistency of glue and was gritty. "I can't." My throat was too dry, too sore. I'd never be able to choke that down.

My mom rubbed my back. "You can do it."

My mom believed I could do anything. So I did. I gagged the charcoal down.

And then the vomiting began again.

One of the few things I learned secondhand and not from direct experience came from my mom. She told me that after I drank the charcoal, I was too sick to care about the ice chips anymore. I was crying and puking up this black, tarry nightmare. The nurse, whose calm, friendly smile hadn't wavered since the moment I'd been wheeled in by the paramedics, not even when she was threatening me with a stomach tube, stepped outside the room, went around the corner, and cried.

I never saw it. I never saw her cry. I never saw the pain I was inflicting on her. I loved her because she was kind and I hated her because she made me drink that charcoal, but I never knew she cared back.

Eventually the doctor arrived and explained that Tylenol doesn't kill quickly. It's metabolized in the liver, and an overdose causes liver toxicity. If I hadn't called 911, I could have lingered for a long time while my poisoned liver died. According to my blood test results, my liver enzymes were around 4,800 when they should have been somewhere between seven and fifty. I'd waited too long, so pumping my stomach wasn't an option, and the charcoal wasn't going to help much. My only remaining option was a medication called Mucomyst.

"It's most effective if administered within eight hours of the overdose. But we'll try it." It'd been nearly twenty-four hours since I'd taken the Tylenol, and the doctor did *not* sound optimistic about my chances. Like he'd given up before the first dose but wasn't willing to say it outright.

When my nurse brought me the little cup of Mucomyst, I figured it couldn't be any worse than the charcoal. I was wrong. I was *so* ridiculously wrong.

It smelled like rotten eggs. Rotten eggs that had been left out in the Florida summer sun for a week. Sun-rotted eggs that some wild animal had tried to eat but had died on, and now their putrefying carcass was marinating it. Rotting roadkill eggs that had been steeped in a truck stop septic tank and then bathed in sulfur. Because, yes. The rotten roadkill truck stop shit eggs also reeked of sulfur.

And I had to drink it.

But the nurse didn't have to threaten me this time. I didn't know how I was feeling about being alive, but I couldn't give up while my mom was sitting beside me. I might not have believed in hell, but I did worry the universe might not look too kindly on a guy who gives up on life while sitting in the emergency room with his mother.

I clenched my free hand into a fist and tossed the Mucomyst back like a shot. The cool, disgusting liquid hit my throat, and I gagged but managed to keep it down. The stuff tasted at least as awful as it smelled, but I smiled proudly.

The nurse took the empty cup, but she wasn't smiling. She turned around and handed me another. "The first dose is a double."

I lost it and started crying again, but eventually I got the medicine down.

Not long after that, they moved me into the ICU, and the charcoal diarrhea began.

ICU

March 1998

I WAS GIVEN A DOSE OF MUCOMYST EVERY FOUR HOURS until I'd completed seventeen doses, with the warning that if I threw any of them up, I'd have to take them again. The doctors kept an eye on my liver enzymes. My mom discussed the possibility of them testing her to see if she'd be a match for a liver transplant. The days in the ICU blurred. I watched TV and listened to the parade of people tell me how lucky I was to be alive.

A psychiatrist stopped by one day to talk to me. I don't remember his name, so I'm going to call him Dr. Smith.

"How're you feeling today, Shaun?"

I'd just taken another dose of Mucomyst, and I had charcoal leaking out of my ass. "Just great."

Dr. Smith wore a fake smile. I'm sure the nurse in the ER had been faking her smiles too, but I could tell Dr. Smith was faking.

"That's good. That's good." He glanced at my chart. "It looks like your liver enzymes are beginning to come down."

I wasn't out of the woods, but I'd been healthy prior to my overdose, hadn't drunk much or done any drugs, so my doctors were feeling cautiously optimistic about my progress. They were even talking about moving me out of the ICU if my levels continued dropping once I'd finished my Mucomyst treatment.

"Yep."

"Do you know why I'm here?"

I shrugged. The initial surge of joy at living had already begun to fade.

"I'm here to talk to you about why you attempted to take your own life. Do you want to talk about that with me?"

"Not really."

Dr. Smith laughed. It was a stupid, fake laugh. "Totally understandable. But we do need to discuss it."

"Look, if you want me to tell you I'm sorry I tried to kill myself and that I won't do it again, I will. I'll pinky-swear it."

"I don't want you to say it," he said. "I want you to mean it."

I opened my mouth to say that I did, but nothing came out. I didn't believe I'd try to kill myself again if given the opportunity, but I also couldn't say with any certainty that I was happy to be alive. I was ashamed of what I'd done. I was embarrassed. In the last seventy-two hours I'd had paramedics bust into my dorm room, I'd cried in the ER, I'd shit charcoal in my bed and had been forced to lay there while nurses cleaned me and my sheets, I'd put my mom through hell, I'd put my friends through hell. I'd made a mess of everything because I was too weak to live and too stupid to die.

"Here's the thing," Dr. Smith said. "I can have you placed on an involuntary seventy-two-hour psychiatric hold for evaluation to make sure you're no longer a harm to yourself or others. But I'd rather not do that."

I didn't want that either. Stigma surrounding mental health was and is awful. When Dr. Smith talked about a psychiatric hold, I pictured straightjackets and padded cells and every wrongheaded stereotype I'd ever seen in a movie.

"What's the alternative?"

"You voluntarily admit yourself to a psychiatric treatment facility."

So I did. My parents found one called Fair Oaks that was nearby and started the paperwork. As soon as I was discharged from the hospital, that's where I'd go for a while.

But I wasn't out of the hospital yet. I wasn't even out of the ICU.

Madelyne came to visit me while I was still in the ICU. I'm not sure how she convinced them to let her in, but there she was. I didn't know what day it was, who had called her, if she'd cut her trip to Illinois short to come to the hospital. But as soon as I saw her, I started to cry.

"I'm sorry I didn't give you a twenty-four-hour notice."

Maddie stood at the edge of my bed and smiled. "It's okay."

But it wasn't okay. I could see that in her eyes. From the

moment we'd been cast as father and son in *Aladdin* all the way back in tenth grade, Madelyne had been there for me. She would have done anything to protect me, anything to help me. But I hadn't given her the chance. I hadn't just attempted to end my life, I'd broken a promise to my best friend, and I couldn't undo that. I'd wounded her deeply. Breaking my promise fundamentally changed our friendship. I believed she'd still be there for me, she'd still help me and support me and love me, but I doubted she would ever trust me again.

"God, I love you, Maddie, and I'm so sorry."

"I love you too, pookie bear. But next time you don't want me to go away for spring break, just tell me."

WHY

March 1998

AFTER NEARLY A WEEK IN THE ICU, I WAS MOVED INTO A regular room where my parents or a hired nurse were required to stay with me at all times to make sure I didn't hurt myself again. I hadn't been alone in almost two weeks. I hadn't shaved or showered. I hadn't gone to the bathroom without someone hovering outside the door, which I was required to leave open. I hadn't talked about what had happened either, and I wasn't planning to start anytime soon.

My liver enzymes continued to drop, but I was informed that it would be months before I was completely in the clear, and I'd need to continue to have my liver function tested regularly and stay away from alcohol.

Carlos popped his head into my room. He was the last person I'd expected to see. "Hola! You look like shit, man."

The nurse glanced at him, then at me questioningly. "He's a friend," I said. "And he's not wrong."

"My babysitter," I said to Carlos after the nurse left. She made him promise not to leave until she returned or someone else showed up to stand guard. Carlos made everything into a joke, but he didn't joke about that.

"Everyone at the store's asking about you."

"You didn't tell them—"

Carlos shook his head. "C'mon, man, who do you think you're talking to?" He stood near the foot of the bed, fidgeting and looking around nervously.

"Sorry for messing up the schedule." I'd been desperate to see someone other than the doctors and nurses and my parents, but now that Carlos was there, I wanted him to leave. I didn't know how much my parents had told him about why I was in the hospital, but I assumed he knew I'd tried to kill myself, which was mortifying, though I wasn't sure whether I was embarrassed because I'd made the attempt or because I'd failed.

"We'll be fine without you."

I flashed him a wry smile. "Thanks."

"You know what I mean."

"I don't know when I'll be back."

"Candy told me." Candy was my mom. Candyce. She and Carlos adored each other, which wasn't unusual since most people loved both of them. What surprised me was that either of them cared about me. "They feed you in here?"

"At least three nurses have tried to insist that I must have an eating disorder, and they keep trying to force me to eat." I was five foot eleven and weighed about a hundred and twenty-five pounds despite eating anything and everything I could stuff into my mouth.

"Do they bring you extra Jell-O?"

"Pudding."

"Lucky."

"You know you can buy pudding at Publix, right?"

Carlos rolled his eyes. "Yes, Shaun. I know." He stuck around for a while and regaled me with stories from the store. He could turn even the most mundane interaction into a hilarious tale guaranteed to leave me crying. It was part of his charm. I don't remember how long he stayed, but when he was ready to leave, he stared quietly for a moment and then said, "Why'd you do it?"

My smile faded. My muscles clenched. I couldn't look Carlos in the eyes. The paramedics had asked me why. So had the ER doctors and nurses and the psychiatrist who'd stopped by the ICU. But every person who'd asked had done so wearing an expression and holding their breath like I was a faulty grenade that could explode at the slightest jiggle. They asked out of duty, but they were hoping I wouldn't answer because I was fragile and weak.

But Carlos had never treated me that way, and he wasn't about to start now. So he waited for an answer. Finally, I said, "I don't know."

Right then, at that moment, it was the best I could come up with.

FAIR OAKS

March 1998

CARLOS WAS THE LAST PERSON TO VISIT ME BEFORE I WAS finally released to check myself into Fair Oaks. My parents had convinced Dr. Smith to let them drive me from the hospital to Fair Oaks, so that we could stop for lunch on the way. I'm sure my mom spent the entire time wondering if she could kidnap me, lock me in a room, and never let me leave so that she could be certain I never hurt myself again, but since that wasn't an option, we went to Cracker Barrel. Their okra and homophobia may have been shameful, but I loved their Chicken n' Dumplins.

I may have taken advantage of the situation to break it to my parents that I'd started smoking. They were both disappointed, but they weren't going to yell at me on the way to a psychiatric hospital. I even got them to stop and buy me cigarettes so that I could smoke on the way.

I don't know how my mom didn't cry when she checked me in, but she held it together. At least for me she did.

When my parents left, I was led to an exam room by a nurse who hit me with a ton of questions. Had I ever been depressed? Was this the first time I'd tried to kill myself? Had I ever hurt myself before? Was I anorexic or bulimic? Honestly, no matter how many times I told them I wasn't, no one believed me.

My parents had gone to my dorm and cleaned out my stuff, which I was grateful for because I didn't think I could handle seeing Jason or Carly or any of the people who lived there. They'd also packed me a bag with some clothes and toiletries.

The nurse dug through my belongings and took my shaving razor, my shoelaces, my belt, the cord from my hoodie, and my pen. I was allowed to keep some loose sheets of paper and a pencil.

"Now I need you to take off your clothes," the nurse said.

"Excuse me?"

"To check for scars and other injuries you might have caused yourself." The nurse was nice and friendly, but I had no desire to strip for him. "Trust me, you've got nothing I haven't seen, and you can leave your underwear on."

Slowly, I pulled off my shirt and then my shoes and jeans. I was humiliated. At least when I'd been forced to let the nurses sponge-bathe my charcoal-shitting ass, I hadn't been in control or particularly lucid. This was deliberate.

The nurse immediately began to catalog my scabs and scars. "You do these to yourself?"

I nodded. "Sometimes with a Swiss Army knife. Sometimes

with a razor." I watched as he marked them down on an outline of a body, front and back. He made a mark for each place I'd hurt myself. There were so many. Most were concentrated on my upper right arm, which made sense since I'm left-handed, but there were marks on the underside of my right wrist and left wrist and upper thighs and chest.

"This one on your knee?"

I laughed. "No. I fell when I was eight and my front tooth went into my kneecap."

He frowned, looking at me skeptically.

"I swear," I said. "I had these giant buck teeth when I was young, and I was really clumsy."

Finally, he moved on, but I'm still not sure he believed me. "What about your knuckles?"

The pinky knuckle of my right hand was deformed and scabbed. "Sometimes I punch things." The nurse looked up, so I added, "Never people. Just walls. And filing cabinets."

"Filing cabinets?"

"One filing cabinet."

"And the burns?"

"Cigarettes."

The nurse marked where the burn scars on the top of my hand and underside of my arm were.

"You'll be allowed to smoke while you're here, but we'll keep your cigarettes, and you won't be allowed to have your own lighter. And someone will be with you, watching while you smoke. If you try to burn yourself, you'll lose smoking privileges."

I nodded. "Got it."

"Anything else you want to tell me?"

"I'm gay," I said. I don't know why. But I was standing in that room mostly naked, cold and humiliated while the nurse recorded the story of my life that I'd been writing on my body, and I'd never felt so exposed. I couldn't lie to him; I couldn't hide anything. He knew I'd tried to kill myself, he knew I was clumsy, he knew I'd cut and punched and burned myself, he knew what I looked like in my underwear. He might as well know I was gay too.

"Uh, cool, but I don't really need that for the file." He nodded and shuffled the papers. "You can get dressed now."

Because I was privileged enough to have good insurance through my stepdad's job, and parents who were willing to pay the deductibles, I got to stay in a really nice treatment facility. I shared a room with a guy named Jose, who rarely got out of bed, I ate three decent meals a day while the nurses watched to make sure I cleaned my plate, and I attended solo therapy sessions as well as group therapy.

My first night at Fair Oaks, I was watching television with the others, and one of the nurses brought a young woman back who'd undergone ECT—electroconvulsive therapy. She spent the rest of the evening staring at the television and not saying a word. I didn't know anything about ECT at the time other than what I'd seen in movies, so I didn't know that it had gotten a bad reputation but actually has a lot of therapeutic value in cases where medication proves ineffective. All I saw was a young woman who appeared catatonic and empty. Because of the damage to my liver, the doctors at Fair Oaks weren't allowed to put me on any type of medications for depression, and I feared they'd subject me to ECT if I didn't get "better" quickly enough.

There was no ECT for me, though. My treatment mostly involved talking. My main doctor, Dr. Lewis, was a plainspoken older man who made very little of an impression on me. I know we discussed why I'd taken the Tylenol, and he attempted to provide me with some strategies for dealing with my depression when it got bad, but I quickly understood what it was he wanted to hear and what it would take to get released, so I said those things.

During one of my cigarette breaks, I was standing outside smoking when a nurse walked up behind me and put his hand on my shoulder. His name was Ed, and he was lanky and bald and had loaned me a couple of smokes when I ran out to tide me over until my parents could bring me more.

"How's it going in here?"

I shrugged. "It's kind of boring."

There wasn't much to do other than watch TV. I'd gotten to know some of the other patients, but I didn't intend to spend any longer than necessary in Fair Oaks.

Ed laughed. "Sometimes. That's why so many people smoke."

The patio we smoked on was in a sad state of disrepair. Most of the plants were dead or dying, and there were cigarette butts everywhere.

"I just can't wait to get out of here."

"Already?"

"I mean, yeah. Isn't that a good thing?"

"Depends on why you want out."

Having my cigarette breaks regulated caused me to smoke faster so that I could squeeze two cigarettes into one break. "I'm not gonna kill myself, if that's what you're asking."

"Just . . . I heard you're gay," he said. "Me too."

I froze when he said it, suddenly aware of how close he was standing to me, of how he'd touched my shoulder earlier, of where everyone else on the patio was standing. Had they overheard us talking? Had they heard Ed say the word "gay"?

"Uh, yeah."

"Don't worry about it," he said. "I know it's rough, but you'll find your people."

I didn't know what he meant. Honestly, as soon as he told me he was gay, I became suspicious of him. I assumed he was only being nice to me in exchange for sex. He never tried anything, nor had he actually given me any reason to believe he wanted to sleep with me, but that's where my brain went. I firmly believed my worth to the gay community depended on my willingness to party and sleep with every man who wanted me. As a result, I became standoffish to Ed. I'm not sure if he noticed that I avoided him after that, but I really hope he didn't take it personally. I was just a confused kid who'd learned the vocabulary of being gay from a world that hated fags.

One of the few people I became friendly with was an older woman named Emily. Emily was a mother and an executive, and she had a wonderful, warm smile. She was admitted a couple of days after I was, and we immediately bonded.

We were sitting in the common room playing cards. "When are your parents coming to visit?" Emily asked.

"I don't know," I said. "I'm not sure I want them to see me here."

"You should let them."

"Why?"

"Because they have to recover too. Seeing that you're getting better will help with that."

While I was deeply ashamed of what I'd put my family and friends through, I still hadn't spent a lot of time looking at my suicide attempt through their eyes. I was pretty much focused on myself.

"What if I'm not getting better?"

"You don't think you are?"

"I don't know," I said. "I mean, I guess I don't want to kill myself right now, but I didn't want to kill myself before either. Until I did."

Emily was the first person I'd actually opened up to since I'd attempted suicide. All the doctors and nurses had gotten bits and pieces of the story, but I told Emily everything, and she just listened and nodded and then gave me a hug.

"The next time you feel like you want to, you ask for help." Emily smiled and declared rummy, laying out her sets for me to see. I tallied the points and shuffled. "I checked myself in here."

"Really?" That caught me by surprise. I'd also checked myself in, but only because Dr. Smith had threatened to commit me if I hadn't. I was having a difficult time imagining anyone willingly checking themselves into a psychiatric facility.

"It's true," Emily said. "My life just became . . ." She paused, looking for the right word. "Overwhelming. I felt like I couldn't handle the stress I was under, and I worried I might do something bad if I didn't get help."

"So you just asked for help? Simple as that?"

"It's not really that simple," she said, laughing. "But yes. I told my husband and kids I needed a mental vacation, and then I checked myself in."

A mental vacation. I'd never heard anyone talk about mental health that way. Emily wasn't ashamed of being in Fair Oaks, she wasn't worried anyone was going to think she was weak for needing help. In fact, she was acting like she'd done something brave by recognizing she needed help and asking for it. And she had.

"Fine," I said. "I'll let my parents come visit."

Emily, it turned out, had a friend who was an editor at a publisher in New York. When we were both out of Fair Oaks, I visited her at her house and met her family, and she sent a copy of a story I'd written to her publisher friend. A couple of months later, the editor sent back my story with a wonderful letter tearing it to shreds but also pointing out my strengths and encouraging me to continue writing. I lost that letter along with a box of other belongings during a move many, many years ago, and therefore don't remember who the editor was, but both she and Emily are among the reasons I'm writing this today.

* * * * *

I know that in books where the narrator ends up in a psychiatric facility, there's usually some kind of epiphany that helps them turn their life around, but that's not how it was for me. I did let my parents come visit, and it was awkward. Now that my life was no longer in immediate danger, I didn't know how to deal with them, and they didn't know how to deal with me. My stepdad isn't comfortable with emotions, and he wanted to put the entire incident behind us. My mom, though, seemed to be fighting competing impulses. One to hug me close and never let me out of her sight, and the other to keep me at arm's length so that I couldn't hurt her again.

We talked about me dropping out of school for a while. I'd already missed close to a month of classes, so I'd blown the semester. I was also taking a leave of absence from work. We avoided discussing the future. Them because I guess they still weren't sure whether I wanted a future, and me because I didn't know where to go from there.

I wasn't better, but I'd decided that I didn't want to die. In a weird way, I felt like living was the punishment I deserved. I didn't tell the doctors that, though. Instead, I told them the things they wanted to hear. That attempting suicide had been a mistake, that I'd gotten really confused and sad, that I would try to find healthier ways to channel my anger and pain than cutting and burning myself. Since I was a master bullshitter, they believed me and signed me out.

When I left Fair Oaks, I was alive but I wasn't "better." I still had the same problems I'd had before I'd tried to take my life. But there was one major difference. I'd begun to realize that my fear of being gay and my depression were two separate issues. I wasn't depressed because I was gay. I was depressed *and* I was gay. Being gay doesn't make a person depressed any more than being depressed makes a person gay. My self-hate was caused by my complete misunderstanding of myself and what being gay meant. My depression simply used it as a way to beat me down. But that's the thing about depression math. $1 + 1 \neq 3$. The numbers never add up, but depression keeps you from showing your work and figuring that out.

It took me a long time to work through it, but understanding that and understanding that there was no shame in asking for help were good first steps.

TWENTY YEARS AND COUNTING

SO WE'RE AT AN END. NOT "THE END," BUT SIMPLY ONE ending. And a beginning.

I wanted to write *Brave Face* because, while I love the message of "It Gets Better," I worry that it's not enough. When does it get better? How long does it take? How does it happen? Those are the unanswered questions I wanted to try to tackle. Because getting better isn't something that happens overnight. It can take years. Sometimes it gets better, then it gets worse, better, worse again, and then better. And sometimes it's not a simple either/or. Sometimes it gets better *and* it gets worse. At the end of the day, what changes isn't life; it's us. Moving to New York City wouldn't have fixed my problems. They would have still been there, but I would have been going through them without the people in my life who cared about me. Without Madelyne and Carlos and my family.

Moving wouldn't have fixed anything. Only I could do that.

It's easy for me to tell you that it gets better because I'm in a good place. I've made a career of doing what I love, I'm financially secure, I've come to terms with who I am, and I actually like that person. I've learned how to manage my depression in a healthy way. But twenty years have passed between when I got out of Fair Oaks and now, and those changes didn't occur right away. It didn't get better immediately.

In some ways, it got worse.

I stopped cutting and burning myself and eventually went back to work. Ed was right; I did end up meeting my people. One of those people, oddly enough, was a younger sister of my old D&D art idol, Tony DiTerlizzi. I didn't just find my people; I found my family. We went dancing on Thursday nights at Respect's in downtown West Palm. I still didn't know who I was, so I tried on a million different faces looking for one that fit, and they accepted them all without hesitation.

I met a boy and moved to Georgia to be with him. But he had issues of his own, and it didn't last. I moved home two months later. I met a ballet dancer who I had to stop seeing after he tried to take his own life. I met a guy I thought I was in love with. I got his name tattooed on my back, we partied until dawn, we moved in together, and I let my life spiral totally out of control. I went back to school. I dropped out of school again.

Madelyne and I got into a massive fight because I'd become the Shaun Who Drinks and Does Drugs and Smokes and Is Trash to His Best Friend, and we stopped speaking to each other.

I moved with my boyfriend to Rhode Island without telling anyone and didn't talk to my family for months, which was a cruel thing to do and is one of the few decisions I've made in my life that I truly regret.

My boyfriend and I broke up because he'd been cheating on me. I fell in love with a boy who went to school in Boston and who eventually contracted HIV. I found a new family in Rhode Island at a gay bar downtown. We sang karaoke on Wednesday nights, and for one of my birthdays the bartender and I sang a duet of "You Don't Bring Me Flowers." I learned that many gay men were exactly like I expected. There were gay men who *were* flamboyant and femme and who loved having sex. There were gay men who spent their nights dancing in clubs, and gay men who couldn't dance their way out of a paper bag. Gay men who reminded me of Hollywood and Nathan Lane. I learned not to judge them for it. I learned that there was nothing better or worse about them. That we were all equal and amazing and the same despite being different. I learned that there were also gay men who were like me. I fell in love with one when he moved in to my apartment building, but I let him get away because I still didn't believe I was worthy of being loved, and that is one more of the things that I truly regret.

My brother and I put our pasts behind us and finally became brothers *and* friends. He'd always been there for me; it simply took me a while to realize it.

I moved back to Florida, went back to school, and suffered another major depressive episode. Though I'd been doing well in college, I quit with one semester left. I had a falling-out with my mom because I was ruining my life again. I'd reconnected with Madelyne, but instead of repairing our friendship, I screwed it up even worse by taking advantage of her better nature.

I got involved in a powerfully destructive relationship that exacerbated my depression. I also met another group of great friends. I'd fallen in with a crowd of lesbians, and they were my life. They helped open my eyes to the queer world beyond gay men. They helped me see that I didn't have to be anyone in particular to fit into the queer community. I didn't have to listen to a specific type of music or dress in particular clothes or act a certain way, because being queer wasn't the nucleus of who I was, it was simply a modifier. I could be punk and queer; I could be a conservative lawyer and queer; I could be an Olympic athlete or a famous comedian or the CEO of the richest company in the world. I could be me, and I'd find a place to belong.

But still, I had no idea who I was.

I tried many different kinds of medications to get my depression under control, but medication didn't seem to work well for me. Effexor made me sleep twenty-three hours a day, Paxil made me obsessively buy underwear. I was drinking a lot and I got fired from my job as a shift manager at Starbucks. I'd started cutting myself again.

One morning I woke up on my bedroom floor, surrounded by broken glass and cuts on my arm. I'd smeared blood across a page in my journal and had written "Somebody help me" over and over.

This time, instead of trying to fight my monsters on my own,

I asked for help. A friend helped me move out of where I was living and into a spare room at her ex-girlfriend's house. I didn't tell anyone where I'd gone, and she didn't tell them either. I let go of the guy I was in love with but who was inadvertently hurting me, his friends, and anyone who was friends with them. I got a job in an office. I focused on me.

And that's what I did for the next five years. I worked my way up to running the IT department for the company where I'd started as an assistant. At night I went through training to become an EMT and a firefighter. I learned how to manage my depression. I moved out and got a place of my own. I slowly rebuilt my relationship with my mom and with Madelyne. My dad found out one of his best friends was gay, and it changed his attitude about everything. I saw a doctor and learned that I was *not* lazy or failing to live up to my potential as I'd always been told; I learned that I had ADHD. When we finally found a treatment that worked, it was like putting on glasses for the first time. The world came into focus.

I wrote and sold my first book. I quit smoking. I peeled away every mask I'd ever worn until the only person left was me. And then I learned to like that person. I learned to love him, and I learned that he deserved to be loved.

One day, Madelyne and I were spending time together. She'd gotten married and was raising two amazing children. I knew I could never undo the damage I'd done to our friendship, but I was grateful for whatever she was willing to offer. We were discussing how much we'd both changed.

"You've come full circle," she said.

"What do you mean?"

"Well, you were a nerd like me. You were into computers, and you loved performing in plays and reading books and watching ridiculous movies. And then you changed. You were smoking and going to clubs and you had all these 'cool' friends, and I didn't fit in."

"And now I'm back to Nerdy Shaun again?"

Maddie nodded. "Yeah, but this time you're comfortable being Nerdy Shaun."

She wasn't wrong. The problem had never been that I didn't know who I was; it was that I'd assumed who I was wasn't good enough. But he was. I was. And you are too.

ONE LAST THING

I WANT TO LEAVE YOU WITH ONE LAST THING. IT TOOK ME a long time to come to terms with being gay and fitting into the community and accepting myself for who I was instead of trying to become who I thought others wanted me to be. And I have been much happier since I got to that point. But none of that made my depression go away. Depression is something I'll always struggle with. The difference is that I understand now what that voice in my head is. It's a fucking liar.

I was with a guy for six years, and then we broke up. The voice in my head spent a lot of time trying to convince me it was because I wasn't worthy of being loved, that I was ugly, that I was a terrible person. But this time, instead of listening, I built a LEGO Millennium Falcon. Instead of cutting myself, I built a LEGO Ghostbusters Firehouse. Instead of letting that voice convince me to ruin my life, I wrote another book. Even now, writing *this* book, dredging up all that pain from twenty years ago, hasn't been easy. So instead of listening to the voice when it told me to quit writing this book, to quit writing completely, I flew across the country to stay with my brother, so that when it was time to write the hard bits, I wouldn't have to do it alone.

That voice is a liar.

There are so many treatments for depression, and I found what works for me. That doesn't always make life easy, but it makes it manageable. And when it gets too bad, I'm not ashamed to ask for help.

The only thing that's permanent in life is death. You won't always be in high school. You won't always have to live with your parents. You can change majors, change jobs, change friends, change relationships. You can move to a whole new country every year, if you like. And if you need help making some changes, all you have to do is ask.

For every bad thing that happened after I got out of the hospital, for every fight and every heartbreak, there were a hundred wonders. I might have let Andy get away, but we also spent the most amazing weekend together at his sister's wedding. A weekend I will never, ever forget. My mom and I might have said some horrible things to each other, but we also became better friends for it, and I got to bum around Europe with her for six weeks. I might have lost some friends because I was an asshole, but I gained new ones, and I learned to appreciate them.

There have been days since I got out of the hospital where I wasn't sure I could go on, where I wasn't sure I was happy I'd survived, but those days pass. There are always better days beyond the bad.

It gets better. Sometimes not as quickly as we'd like, but eventually. *You* get better. You learn and you grow and you accept yourself for who you are and know that you *are* good enough. It takes work, it takes patience, and often it takes help. But it does and *will* get better.

And you don't have to do it alone. You don't have to put on a brave face and pretend that everything's okay. It's okay to hurt, and it's okay to ask for help. You can show people who you really are, and you'll still be worthy of being loved.

ACKNOWLEDGMENTS

From the first moment I began considering this project, I knew I wanted to publish it with Simon Pulse and nowhere else. Over the course of ten years, the team at S&S has supported me and my work; they've performed miracles getting my books into the hands of readers; and even though I'm just one author among many, they've always made me feel special. They treated *Brave Face* with care and compassion, and I am forever in their debt.

I'm so grateful to Jessi Smith for her tireless efforts behind the scenes and for putting up with my forgetfulness in replying to e-mails; Sarah Creech for designing the best cover ever; Casey Burns for taking a photo of teenage me and turning it into an illustration that just blows my mind; Chelsea Morgan, Adam Smith, and Elizabeth Mims for their copyediting brilliance (and for preventing me from looking like a fool on many, many occasions!); Tom Spain and the entire S&S Audio team for giving me the chance to give voice to my story; Michelle Leo and the entire team in the S&S education and library marketing department and Nicole Russo, Caitlin Sweeny, and Anna Jarzab in publicity, marketing, and digital marketing, all of whom do so freaking much to help my books find the readers who need them; and Mara Anastas for always being game to give me a chance.

Ever since I announced I was writing a memoir, I've gotten loads of amazing support from the YA community—readers, writers, librarians, teachers, bloggers—and I can't thank you all enough. Your encouragement helped me keep writing when I wanted to quit.

Dylan Calvert especially has been a huge champion of *Brave Face* and of all my books, and he even loaned me his blog and helped announce this project. Thank you, Dylan. Keep marching on!

Last year, as I was working on the most difficult parts of *Brave Face*, my brother and his husband, Syrus, gamely let me camp out in their living room for a couple of weeks so that I didn't have to be alone. And they even convinced me to move to Seattle! Thank you both, for your support, your couch, the *Drag Race* marathons, and the nightly dinners.

There are a lot of folks I wish I knew how to reach out to so that I could thank them properly—the ER nurse, the 911 operator, the paramedics, Ed from Fair Oaks, the teaching assistant in my creative writing class—but I don't know their names or how to contact them, so I hope, even if they never read this, that they know how much of an impact they had on my life. I hope everyone reading this realizes the impact you can have on someone's life. You might never know it, and you might think you didn't make a difference, but you did.

I also want to thank Becky Albertalli for her kindness and wisdom. Thank you.

Finally, there are four amazing people without whom *Brave Face* would not exist. My editor, Liesa Abrams; my agent, Katie Shea Boutillier; my best friend, Rachel Melcher; and my mom. There aren't enough words to describe the ways in which I'm grateful to them or to list all the ways they helped bring this project to life. So I just want to say thank you.

Thank you, Liesa and Katie, for helping me shape *Brave Face* into a book I'm proud of, and thank you, Rachel and Mom, for helping me become a person I hope *you're* proud of.

Turn the page for a look at an unforgettable novel from Shaun David Hutchinson.

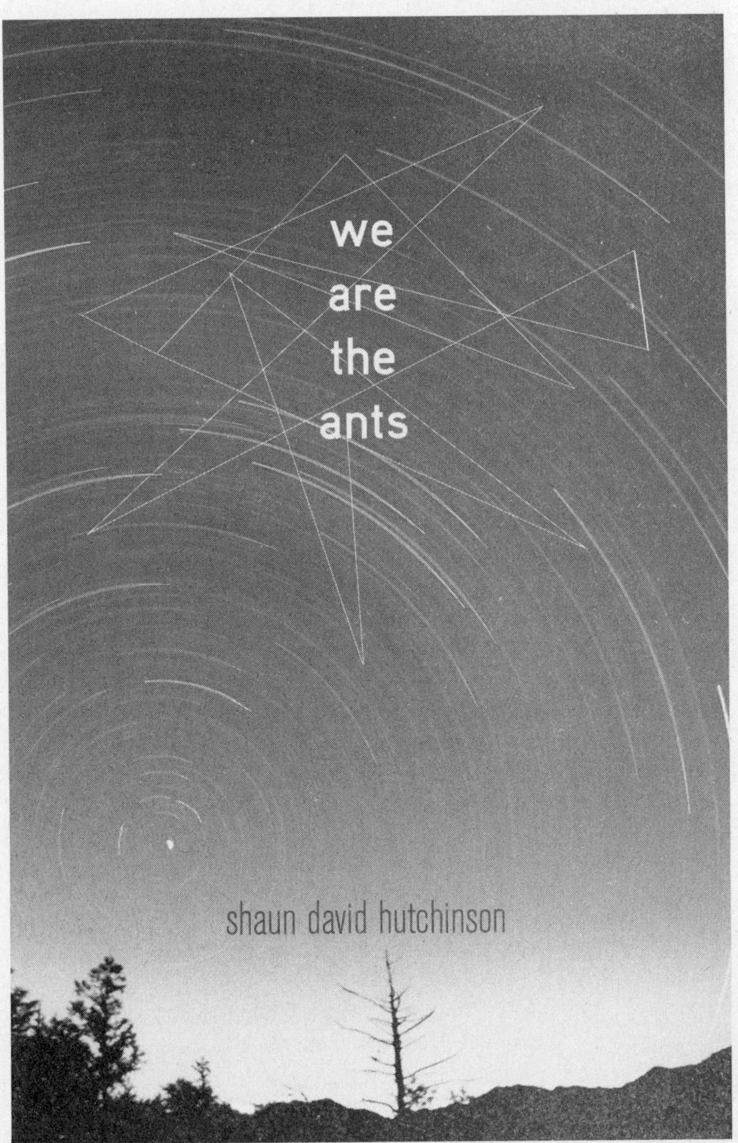

Chemistry: Extra Credit Project

Life is bullshit.

Consider your life for a moment. Think about all those little rituals that sustain you throughout your day—from the moment you wake up until that last, lonely midnight hour when you guzzle a gallon of NyQuil to drown out the persistent voice in your head. The one that whispers you should give up, give in, that tomorrow won't be better than today. Think about the absurdity of brushing your teeth, of arguing with your mother over the appropriateness of what you're wearing to school, of homework, of grade-point averages and boyfriends and hot school lunches.

And life.

Think about the absurdity of life.

When you break down the things we do every day to

their component pieces, you begin to understand how ridiculous they are. Like kissing, for instance. You wouldn't let a stranger off the street spit into your mouth, but you'll swap saliva with the boy or girl who makes your heart race and your pits sweat and gives you boners at the worst fucking times. You'll stick your tongue in his mouth or her mouth or their mouth, and let them reciprocate without stopping to consider where else their tongue has been, or whether they're giving you mouth herpes or mono or leftover morsels of their tuna-salad sandwich.

We shave our legs and pluck our eyebrows and slather our bodies with creams and lotions. We starve ourselves so we can fit into the perfect pair of jeans, we pollute our bodies with drugs to increase our muscles so we'll look ripped without a shirt. We drive fast and party hard and study for exams that don't mean dick in the grand scheme of the cosmos.

Physicists have theorized that we live in an infinite and infinitely expanding universe, and that everything in it will eventually repeat. There are infinite copies of your mom and your dad and your clothes-stealing little sister. There are infinite copies of you. Despite what you've spent your entire life believing, you are not a special snowflake. Somewhere out there, another you is living *your* life. Chances are, they're living it better. They're learning to speak French or screwing their brains out instead of loafing on the couch in their boxers, stuffing their face with bowl after bowl of Fruity Oatholes while wondering why they're all alone on a Friday night. But that's not even the worst part. What's really going to send you running over the side of the nearest bridge is that none of it matters. I'll die, you'll die, we'll all die, and the things we've done, the choices we've made, will amount to nothing.

Out in the world, crawling in a field at the edge of some bullshit town with a name like Shoshoni or Medicine Bow, is an ant. You weren't aware of it. Didn't know whether it was a soldier, a drone, or the queen. Didn't care if it was scouting for food to drag back to the nest or building new tunnels for wriggly ant larvae. Until now that ant simply didn't exist for you. If I hadn't mentioned it, you would have continued on with your life, pinballing from one tedious task to the next—shoving your tongue into the bacterial minefield of your girlfriend's mouth, doodling the variations of your combined names on the cover of your notebook—waiting for electronic bits to zoom through the air and tell you that someone was thinking about you. That for one fleeting moment you were the most significant person in someone else's insignificant life. But whether you knew about it or not, that ant is still out there doing ant things while you wait for the next text message to prove that out of the seven billion self-centered people on this planet, *you* are important. Your entire sense of self-worth is predicated upon your belief that you matter, that you matter to the universe.

But you don't.

Because we are the ants.

I didn't waste time thinking about the future until the night the sluggers abducted me and told me the world was going to end.

I'm not insane. When I tell you the human race is toast, I'm not speaking hyperbolically the way people do when they say we're all dying from the moment our mothers evict us from their bodies into a world where everything feels heavier and brighter and far too loud. I'm telling you that tomorrow—January 29, 2016—you can kiss your Chipotle-eating, Frappuccino-drinking, fat ass good-bye.

You probably don't believe me—I wouldn't in your place—but I've had 143 days to come to terms with our inevitable destruction, and I've spent most of those days thinking about the future. Wondering whether I have or want one, trying to decide if the end of existence is a tragedy, a comedy, or as inconsequential as that chem lab I forgot to turn in last week.

But the real joke isn't that the sluggers revealed to me the date of Earth's demise; it's that they offered me the choice to prevent it.

You asked for a story, so here it is. I'll begin with the night the sluggers told me the world was toast, and when I'm finished, we can wait for the end together.

7 September 2015

The biggest letdown about being abducted by aliens is the abundance of gravity on the spaceship. We spend our first nine months of life floating, weightless and blind, in an amniotic sac before we become gravity's bitch, and the seductive lure of space travel is the promise of returning to that perfect state of grace. But it's a sham. Gravity is jealous, sadistic, and infinite.

Sometimes I think gravity may be death in disguise. Other times I think gravity is love, which is why love's only demand is that we fall.

Sluggers aren't gray. They don't have saucer-wide eyes or thin lipless mouths. As far as I know, they don't have mouths at all. Their skin is rough like wet leather and is all the colors of an algae bloom. Their black spherical eyes are mounted atop their heads on wobbly stalks. Instead of arms, they have appendages that grow from their bodies when required. If their UFO keys fall off the console—*boom!*—instant arm. If they need to restrain me or silence my terrified howls, they can sprout a dozen tentacles to accomplish the task. It's very efficient.

Oddly enough, sluggers do have nipples. Small brown buttons that appear to be as useless to them as most men's. It's comforting to know that regardless of our vast differences and the light-years that separate our worlds, we'll always have nipples in common.

I should slap that on a bumper sticker, © HENRY JEROME DENTON.

Before you ask: no, the sluggers have never probed my anus. I'm fairly certain they reserve that special treat for people who talk on their phones during movies, or text while driving.

Here's how it happens: abductions always begin with shadows. Even in a dark room, with the windows closed and the curtains drawn, the shadows descend, circling like buzzards over a reeking lunch.

Then a heaviness in my crotch like I have to pee, growing

painfully insistent regardless of how much I beg my brain to ignore it.

After that, helplessness. Paralysis. The inability to struggle. Fight. Breathe.

The inability to scream.

At some point the sluggers move me to the examination room. I've been abducted at least a dozen times, and I still don't know how they transport me from my bedroom to their spaceship. It happens in the dark space between blinks, in the void between breaths.

Once aboard, they begin the experiments.

That's what I assume they're doing. Trying to fathom the motives of an advanced alien race who possess the technological capacity to travel through the universe is like the frog I dissected in ninth grade trying to understand why I cut it open and pinned its guts to the table. The sluggers could be blasting me with deadly radiation or stuffing me full of slugger eggs just to see what happens. Hell, I could be some slugger kid's science fair project.

I doubt I'll ever know for certain.

Sluggers don't speak. During those long stretches where my body is beyond my control, I often wonder how they communicate with one another. Maybe they secrete chemicals the way insects do, or perhaps the movements of their eyestalks is a form of language similar to the dance of a bee. They could also be like my mother and father, who communicated exclusively by slamming doors.

I was thirteen the first time the sluggers abducted me. My older brother, Charlie, was snoring his face off in the next room while I lay in bed, translating my parents' fight. You might believe all doors sound the same when slammed, but you'd be wrong.

My father was a classic slammer, maintaining contact with the door until it was totally and completely shut. This gave him control over the volume and pitch, and produced a deep, solid bang capable of shaking the door, the frame, and the wall.

Mom preferred variety. Sometimes she went for the dramatic fling; other times she favored the heel-kick slam. That night, she relied on the multismash, which was loud and effective but lacked subtlety.

The sluggers abducted me before I learned what my parents were arguing about. Police found me two days later, wandering the dirt roads west of Calypso, wearing a grocery bag for underwear and covered in hickies I couldn't explain. My father left three weeks after that, slamming the door behind him one final time. No translation necessary.

• • •

I've never grown comfortable being naked around the aliens. Jesse Franklin frequently saw me naked and claimed to enjoy it, but he was my boyfriend, so it doesn't count. I'm self-conscious about being too skinny, and I imagine the sluggers judge me for my flaws—the mole in the center of my chest shaped like Abraham Lincoln or the way my collarbone protrudes or my tragically flat ass. Once, while standing in the lunch line waiting for shepherd's pie, Elle Smith told me I had the flattest ass she'd ever seen. I wasn't sure how many asses a twelve-year-old girl from Calypso realistically could have been exposed to, but the comment infected me like a cold sore, bursting to the surface from time to time, ensuring I never forgot my place.

SHAUN DAVID HUTCHINSON

"A writer to watch." —*Booklist*

★ "Bitterly funny, with a ray of hope amid bleakness."
—*Kirkus Reviews*, starred review, on *We Are the Ants*

★ "Hutchinson artfully blends the realistic and the surreal. . . .
An entirely original take on apocalyptic fiction."
—*SLJ*, starred review, on *The Apocalypse of Elena Mendoza*

EBOOK EDITIONS ALSO AVAILABLE

Simon Pulse

simonandschuster.com/teen